COLLEGE AND CAREER READINESS:

Writing

Level 10

Writers:
Bill McMahon and Douglas Grudzina

Senior Editor:
Paul Moliken

Cover and Text Design:
Maria J. Mendoza

Layout and Production:
Jeremy Clark

PRESTWICK HOUSE, INC.
"Proud to Be on the Teacher's Side"

P.O. Box 658
Clayton • Delaware 19938

Tel: 1.888.932.4593

Fax: 1.888.718.9333

Web: www.prestwickhouse.com

ISBN: 978-0-9823096-3-6

TABLE OF CONTENTS

STANDARDS-BASED SCORING RUBRIC FOR GRADE 10

TOPIC		
5	Topic is **clear and sufficiently narrow** for the nature of the writing.	Topic is **sufficiently complex** and is **suitable to** fulfilling **the purpose** of the writing (e.g., persuasive versus informational).
4	Topic is **clear and sufficiently narrow** for the nature of the writing.	Topic is **sufficiently complex** and is **suitable to** fulfilling **the purpose** of the writing (e.g., persuasive versus informational).
3	Topic is **clear** and reveals a **strong attempt** to **narrow** it sufficiently for the nature of the writing.	Topic may be **too simple or general** for **the purpose** of the writing (e.g., persuasive versus informational).
2	Topic is **clear but either too broad or too narrow** for the nature of the writing.	Topic may be **too simple or general** for **the purpose** of the writing (e.g., persuasive versus informational).
1	Topic is **clear but either too broad or too narrow** for the nature of the writing.	Topic may be **too simple or general** for **the purpose** of the writing (e.g., persuasive versus informational).

	CRAFTSMANSHIP	
5	Writing is **competent and confident. Tone and style** seem **natural and appropriate** to the topic, purpose, and audience of the piece.	• **All claims** or points being explored are **expressed clearly**. • The **distinctions** between the student's ideas and those from other sources **are evident**. • **All claims** (both the students' and others') are **presented accurately**, with **strong evidence** of an **attempt** to present **others' claims fully and accurately** as appropriate to the topic, audience, and purpose. • If appropriate to the topic, audience, and purpose, **narrative techniques are used for variety** and **effect**.
4	**Writing** is **competent. Tone and style** are **consistent and appropriate** to the topic, purpose, and audience of the piece.	• **All claims** or points being explored are **expressed clearly**. • The **distinctions** between the students' ideas and those from other sources **are evident**. • A **strong attempt to present all claims** (both the students' and others') is apparent, and there is **evidence** of an **attempt** to present **others' claims fully and accurately** as appropriate to the topic, audience, and purpose. • If appropriate to the topic, audience, and purpose, **narrative techniques are used for variety** and **effect**.

CRAFTSMANSHIP (CONT.)		
3	**Tone and style** are **consistent** and **appropriate** to the topic, purpose, and audience.	• **Most claims** or points being explored are **expressed**, while **some** may be **suggested or implied**. • The **distinctions** between the students' ideas and those from other sources **are clearly suggested**. • The writing exhibits **some effort** to present **all claims** (both the students' and others') **accurately**. • **Omissions** in either strengths or limitations **suggest bias** and/or **faulty reasoning**. • If appropriate to the topic, audience, and purpose, **narrative techniques are used for variety** and **effect**.

CRAFTSMANSHIP (CONT.)		
2	**Tone and style** are, for the **most part, appropriate** to the topic, purpose, and audience with a **few minor lapses.**	• **Some claims** or points being explored **are specified,** but **many are implied** or are **stated ambiguously.** • **The distinctions** between the students' ideas and those from other sources **are usually apparent.** • The writing suggests **tentative attempts to present all claims** (both the students' and others') **accurately,** but **obvious omissions** in either strengths or limitations **suggest bias and/or faulty reasoning.** • **Narrative devices** that would make the writing clearer or more powerful **are missing.**
1	**Tone and style** are **inconsistent.**	• **Claims** or points being explored are **expressed clearly.** • There is **minimal distinction** between the student's ideas and those from other sources. • The writing suggests **minimal attempts to present all claims** (both the students' and others') accurately. • **Narrative devices** that would make the writing clearer or more powerful **are missing.**

ELABORATION, DEVELOPMENT, AND SUPPORT		
5	All **claims**, inferences, and analyses are **supported with evidence** from literary or informational texts, as appropriate to the topic, audience, and purpose.	• **Facts**, examples, and/or details are **well-chosen, relevant, and sufficient to establish the purpose** of the writing and meet the needs of the audience. • When appropriate to the topic, audience, and purpose, **sensory language** helps to create desired **images and impressions**.
4	**For the most part, claims,** inferences, and analyses are **supported with evidence** from literary or informational texts, as appropriate to the topic, audience, and purpose.	• **Facts**, examples, and/or details are **well-chosen, relevant, and sufficient to establish the purpose** of the writing and meet the needs of the audience. • When appropriate to the topic, audience, and purpose, **sensory language** helps to create desired **images and impressions**.
3	Most **claims**, inferences, and analyses are **supported with evidence** from literary or informational texts, as appropriate to the topic, audience, and purpose.	• **Facts**, examples, and/or details are **well-chosen and relevant** and **help to establish the purpose** of the writing and meet the needs of the audience. • A **strong attempt to use appropriate sensory language** contributes to the creation of desired **images and impressions**. **Sensory language** may **occasionally give way** to less powerful **adjectives and adverbs**.

	ELABORATION, DEVELOPMENT, AND SUPPORT (CONT.)	
2	**Most claims**, inferences, and analyses are **supported with evidence** from literary or informational texts, as appropriate to the topic, audience, and purpose.	• **Facts**, examples, and/or details are **generally relevant with occasional minor irrelevancies**. • **Facts**, examples, and/or details **may be generally relevant, but** are **insufficient to establish the purpose** of the writing and/or meet the needs of the audience. • **Sensory language generally gives way** to less powerful **adjectives and adverbs**.
1	**Lack of adequate support** for one or more claims, inferences, or analyses **weakens the overall impact** of the writing.	• **Evidence** is characterized by **trivial or irrelevant** facts or details. Examples may be **tangential**. • **Ineffective or over use of common adjectives and adverbs** undermines attempts to create images and impressions.

ORGANIZATION		
5	**Introduction**, thesis, lead, etc., **explicitly orients** the reader to the **nature and purpose** of the piece to follow.	• **Conclusion follows logically from** the information presented. • **Order** of ideas and the use of **transitional elements** establish the **relationships** between **claims and reasons**, between **reasons and evidence**, and between **claims and counterclaims**.
4	**Introduction**, thesis, lead, etc., **explicitly orients** the reader to the **nature and purpose** of the piece to follow.	• **Conclusion follows logically from** the information presented. • **Order** of ideas and the use of **transitional elements** establish the **relationships** between **claims and reasons**, between **reasons and evidence**, and between **claims and counterclaims**.
3	**Introduction**, thesis, lead, etc., **orients** the reader to the **nature and purpose** of the piece to follow.	• **Conclusion follows logically from** the information presented. • **Order** of ideas and the use of **transitional elements** suggest the **relationships** between **claims and reasons**, between **reasons and evidence**, and between **claims and counterclaims**.

ORGANIZATION (CONT.)		
2	Introduction, thesis, lead, etc. **suggests** the **nature and purpose** of the piece to follow.	• **Conclusion is largely drawn from** the information presented. • **Relationships** between claim(s) and reasons, between reasons and evidence, and between claim(s) and counterclaims **can be inferred** but **are not necessarily established** by the **order** of ideas or the use of **transitional elements**.
1	Introduction, thesis, lead, etc., leaves the **nature and purpose** of the piece unclear.	• **Conclusion essentially recaps** the information presented. • **Order** of ideas and the use of **transitional elements fail to establish relationships** between claim(s) and reasons, between reasons and evidence, and between claim(s) and counterclaims.

FORMS AND CONVENTIONS		
5	Word choice is **intentional and precise** and clearly conveys the student's **meaning**.	• When appropriate, **academic and domain-specific words and phrases are used accurately and effectively**. • **Writing** is **free of** spelling and/or typographical **errors**. • **Writing** is **free of** grammatical and **mechanical errors**. • The piece **clearly reflects the student's own thinking** and writing, with **all material** or ideas derived **from outside sources clearly identified** and **carefully cited**. • **All citations** and notations **conform** to the teacher's or school's prescribed style manual (MLA, APA, Turabian, etc.).
4	Word choice is **intentional and precise** and conveys student's **specific meaning** and add **variety and interest** to the writing.	• When appropriate, **academic and domain-specific words** and phrases are used **accurately and effectively**. • **Writing** is **free of** spelling and/or typographical **errors**. • **Writing** is **free of** grammatical and mechanical **errors**. • The piece **clearly reflects the student's own thinking** and writing, with **all material** or ideas derived **from outside sources clearly identified** and **carefully cited**. • **All citations** and notations **conform** to the teacher's or school's prescribed style manual (MLA, APA, Turabian, etc.).

FORMS AND CONVENTIONS (CONT.)

3	Word choice is **careful** and conveys the **student's meaning**.	• The use of **academic and domain-specific words** and phrases **occasionally reflects a growing understanding** of the term's meaning or appropriate application.
		• Spelling and/or typographical **errors** are **infrequent** and **do not interfere** with the reader's ability to understand the writing.
		• Grammatical and mechanical **errors** are **infrequent** and **do not interfere** with the reader's ability to understand the writing.
		• The piece **clearly reflects the student's own thinking** and writing, with **all material** or ideas derived **from outside sources clearly identified** and **carefully cited**.
		• **All citations** and notations **conform** to the teacher's or school's prescribed style manual (MLA, APA, Turabian, etc.).

FORMS AND CONVENTIONS (CONT.)

2	Word choice is **mostly adequate** to convey the **writer's meaning**. Use of **ambiguous or vague words** and **occasional misuse of key words** contributes to **reader confusion**.	• **Academic and domain-specific words** and phrases are used **unnecessarily** or **incorrectly**. • Spelling and/or typographical **errors** are **infrequent** and **do not interfere** with the reader's ability to understand the writing. • Grammatical and mechanical **errors are noticeable** and **distracting** but **do not interfere** with the reader's ability to understand the writing. • The piece **clearly reflects the student's thinking** and writing, with **material** and ideas derived **from outside sources identified** and **cited** with only **occasional lapses**. • **All citations** and notations **conform** to the teacher's or school's prescribed style manual (MLA, APA, Turabian, etc.).

FORMS AND CONVENTIONS (CONT.)		
1	Word choice is adequate to convey the student's meaning.	• Academic and domain-specific words and phrases are used unnecessarily or incorrectly, or they are not used when their application is indicated. • Spelling and/or typographical errors are noticeable and distracting but do not interfere with the reader's ability to understand the writing. • Grammatical and mechanical errors are noticeable and distracting but do not interfere with the reader's ability to understand the writing. • Material and/or ideas derived from outside sources are identified and cited carelessly and erratically. • Citations and notations generally conform to the teacher's or school's prescribed style manual.

PART I:

Personal Writing

[conveying what students have experienced, imagined, thought, and felt]

The occasion might be as dull as the clichéd first writing assignment of the new school year: *How I Spent My Summer Vacation.* Perhaps your new English teacher has assigned you to write "a paragraph or two introducing yourself" to her.

Then again, this might be an immensely important essay: your college application "personal statement" or an essay to accompany your request for financial aid, employment, or some form of honor or special recognition.

Whatever the case, the next several years will probably provide you with a number of occasions on which you will be asked to write about yourself, to sell yourself, to make yourself stand out in the minds of men and women who will be reading thousands of statements just like yours. And these readers will be deciding whether or not to admit you to their school or program, give you money, give you a job, or present you with that award.

This book begins with personal writing, not because personal writing is "easier" than the other purposes—it is no easy task to make your "Why I Think I Deserve Your $500 Book Scholarship" essay stand out from the thousands of other essays the scholarship committee has already read and the 500 it will read after yours—but because personal writing requires the least outside research and, therefore, allows us to focus completely on the craft of writing the essay.

After all, you should not have to devote too much time to gathering information about your experiences, thoughts, and feelings. Instead, you can devote your time and energy to developing the best, most effective means of communicating that information.

Common elements of good personal essays (actually, common elements of good writing):

- **A point**: This is your answer to your reader's question, *Why are you telling me this?*

- **An angle**: What makes your account of your day at the beach, your first job, the day you got cut from the team *more meaningful, moving, or memorable* than those of the hundreds of other teenagers who visited beaches, worked first jobs, or got cut from teams?

- **A voice**: How do you want to sound to your reader? Confident but not cocky? Respectful but not subservient? Witty but not caustic? Along with your angle, a voice is what will give your reader a sense of you beyond the mere facts of your narrative.

- **Substance**: Vague generalities and abstract concepts might suggest ideas to your reader, but they will do little to recreate the physical, psychological, emotional, and spiritual effects that will make the reader take notice of your account.

Remember your writing process. We cannot stress enough that, except for the most personal writing, good writing does not simply flow spontaneously from brain through the pen onto the paper (or fingers to keyboard). It is planned, often over long periods of time. The more important the writing, the more carefully you want to plan it.

For the most part, you'll want to leave yourself time to accomplish these steps in the process of crafting the final draft of something you're writing for an audience:

STEP 1: Select a topic

STEP 2: Develop a(n) slant/angle/hook

STEP 3: Brainstorm, discuss, research

STEP 4: Outline

STEP 5: Write your first draft

STEP 6: Peer edit

STEP 7: Revised/final draft

POSSIBLE STEP 8: Second edit and final revision

A S S I G N M E N T   1 :

The "significant experience" essay

As we've said, the personal essay is often the means by which you will introduce yourself to a potential employer, scholarship giver, or college admissions officer. All of these people will have access to your transcript and information like your attendance record and class rank. But consider how many students, even in your school, have taken the same courses as you and have earned similar grades. Chances are, you are tied or nearly tied with at least one or two other people for your class rank; and even if you are at the top of your class, every high school graduating class has a valedictorian and salutatorian.

The fact that you got "straight As" and are tied for #1 ranking in your class does not make you unique. This information does not give the person reviewing your file a sense of you as a person.

Neither does the fact that you have more "credits" than are mandated by your school, district, and state for graduation.

Your personal essay is really the only way to show yourself to the reviewer. The goal of this essay is to get your file from the big pile of "Everyone Who Applied" into the smaller pile of "People They Are Still Considering."

Here is a typical writing prompt on college and scholarship applications:

> Evaluate a significant experience, achievement, risk you have taken, or ethical dilemma you have faced and its impact on you.

"**Kyle**" is a first-semester tenth-grader in a large, urban high school. He does plan to attend college, and he believes he has the grades (and will also have the test scores) to attend an Ivy League school. He knows he will need scholarship and grant money, however, if he is going to achieve that dream.

Here is a recreation of the process Kyle followed when faced with the "Evaluate a significant experience" prompt:

STEP 1: Select a topic

First, Kyle paid close attention to the actual wording of the prompt and brainstormed as many experiences or events as he could think of.

- **Significant experiences**: learning to ride a bicycle? learning to drive? first summer job? grandfather's funeral?
- **Achievements**: finishing my first marathon?
- **Risks**: not sure what kind of "risk" they mean? Jumping off a cliff? Standing up for someone being bullied?
- **Ethical dilemmas**: when I saw Maxie cheating?

He then evaluated the topics on his list to determine which ones would give him the most material and the most interesting angle.

- **learning to ride a bicycle**—not very unique. I was glad to learn, but it wasn't really a challenge.
- **learning to drive**—not unique either. Gained freedom—but isn't that what everyone says? Also not much of a challenge. Did I overcome anything or learn anything?
- **first summer job**— Did I overcome anything or learn anything? Yes...I didn't want to look stupid in front of Nick, and it ended up that I looked even more stupid. I can say that I'm a different person now because I've learned how to ask for help...or something.
- **grandfather's funeral**—it was kind of hard for me to be a pall-bearer. I was afraid I'd trip and fall or something. Okay...am I different now because I did it? Maybe I'm more confident. How unique is that?
- **finishing my first marathon**—same thing. What's unique? Not everyone runs a marathon. I trained hard. Learned the "benefit of dedication and hard work"?
- **when I saw Maxie cheating**—this could be a good one. There's the whole friendship versus what's the right thing to do? Maybe I could bring in a mention of Julius Caesar. But would they see me as a tattletale or something? What if they disagree with the decision I made? Do I even still believe I did the right thing? But maybe I could talk about that...not knowing whether I did the right thing or not.

Finally, Kyle narrowed his list down to the summer job and the friend cheating. Unable to make his final decision, he decided to move to the next step and see whether his possible slant or angle would help him eliminate one of the two.

STEP 2: Develop a(n) slant/angle/hook

WHAT CAN MY ANGLE BE?

- **Cheating**—not sure what the right thing is. Right versus wrong; good versus evil. Is friendship an important ideal? Brutus was a tragic hero because he thought there was something higher than the ideal of friendship. But Maxie hasn't spoken to me since, and I do not feel good about what I did. Can I write a good essay about something that I guess I haven't really figured out yet?

- **Summer job**—I like the irony of making myself look more stupid by not wanting to look stupid to begin with. If I'm willing to look stupid (admit I don't know something), maybe that makes me more ready to learn. Like you've got to admit you're sick to go to the doctor and get healed. <u>So maybe that's a good thing to say to the college admission people: I'm able to learn because I'm not too proud and afraid to look stupid and ask questions.</u>

WHERE WOULD I BEGIN MY EVALUATION?

- I guess I'll begin at the beginning, tell the story and then talk about what I learned.

> Note: This is an early choice that Kyle will eventually change to make his essay better address the prompt's instruction to evaluate the experience and its impact.

WHAT TYPE OR TONE OF VOICE DO I WANT TO CREATE IN MY READER'S MIND?

- I want to impress these guys, so I guess I'll try for a formal tone, something that shows them I am intelligent and a good student.

> Note: This is another early choice that Kyle will eventually change. As his own voice emerges, and he begins to trust his understanding that the committee members want to get to know him as a person, he allows himself to sound like himself.

STEP 3: Brainstorm, discuss, research

Thinking about his potential angles helped Kyle realize that he wasn't ready to write about the cheating incident. He also realized he had some good ideas for an essay about what he learned as a result of his first summer job. That is the topic he chose for this essay.

Now, having selected a topic he is excited about, he knows he must make note of the specific details, facts, etc., that will make his experience real to his readers.

- The tools: the gas-powered weed-whacker, the lawn mower. Why couldn't I start the weed-whacker? There was the starter-rope. The primer bulb, and the choke lever. The buttons on the truck's lift: red, green, blue, yellow, and the black lever.
- The lush green of the lawns. The nauseating smell of the exhaust from the tools. The noise.
- The houses: brown and gray stone. Brick (brown and red). Raised flowerbeds in stone or brick retaining walls. Brown and red paver driveways. The mulch. Some smelled fresh—like Christmas? Some smelled foul—like [what would be the best word?] excrement? feces?
- Nick's voice: deep, grating. Sort of mush-mouthed, mumbling. With kind of a Southern accent. Or Western drawl?
- Nick, tall and really skinny. Stoop-shouldered. Dark blue-gray pants. Lighter gray shirt with "Nick" in red over the breast pocket. Clean-shaven to look professional. Baseball cap with name of lawn company embroidered on it.
- I did not have a uniform. Khaki pants and dress shirt.
- Some of the customers/clients were nice. Some were really snobby.
- Blue sky. Gray sky. Overcast days. Hot and humid days. Bugs.
- Loved rainy days because we did not work, but I did not get paid for days we did not work.

> Kyle is definitely giving himself more material than he is going to need. Remember that it is always easier to delete excess material than to run out while writing and have to come back to this step. Notice also, however, that some of these details are fairly well developed while others do nothing more than name a tool or article of clothing, etc.

STEP 4: Outline

Because at this point Kyle thinks he is going to write a chronological narrative, he has chosen something that looks like an academic outline, with each Roman numeral representing a distinct step in the narrative sequence.

I. How I got the job.

   A. Client of Dad's uses this service

   B. Recommended me

   C. I sort of lied and said I had experience

II. My first day

   A. First house

     1. Nick tells me to unload truck

     2. I can't operate the lift

       a. describe the buttons and levers

     3. Nick grumbles at me

     4. I can't start the weed whacker

       a. describe the primer bulb, starter cord, and choke lever

     5. Nick grumbles at me again

III. What I learned

   A. I was afraid of looking stupid

     1. Everyone in my family is smarter and more accomplished than me

     2. Yard work should be easy and not require knowledge

   B. I looked more stupid by pretending I knew what I didn't know

---

Note: This is a flawed outline that can lead only to a flawed essay. If Kyle were to share the prompt and this outline with a sharp reader, the reader would tell him that this outline focuses too much on the story of the job and not enough on the evaluation of the experience and its impact.

STEP 5: Write your first draft

Even though Kyle believes he has a strong topic, more-than-adequate notes, and a sound outline, he knows that this is only the first draft of his essay. Even so, however, he strives to make this as polished as he can. Given his notes and outline, he is beyond the stage of this draft's being simply a rough "mind-dump."

Here is Kyle's first draft. Read it and consider its strengths and weaknesses. How successfully has Kyle responded to the prompt and drafted an essay that will be noticed by the admissions committee of the college he hopes to attend?

The essay starts out pretty weakly. We can guess the "significant experience" has to do with Kyle's first summer job, but we don't yet have a clue to why it is significant or what its impact has been.

The significance is still unclear. Is this essay going to be about the difficulty in finding a job? The father's help?

With each paragraph, this essay seems to be developing into a description of the job. Kyle needs to be reminded that the prompt instructs him to evaluate the experience, not merely narrate it.

It was my first summer job. I knew I had to work because that was how it was in my family. All of my older brothers started working summers the summer they turned fifteen. I was the youngest of five sons. I had four older brothers.

I did try to find a job on my own, but a lot of places won't hire you until you're sixteen or seventeen, so it was hard. My Dad decided to help me out. A client of his (he's a lawyer) used a lawn service, and the guy who did his lawn said he needed some extra help for the summer. My father asked if I thought I could handle yard work for the summer, and I thought I could.

How hard could it be? My job would be to do the "edgework." That meant I would swing the weed-whacker around flowerbeds and stone walls, guide the edger along driveways and sidewalks, and the walking mower around places where the riding mower wouldn't fit.

The guy who owned the lawn service didn't ask if I thought I could do it. He asked if I had experience. He meant had I actually used a weed-whacker, an edger, and a lawn mower. I said yes even though I never had. I didn't think they were chores that required a lot of skill or training. He hired me, and I was partnered with "Nick."

Nick was tall, much taller than me, and really, really skinny. But he didn't look emaciated

- 8 -

like someone who was sick. He looked wiry and strong. He wore the company's uniform, dark gray khaki pants and a lighter gray shirt with his name embroidered in red over the shirt's breast pocket. He was clean-shaven and wore the company's baseball cap. Because I was only temporary, I didn't have a company shirt with my name on it. They told me to wear khaki pants and a dress shirt every day.

The company's territory was huge, and we serviced lawns not only in the nicest neighborhoods of my city, but we went several miles out into the suburbs. Many nights that summer, I didn't get home from work until 10:00, and then I had to be at work by 8:00 a.m. the next morning. I loved rainy days because we didn't work in the rain, but of course we didn't get paid for days we didn't work, so that wasn't so good.

My first day at work was the hardest, and that's when I learned an important lesson.

When we got to the first house, Nick told me to open the gate at the back of the truck, so we could get out the equipment. I didn't know how to operate it! It was a gate and a lift elevator because the riding mower was really heavy. There were four buttons on the control: red, green, blue, and yellow, as well as a black lever and a silver toggle switch. Nothing was labeled.

Finally, grumbling what I think were curses, Nick jumped off the truck and lowered the gate. He looked at me and said that I should have asked how to operate the gate. His voice was low and mumbly. I replied that I didn't want to seem stupid.

He handed me the weed-whacker and asked if I knew how to start it. I knew he was mocking me.

I nodded and walked over to the brick retaining wall where I was supposed to begin trimming the

These details are from Kyle's pre-writing work, but they don't seem relevant. Of course, without yet knowing what specifically is Kyle's point, it is hard to assess the relevance of any details he chooses to include.

Again, we don't yet know Kyle's focus, and we do question the relevance of this information.

This is the seventh paragraph. We're more than a page into Kyle's essay, and this is the first suggestion of what the significance of this experience—the impact—is going to be. It is, however, a very vague reference to an impact.

Now the essay seems to have returned to a simple narrative.

grass that Nick would not be able to get to. The weed-whacker was heavier than I expected, and it wasn't until I thought I'd forgotten the extension cord that I realized it was gasoline-powered. I did not know how to start it.

I did not know what the rubber primer bulb was for. I did not know how to operate the choke. I knew I had to pull on the starter cord, but my strongest attempts didn't even produce a sputter. I was so intent on studying the contraption and trying to figure out what to do with the different parts that I didn't hear Nick walk up to me.

The reader might guess that Kyle's point has something to do with feeling stupid and needing to ask for help, but Kyle does not make it at all clear.

Back to narrative.

This is the third reference to Nick's insistence that Kyle should have asked. We are probably certain that that is the "important lesson" Kyle learned that day, but he has not made it explicit at all.

Finally, in the next-to-last paragraph, Kyle specifies his point. By now, however, it is too late. Whatever relevance or significance any of the previous details has is lost in our not knowing this point. Kyle has essentially failed to "Engage and orient [his] reader by setting out a problem, situation, or observation ..." from the beginning.

This is a rather silly statement since we know that Kyle is in the first semester of his sophomore year. That means this important lesson has stuck with him for, maybe, two or three months at the most.

There is nothing wrong with an analogy, but a doctor/patient comparison does not fit in the context of Nick and the landscape company.

We finally have some statement of significance, but it is too little too late. The prompt did not instruct Kyle to narrate an experience but to evaluate it. He was also instructed, not only to state the impact of the experience, but also to evaluate its impact. Why is this an important lesson for Kyle to have learned? In what ways is it important?

Again, he told me that I should have asked how to start the thing.

He laid the machine on the ground, opened the choke, squeezed the bulb a couple of times, gave one quick pull on the rope and the machine roared. Nick shook his head, and returned to his work.

The rest of the day was a little better. I did know how to start the lawn mower. Now that I knew how to control the truck's gate and start the weed-whacker, I was able to work without any more help. But all day long, I could hear Nick grumbling that I should have asked.

That was when I realized that it wasn't the fact that I didn't know how to do it that made me look stupid; it was the fact that I pretended to know how when I didn't.

I learned an important lesson that day that lasted the entire summer and still stays with me. I won't learn anything if foolish pride makes me pretend I already know it. Like a person who has to admit he's sick and go to the doctor, I have to admit I don't know something. Then someone can teach me what I need to know, and I can learn.

Analysis of First Draft

What is this writer's point? A single, identifiable point is hard to isolate. At first, it seems as if the writer is going to tell a story about the difficulty of getting a job. Much of the essay is simple narrative, a chronological retelling of the events of his first day. Eventually, it seems as if the point has something to do with admitting when you don't know something and asking for instruction.

What is his angle? As unclear as the point is, the angle is even less clear. Everyone who works has a first job and a first day on that job. Most of those first days involved making mistakes and feeling stupid. There is nothing new or different or unique in this telling of this experience to make the reader like, dislike, pity, or admire the narrator.

What type or tone of voice has he created in his reader's mind? The voice and tone in this essay are not particularly distinctive, but there are a few attempts at a glibness or mild humor. The writer generally maintains an informal, conversational tone.

What techniques has this writer used to create this voice? This essay does not give the overall impression of control. While there is nothing particularly bad about this writer's voice, there is nothing particularly distinctive, either.

What specific details, facts, etc., make this experience real? One problem with this draft is that it contains quite a few details, most notably physical descriptions of Nick, the company uniform, and the machinery; but since there is no clearly discernable point, it is difficult to assess the relevance of these particular details. As it becomes more clear that the point has to do with the writer's learning a lesson about admitting what he does not know, some of these particular details do not seem relevant to the point. What did Nick's tallness, or thinness, or the name embroidered in red on his shirt have to do with the lesson the writer learned?

NOW you will plan your own essay to the same prompt. You will probably find it helpful to follow the process by which Kyle arrived at his first draft. Remember that Kyle brainstormed, took notes on several possible topics, and developed each of them to see which one would yield the best essay.

> Evaluate a significant experience, achievement, risk you have taken, or ethical dilemma you have faced and its impact on you.

STEP 1: Select a topic

What experiences lend themselves to a successful evaluation?

What point would you want to make in evaluating each of these potential topics?

> Go back and look at Kyle's thoughts in this step. Even in the selection of topics, you need to think about things like an interesting angle and sufficient and relevant details.

STEP 2: Develop a(n) slant/angle/hook

What will your angle be?

Where might you begin your evaluation?

What type or tone of voice do you want to create in your reader's mind?

STEP 3: Brainstorm, discuss, research

What specific details, facts, etc., will make this experience real and not merely hypothetical?

STEP 4: Outline

Remember, a variety of outline forms is available to you, and you should practice with as many as possible to find which one(s) work best for you.

STEP 5: Write your first draft

> Be your own first editor. Go back and look at the scorer's notes and analysis of Kyle's first draft and see if you can avoid some of the first-draft blunders Kyle has committed, especially those concerning clarifying the point early in the essay and selecting only the most relevant details.

STEP 6: Peer edit

You and your partner might find it helpful to use the same questions Kyle and his partner used:

What is this writer's point?

What is his/her angle?

What type or tone of voice has he/she created in his/her reader's mind?

What techniques has this writer used to create this voice?

What specific details, facts, etc., make this experience real?

STEP 7: Revised/final draft

After the peer edit, it's time to write a second draft. In many cases, due to time limitations, this second draft may have to be your final draft. That's why it's so important to make the first draft really count.

The first step in revising your draft, of course, should be to consider all of your editor's comments on your first draft and determine how to deal with them.

Remember that anyone you give your draft to for review and editing help wants only for you to succeed with this essay (otherwise, why else would you choose this person to review your essay?). You should, therefore, consider everything your editor has said and respond to it, even if your response is to explain why you are not changing something or are changing it in a different way from the one suggested. The final decision on any revision is yours, but *you must have a valid reason that you can explain in your own words* for disregarding an observation or suggestion made by your editor.

Here are Kyle's editor's comments and analysis, as well as Kyle's responses. The responses do not need to be written, but you must know that you understand what your editor is telling you, and you must know whether or not you are going to revise your essay accordingly (and why).

- The essay starts out pretty weakly. We can guess the "significant experience" has to do with Kyle's first summer job, but we don't yet have a clue to why it is significant or what its impact has been.

- The significance is still unclear. Is this essay going to be about the difficulty in finding a job? The father's help?

- With each paragraph, this essay seems to be developing into a description of the job. Kyle needs to be reminded that the prompt instructs him to *evaluate* the experience, not merely *narrate* it.

- These details are from Kyle's pre-writing work, but they don't seem relevant. Of course, without yet knowing what specifically is Kyle's point, it is hard to assess the relevance of any details he chooses to include.

- Again, we don't yet know Kyle's focus, and we do question the relevance of this information.

- This is the seventh paragraph. We're more than a page into Kyle's essay, and this is the first suggestion of what the significance of this experience—the impact—is going to be. It is, however, a very vague reference to an impact.

- Now the essay seems to have returned to a simple narrative.

- The reader might *guess* that Kyle's point has something to do with feeling stupid and needing to ask for help, but Kyle does not make it at all clear.

- Back to narrative.

- This is the third reference to Nick's insistence that Kyle should have asked. We are probably certain that that is the "important lesson" Kyle learned that day, but he has not made it explicit at all.

- Finally, in the next-to-last paragraph, Kyle specifies his point. By now, however, it is too late. Whatever relevance or significance any of the previous details has is lost in our not knowing this point. Kyle has essentially failed to "Engage and orient [his] reader by setting out a problem, situation, or observation ..." from the beginning.

- This is a rather silly statement since we know that Kyle is in the first semester of his sophomore year. That means this important lesson has stuck with him for, maybe, two or three months at the most.

- There is nothing wrong with an analogy, but a doctor/patient comparison does not fit in the context of Nick and the landscape company.

- We finally have some statement of significance, but it is too little too late. The prompt did not instruct Kyle to narrate an experience but to evaluate it. He was also instructed, not only to state the impact of the experience, but to evaluate its impact. Why is this an important lesson for Kyle to have learned? In what ways is it important?

And here is Kyle's reaction:

> The biggest problem seems to be with making my point clearer from the very beginning. I want this essay to be about the irony of making myself look stupid by not wanting to look stupid. I probably need to state that right in the first paragraph.
>
> I think that, if I take care of that point, the other problems will be easy fixes. I can include only details that show my stupidity...like why I didn't know how to start the weed-whacker.
>
> I think I understand the comments about the narrative. In most of my essay, I am simply telling the story. And the prompt says to "evaluate," not "describe." I think making my point earlier will also help me to cut out a lot of the narrative.
>
> The other comments I understand, too. The doctor analogy doesn't fit, and I have to explain why realizing I had made myself look stupid was important.

Analysis of First Draft

What is this writer's point? A single, identifiable point is hard to isolate. At first, it seems as if the writer is going to tell a story about the difficulty of getting a job. Much of the essay is simple narrative, a chronological retelling of the events of his first day. Eventually, it seems as if the point has something to do with admitting when you don't know something and asking for instruction.

> My point is that I was afraid of looking stupid, and so I ended up looking even more stupid by pretending I knew how to do things I didn't know how to do. I know I need to make that clear earlier.

What is his angle? As unclear as the point is, the angle is even less clear. Everyone who works has a first job and a first day on that job. Most of those first days involved making mistakes and feeling stupid. There is nothing new or different or unique in this telling of this experience to make the reader like, dislike, pity, or admire the narrator.

> Why was I so afraid of looking stupid? Because all of my older brothers are smarter and more accomplished than I am.
>
> What difference does it make that I had this experience and learned this lesson? Admitting what I don't know and asking is what is necessary to really learn in school... so this experience means I will do well in college.

What type or tone of voice has he created in his reader's mind? The voice and tone in this essay are not particularly distinctive, but there are a few attempts at a glibness or mild humor. The writer generally maintains an informal, conversational tone.

> I want the tone to be conversational and informal. Everyone has felt stupid at some time, and no one likes to feel stupid, so this is an experience everyone should be able to relate to.

What techniques has this writer used to create this voice? This essay does not give the overall impression of control. While there is nothing particularly bad about this writer's voice, there is nothing particularly distinctive, either.

> Contractions. Shorter sentences and paragraph. Maybe some direct address to the reader?

What specific details, facts, etc., make this experience real? One problem with this draft is that it contains quite a few details, most notably physical descriptions of Nick, the company uniform, and the machinery; but since there is no clearly discernable point, it is difficult to assess the relevance of these particular details. As it becomes more clear that the point has to do with the writer's learning a lesson about admitting what he does not know, some of these particular details do not seem relevant to the point. What did Nick's tallness, or thinness, or the name embroidered in red on his shirt have to do with the lesson the writer learned?

> The description of Nick isn't important, but I still think the description of the colored buttons and the parts of the weed-whacker are because they show how and why I was confused.
>
> To make the experience really seem real, maybe I should use some dialogue...maybe "describe" Nick through the way he talks...direct quotation...maybe even dialect.

Here is Kyle's revised draft. Notice how he has addressed the comments and suggestions his peer editor made. Read the essay and consider how it is stronger and more likely to make a positive impression on the admissions committee.

> Evaluate a significant experience, achievement, risk you have taken, or ethical dilemma you have faced and its impact on you.

No one likes to feel stupid, and if you're the youngest of five sons, and your older brothers include a chief surgical resident, a physics professor, and a first-year Harvard Law student, you already feel dumb enough without completely screwing up your first day at a new part-time job. I would be working for a lawn service, doing "edgework." That meant I would swing the weed-whacker around flower beds and stone walls, guide the edger along driveways and sidewalks, and the walking mower around places where the riding mower wouldn't fit.

This strong first sentence mentions the experience and suggests the terms by which it is going to be evaluated.

How hard could it be?

This one-sentence paragraph may work to establish voice, or it may distract the reader.

We got to the first house, and "Nick" expected me to know something about how to open the gate at the back of the truck and operate the elevator mechanism that lowered the riding mower out of the truck and raised it back in again. If it had been a matter of a couple of buttons—red for down and green for up or something—that would have been fine. But there were four buttons, red, green, blue, and yellow. And there was a black lever and a silver toggle switch. Nothing was labeled.

Nothing happened as I flipped the toggle switch back and forth, fiddled with the lever and pushed the buttons in every order I could think of. I think Nick sat on the mower waiting for his ride to the street for a full fifteen minutes before, grumbling what I think were curses, he jumped off the truck and lowered the gate.

It turns out the toggle switch controlled the power—on and off. The red button was indeed for down and green for up. The lever tilted the gate up when everything was stowed on the truck, and it was time to go to the next house. I never learned what the yellow and blue buttons were supposed to do.

"Ya' should of asked if ya' didn't know how to do it," Nick grumbled.

I just kind of shrugged my shoulders and muttered that I didn't want to seem stupid.

He handed me the weed-whacker. "Ya' know how to start it?" I think I heard more mockery in his voice than was actually there.

I nodded and walked over to the brick retaining wall where I was supposed to begin trimming the grass that Nick would not be able to get to. The weed-whacker was heavier than I expected, and it wasn't until I thought I'd forgotten the extension cord that I realized it was a gasoline-powered tool. I had no idea how to start it.

There was a little rubber bulb, a choke, and the cord to pull. I was so intent on studying the contraption and trying to figure out what to do with what that I didn't hear Nick huffing and puffing toward me.

"Ya' should of asked if ya' didn't know how to do it," he grumbled.

He laid the machine on the ground, opened the choke, squeezed the bulb a couple of times, gave one quick pull on the rope and the machine sputtered and smoked and roared. Shaking his head, Nick returned to his riding mower.

The rest of the day was a little better. I did know how to start the gasoline-powered walking mower, and once he showed me how to

This comment is very important. The prompt instructs the student to "evaluate" the experience, not to "narrate" the experience. This sentence brings the focus back to the theme of feeling stupid.

operate the truck's gate and start the weed-whacker, I was able to it without any more help. But all day long, sitting next to Nick in the truck and feeling stupid, I could hear him grumbling to me, Ya' should of asked if ya' didn't know how to do it.

I knew he was right. And it wasn't the fact that I didn't know how to do it that made me look stupid; it was the fact that I pretended to know how when I didn't.

The student makes certain to specify the point.

This isn't an essay about how, by the end of the summer, Nick and I became best friends and when my first son was born I named him Nick and my wife and I go to his house every Sunday for dinner. I don't think he ever liked me. Maybe he really did think I was stupid, or lazy, or something. Maybe he felt that I didn't keep up my end of the work, and he had to work harder that summer because of me.

This paragraph might be an unnecessary tangent, or it might help the student to establish his voice, give the reader a sense of the person behind the essay.

But I will always remember the important lesson he taught me my first day: I should ask if I don't know how to do something. At the end of the summer when school started again, I was in a chemistry lab. There was a lot I didn't know how to do. But I knew enough to ask.

This is a college application essay. This statement explains why this particular experience is relevant to the occasion.

I think I'll do well in college. I'm sure I'll face things I don't know or don't know how to do.

But I now know enough to ask.

Thanks to a disastrous first day at work and the fear of looking stupid.

This last sentence might be unnecessary. The student's point and the relevance of the chosen significant experience are already clear.

Analysis of Final Draft

What is this writer's point? The writer wants to establish that he has mastered the one crucial element of being educated—the ability to ask questions.

What is his angle? By providing the little bit of background about his successful older brothers and beginning with the admission that he is more or less afraid of feeling stupid, this writer makes himself a little vulnerable. This vulnerability is intended to emphasize that the writer is a real person, a high school student, someone who is still learning and growing.

What type or tone of voice has he created in his reader's mind? The voice and tone in this essay are not particularly distinctive, but there are a few attempts at a glibness or mild humor. The writer generally maintains an informal, conversational tone.

What techniques has this writer used to create this voice? The glibness is most apparent in the few single-sentence paragraphs, especially the second paragraph, "How hard could it be?" The rhetorical question reinforces the humorous intent. Relatively short paragraphs, attempts at recreating, "Nick's" voice and manner of speaking, and the use of contractions all contribute to an overall informal tone.

What specific details, facts, etc., make this experience real? Recreating Nick's actual words and manner of speaking is a powerful tool to help the writer recreate this experience. Listing specific components of the two machines that puzzled the writer—the colored buttons, silver toggle switch, the rubber bulb on the weed-whacker—allows the reader to experience the writer's confusion, not merely know the writer was confused.

POSSIBLE STEP 8: Rewrite Opportunity

MINI LESSON 1:

Journal Writing

Journal writing can be the most personal of all personal writing because it can indeed be intended never to be read by anyone other than the writer. Private journals can be written in any form, and journal writers often create their own conventions, even their own languages, to record thoughts, feelings, daily events, or impressions of the time period in which they live.

Because journal assignments tend to be short and informal—and some teachers require some kind of journal writing every day—you may be tempted to pass these writing opportunities off as throwaways. They can, however, be important tools to help you improve your overall writing.

Last year, we advised you to look at a journal opportunity from three different viewpoints: as a free-writing exercise, as light practice, or as heavy training— similar to the way an athlete or performer keeps in shape or prepares for a major event. All three purposes are worthwhile, and it is important for you to know what your goal is for each kind of exercise.

Journal as Free-writing Exercise

Free-writing, of course, involves the least planning of any type of writing. It is essentially a "mind-dump" of ideas on the assigned topic. Of course, you wouldn't necessarily intend anyone else to read a free-writing exercise, and you certainly wouldn't submit it for evaluation or grading.

Like Kyle, "**Maya**" plans to attend college. The daughter of two lawyers—her mother words for a non-profit legal aid organization, and her father is a public defender—she also intends to study law and maybe enter politics. Near the beginning of her school's second marking period, she arrived in her English class knowing that they were going to begin a new unit, reading William Shakespeare's *Macbeth*. As the teacher distributed copies of the play, students were instructed to respond in their journals to the following prompt, which was displayed in the front of the room.

> Renaissance philosopher and political scientist Niccolò Machiavelli is usually credited with the maxim "The end justifies the means," which is usually interpreted to mean that a minor immoral act is excusable if it is committed in order to achieve a greater good. How do you respond to this philosophy? What examples from your education or your own experiences can you provide to explain your view?

In the past, students have been invited to review the ideas recorded in their journals to inform more formal essays and their participation in class discussion, but Maya knows that journal entries are not graded. She also knows she has probably only fifteen or twenty minutes to write her entry, so she decides to simply free-write her response without following a "process."

Here is her entry:

This is a good example of a free-written paragraph. Maya is off to a quick start with her statement of disagreement and an example.

One benefit of this free-writing exercise is that Maya processes her thoughts and refines her ideas as she goes along. She knows she will not be penalized for changing her mind or not expressing herself perfectly.

Whatever ideas Maya can include can only help. In a free-write, she does not have to worry about organization, coherence, grammar, etc.

I do not agree that the end justifies the means. Look at what happened a couple of years ago when the banks collapsed. The executives of these banks sold bad loans to other banks, knowing those loans would fail, but they made enormous profits for their own banks. The banks that bought the loans lost a lot of money, and people who had invested in those banks lost their savings, their pensions, and sometimes their houses. But the immoral act of selling the bad loans was justified by the executives saying their actions were justified by the profits they made for their own banks. Another good example that hits closer to home would be cheating in school. Cheating is definitely wrong, but many students claim they do it only to raise their grades so they can get into a good college and have good careers. But a career based on cheating isn't really a "greater good." All of the patients of the doctor who cheated in school are cheated out of having a good doctor. All of the clients of a lawyer who cheated in school are cheated by not having a good lawyer. I think maybe a lot of revolutions and wars are also based on the false philosophy that the end justifies the means. A government sends young men and women to be killed for a "greater good." Some countries even take away their citizens' rights for the sake of a "greater good" like security or law and order. Benjamin Franklin even said something about a people willing to sacrifice their freedom for the sake of security deserved neither freedom nor security. He was sort of saying that the end of peace or security does not justify the means of imprisoning people illegally or limiting their freedom of speech or religion and so on. Maybe the point is that the end that is supposed to come about by immoral means never really comes about. The French Revolution did not create rights and prosperity for the people of France. The Russian Revolution did not improve the lives of most of the Russian peasants. A suspension of, like, the right to free speech or assembly will not make us any safer in the long run...only silenced, oppressed, and afraid. Like prisoners.

Time has run out, and Maya's teacher has begun the lesson. Still, Maya has managed to come around to a clear understanding of the maxim and her reasons for disagreeing.

Analysis of Free-write Journal Entry

What is this writer's point? Responding to the question of whether she agrees or disagrees with the "Machiavellian" principle that the end justifies the means, Maya clearly establishes her disagreement.

What is his/her angle? Maya draws on both historical, relatively current, and personal experiences to illustrate the reasons for her disagreement.

What type or tone of voice has he created in his reader's mind? This is a free-write, so there is no intentional attempt at tone or voice.

What techniques has this writer used to create this voice? N/A

What specific details, facts, etc., help this writer establish his/her point? Maya refers to the 2006–2007 economic crisis, the French and Russian Revolutions, and the current cheating trend in United States schools.

Journal as Light Practice

Last year, we compared the "Journal-as-light-practice" exercise to a person who exercises to keep in shape, or a person who dances, paints, sings, etc., as a hobby. Hobbyists and enthusiasts practice their art or skill essentially every day, and they achieve a certain degree of expertise. Their daily practice is not as intense as if they were preparing for a competition, but they strive to maintain— probably even increase—their skill.

Kyle's school is only a few weeks away from its state-mandated writing assessment, so his teacher is having the class practice every day by assigning a journal entry prompt. Her intent is to give the students opportunities to write under a tight deadline and without the benefit of preparation or time for editing and revision. Kyle knows his response to these prompts will not be graded, but he also knows that the essays he writes on the state assessment will be scored. He wants to do well on the assessment, so he does his best to make his journal entries not simply free-writes but actual attempts at organized and coherent essays.

Here is one of the daily prompts Kyle's teacher assigned:

> Explain the meaning of the proverb, "He who will not read is no better off than he who cannot read." Does your experience lead you to believe this to be true? Why or why not?

Here is Kyle's response:

So far, not a bad start for Kyle. He wastes no time explaining the meaning of the adage as the prompt assigns.

The adage "He who will not read is no better off than he who cannot read" is a comment on people's willful ignorance. It says that, even if you have been to school and consider yourself "educated," if you act stupidly or follow the crowd instead of being yourself, you are no different than someone who has never been to school. It's like the saying Forrest Gump made famous in his movie, "Stupid is as stupid does." From people I know in my own family and school, I would have to say that I think the saying is true. Stupid is as stupid does, and people who will not use the skill or knowledge they got in school might just as well have never gone to school in the first place. I see this especially in my uncle, who gets all of his opinions from one television source even though he has a Master's Degree and is a teacher in a private school. Some of the students in my school are just as stupid. A lot of our politicians also brag about their impressive degrees but will not listen to someone else or consider an opposing opinion, so that they are no better than people who have never had the opportunity to have their minds expanded by an education. In other words, if you can read, and you don't, then you're really no different than a person who never learned to read in the first place.

My uncle claims to be a well-educated man. He even brags that he is an educator, helping to shape the minds of tomorrow's citizens. He does have a Master's Degree from a decent school, but he teaches in a small private school that allows for only one viewpoint—no discussion, no exploration of other ideas, no room to question the official view. This same uncle, even though he must have read a lot while in college and graduate school, insists that schools today don't teach but indoctrinate. To me, though, indoctrination is what happens when you only get one view and you get graded on how well you can explain why you agree with it. When he is at home, my uncle watches only one news channel and soaks up everything the newscasters and commentators say. If anyone tries to watch another channel, my uncle yells insults at the other commentators. You cannot have a discussion with him about politics or religion. All you can do is let him talk while you nod. If you say anything, he gets angry, and the conversations turns into a shouting match.

A lot of kids in school are almost as bad as my uncle. The books and articles we read and the films and programs we watch expose us to all sorts of ideas and different views of the same topic. I don't think our teachers require us to agree with any particular ones or disagree with others, but we are always told to point out the strengths and weaknesses of someone's view or argument. To say that the argument is strong is not the same thing as agreeing with it. But a lot of kids only find strengths in arguments they already agree with, and they find weaknesses only in arguments they already disagree with. They're supposed to be getting an education—sort of metaphorically

It appears that Kyle has defaulted to a five-paragraph-essay structure, which is a good skill to practice for times when a timed, on-demand essay is assigned.

Typical of the five-paragraph essay, the first body paragraph will apparently elaborate on the first point mentioned in the introduction.

Kyle has a great deal of elaboration here, but the paragraph becomes something of a rant.

The use of slang is all right for this journal entry, but Kyle will have to be more careful of his word choice in an actual assessment essay.

The use of the word "metaphoric" is very effective and helps Kyle firmly establish his criticism on non-readers.

learning to read—but instead they choose to remain uneducated. They choose not to read.

Most of the politicians in today's government are no better. They have all been to school. Some have Doctorates or Law Degrees, and many attended Ivy League schools. But they don't act as if they have any more knowledge or understanding than kindergarteners or middle-school drop-outs. Like my uncle and the kids at school, these politicians only support bills they already agree with. There is no debate. They do not listen to each other. They do not try to learn from each other to understand why they believe the way they do. Why bother spending the time and money to get an education if you're not going to let that education make a difference in how you make your decisions and do your job?

This is a pretty strong conclusion, especially for a timed, on-demand journal entry.

This is what I think it means when they say, "The man who will not read is no better off than the man who cannot read." And I think it's true.

Analysis of "Light practice" Journal Entry

What is this writer's point? Kyle explains that he believes the adage speaks of the irony of educated people's acting in foolish and unenlightened manners. He provides examples from his family, his school, and society in general to support his contention that people do, indeed, hold on to their ignorance despite opportunities to learn and grow.

What is his/her angle? Kyle draws on both family, school, and society for his examples.

What type or tone of voice has he created in his reader's mind? The tone is somewhat casual—possibly too casual if this were an essay that was actually scored.

What techniques has this writer used to create this voice? In this case, they are not "techniques" as much as they are errors Kyle should pay attention to if he wants a more formal tone. Kyle uses slang ("kids"), second person, and rhetorical questions, all of which contribute to his conversational tone.

What specific details, facts, etc., help this writer establish his/her point? The only specific example is Kyle's uncle. The other examples are probably valid, but are never developed beyond the general category "kids at school" or "politicians in today's government."

Journal as Heavy Training

If some journaling is to the writer what light, daily exercise is to the athlete or performer, there are those times when the writer—still practicing and refining his or her craft—knows that a major event is coming up. The runner facing a marathon, the pianist preparing for an important recital, the singer practicing for a debut performance all practice more intensely than they do for a daily run or a few routine exercises. The practice begins to look like the performance. In some cases, the practice *is more intense* than the final performance.

Maya's teacher has begun assigning the class issue-based journal prompts partly because she wants the students to begin thinking about possible topics for their second-semester social studies research project. Here is one of the daily prompts Maya's teacher assigned:

> Given the current economic crisis and recent cuts to school budgets all across the country, how important is it for public schools to provide athletic and/or arts programs for their students? Why?

Maya knows that most issue questions like this one ask for both an opinion and factual support. As a student, she may feel that athletic programs are important, but she knows that without expert opinion, case studies, statistics, and so on, her opinion is just that—the opinion of a tenth-grader. She also knows that, although she does not have time in the 20 minutes the class has been given to complete this exercise to perform real research and collect actual facts and expert opinions, she wants to use this exercise as practice for her research project. She thinks a little harder and writes with a little more focus than she normally would on a journal exercise.

Here is her response to the prompt:

This poorly worded and factually inaccurate sentence can be forgiven in a journal entry. The point is that Maya does begin to introduce the issue, as stated in the prompt to her reader.

While Maya's writing is far from sophisticated, she does manage to bring her introduction around to the assigned topic.

Maya does establish her thesis, and she mentions the sub-points that she hopes will be developed in the body of the essay.

This is a very important realization. Since Maya is "in training" for her research paper, she is actually thinking in terms of what her research paper would need to include, even though she cannot include it here.

Maya has provided some nice details to illustrate the point she wants to make.

This nation of the United States is experiencing what might be the worst economic crisis in American History since the Great Depression of the 1920s. Everywhere you look, they're talking about budget cuts. Even schools are having to cut their budgets. Teachers and aides are being fired and educational programs are being cut. Some of these programs that are being cut are in the arts departments, art, music, drama, etc. They're regarded as unimportant or "fluff" courses. They are really important, though. Arts courses support what students learn in other courses like physics and math. They give them the chance to practice and really do the theories they learn in the other classes. Therefore, funding for school arts programs should not be cut.

Studies show that students who take band do better in math courses and math exams, especially those that do fractions. (I know that if this was my research paper, this is where I would put information I learned from my research.) Counting measures and keeping rhythm in music is all about fractions. A musician really understands the relationship of a whole note to a half note and a quarter note and so on. If a song is marked that a measure gets four beats, and the quarter-note gets one full beat, the musician has to do the math to figure out that half notes get two beats and eighth-notes get a half a beat. The person who writes the music has to make sure that, with all the half notes, quarter notes, and eighth-notes, each measure does not have more than four beats. So, taking band allows the student to practice these mathematical skills much better than just doing drills and word problems in the math book.

Music students also study things about sound and pitch and frequencies. There are devices they use to tune their instruments and to make sure their instruments are in tune with each other. This is physics. Composers learn music theory where they learn which sound frequencies create what pitches and what pitches will sound good together (harmony) and what will not (discord). This is all physics. (Information here from research. About sound physics and music composition.) And the study of acoustics is physics too.

Arts programs, like band, are important to students. They help them really learn difficult concepts like fractions and physics, and students who take band do better in these classes and on tests. Their funding should not be cut.

This paragraph is not as well developed as the previous one, and it might lead to a digression if this were the actual research paper, but it still shows that Maya understands what she wants to demonstrate in support of her thesis.

If this were an actual research paper, it would be a serious flaw that Maya comes to her conclusion before she has delivered on everything promised in her introduction. This being a journal exercise, however, it is possible that she simply ran out of time. Still, as a conclusion, this is not a bad paragraph. It recaps the material presented and returns to the thesis, which has been established as valid.

Analysis of "Heavy Training" Journal Entry

What is this writer's point? Maya's thesis is that public school arts programs, specifically band, serve an important academic function and should not be cut to accommodate shrinking budgets.

What is his/her angle? Her angle is that the skills students learn and practice in their music classes provide application and practice for the concepts learned in math and physics classes.

What type or tone of voice has he created in his reader's mind? Maya struggles as a writer, and this being a timed journal entry, there are enough problems with fundamental sentence formation and language use to make any discussion of tone or voice premature.

What techniques has this writer used to create this voice? N/A

What specific details, facts, etc., help this writer establish his/her point? The first body paragraph has the most helpful details: the explanations of note values and their relationship to both a whole note and to the overall count of a measure of music. The other paragraphs reveal an awareness of the need for details, but Maya does not succeed in making those discussions as concrete as in her first paragraph.

ASSIGNMENT 2:

The "significant person" essay

One prompt—like the "evaluate a significant experience" essay—can yield dozens of possible essays. Kyle's essay took a positive turn, which is consistent with his personality and overall view of life. Like Kyle, **Maya** (fictional name) is a first-semester sophomore.

She also plans to attend college but wants to stay closer to home and attend one of her state's high-ranking colleges.

Maya chose her essay prompt from the same Common Application page as Kyle, but her experiences and personality drew her to the essay that asks her to talk about a significant person rather than an experience. She did, however, organize the creation of her essay along the same steps as her classmate.

> Indicate a person who has had a significant influence on you, and describe that influence.

STEP 1: Select a Topic

Maya zeroes right in on the directive to "indicate a person…," so she immediately begins to list possible persons to write about. She also lists the persons' influences because she understands that the prompt instructs her to say something about that as well.

- **Uncle Dominic**: his teasing gave me a "thick skin."
- **Cousin Becca**: taught me patience the way she cared for U.J. when he got sick.
- **Mom**: always there for me. The time I had pneumonia and she stayed with me in the hospital for two nights.
- **Mr. Hutcherson, the drama teacher**—taught me to believe in myself and stretch myself.

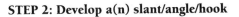

STEP 2: Develop a(n) slant/angle/hook

WHAT CAN MY ANGLE BE?

— **Uncle Dominic**—how I think his meanness was really just a cover because he was so sad and in pain?

— **Becca**—how much I admired her patience. She got teased even more than I did, and sometimes U.J. yelled and cursed at her, but she was the one who was able to show me how to be loving because he was sick and in such pain. But then she was really angry with me that time I babysat Gretchen, but I learned how important it is to think things through and make careful decisions.

— **Mr. Hutcherson**—when he sat down and told me that even though I hadn't auditioned well, I could still be involved, and that's how I started to get interested in light and sound—the tech aspects of theater.

> Note: A few red flags here. Maya has eliminated only one of her potential influential persons, and she is confusing the assigned topic: "Describe the influence" with the angle. Remember that the prompt directs her only to "indicate" the person, but to "describe" the influence.

WHERE DO I BEGIN MY ESSAY?

— I guess I'll begin by describing the person I choose, and then tell the story of how he or she influenced me and what I learned.

> Note: This is an early choice that Maya will eventually change to make her essay address the prompt's instruction to describe the influence.

WHAT TYPE OR TONE OF VOICE DO I WANT TO CREATE IN MY READER'S MIND?

— None of these stories is funny, so I think I'll sound serious.

STEP 3: Brainstorm, discuss, research

Maya is still missing the intent of the prompt. Because this is truly personal writing, she is supposed to reveal something about herself, not provide a character sketch of some other person.

Still, the process of brainstorming details and images helped her decide that an essay about "Uncle Dominic" might disturb her readers, and her relationship with Mr. Hutcherson was a fairly typical mentor-student relationship. Finally, she chose her cousin Becca as her person, and the loss of confidence she experienced after a particularly disastrous babysitting experience.

Becca
   – very independent, very strong-willed, very determined.
   – does not give up and very rarely asks for help.
   – watching how she took care of her father during his last months was a real inspiration to me.
   – left alone to raise daughter and run house (husband deployed).
   – never complained.
   – got married five years ago.
   – small wedding.
   – Uncle Dominic was so sick.
   – only one attendant each.
   – dinner for the immediate families at a nice restaurant.
   – only a weekend trip to Williamsburg for a honeymoon.
   – did not want to be too far away or be gone for too long in case something happened to Uncle Dominic.
   – husband, Travis, is in the Air Force.
   – deployed to Afghanistan a few weeks after their wedding.
   – came home in time to see Gretchen be born, and then he was sent back to Afghanistan.
   – lived in Base Housing.
   – had friends and—support of other AF wives.
   – we had her and Gretchen over a lot.
   – we were not close growing up.
   – almost 10 years older than I am.

The night she called me to babysit.
   – Mom said she wanted me to help out my cousin.
   – I had a test the next day and thought the house would be quiet to study.
   – the time she asked me to babysit—just about the only time she ever asked for help.
   – I felt so bad when I messed up, and she was so angry at me that I decided I would never babysit again.

Her house
- nice but not fancy.
- second-hand furniture did not match.
- sofa in the living room was green and yellow stripes with flowers.
- the one chair was a dull brown faux suede material.

Outside
- red brick exterior.
- bay window with little panes.
- cement and brick stoop.
- overgrown hedges under window, next to stoop.
- cement walk to sidewalk.
- dim streetlight across street.

Games I played with Gretchen
- colored
- stacking blocks
- building blocks

Books I read to Gretchen
- Good Night, Gorilla
- Ten Little Ladybugs
- Caps for Sale
- Good Night, Moon

> Note: Like Kyle, Maya knows she is giving herself more material than she is going to need. It is always easier to delete excess material than to run out while writing and have to come back to this step. Notice also, however, that indeed none of Maya's notes addresses the fact that the prompt directs her to describe the influence her chosen person has had on her.

STEP 4: Outline

Looking at the details she has noted, Maya realized that she has already begun to categorize and organize the ideas and information she thought she'd use in her essay, so she decided to follow an informal outline format. However, her outline that follows still bears a striking resemblance to the formal, academic outline. Notice also that, when she re-examined the exact wording of the prompt, she did rethink some of the ideas she had previously written.

My cousin Becca taught me how to be independent and sensible.
- Her reaction to what happened the one night I ever babysat for her convinced me I'd never babysit again.
- But I learned how important it is to think a problem through.

> This is an idea Maya has added after looking at the prompt again. But it will not be enough simply to add this idea to her introduction without developing it in the body of the essay and making it the focus.

Becca is
- very independent, very strong-willed, very determined.
- does not give up and very rarely asks for help.

She was her father, my Uncle Dominic's, sole caretaker the last two months before he died.
- never complained
- Watching how she took care of her father during his last months was a real inspiration to me.
- had only a small wedding because U.J. was so sick.
- only one attendant each
- dinner for the immediate families at a nice restaurant
- only a weekend trip to Williamsburg for a honeymoon.
- did not want to be too far away or be gone for too long in case something happened to Uncle Dominic.

> Given the assigned prompt, Maya should consider why this is all relevant. Certainly, the reader will need to know something about the influential person, but Maya is still neglecting the directive to "describe the influence."

Her husband, Travis, is in the Air Force.
- deployed to Afghanistan a few weeks after their wedding.
- came home in time to see Gretchen be born, and then he was sent back to Afghanistan.
- left alone to raise daughter and run house (husband deployed).

> Some of this might be relevant, but Maya will need to be careful to point out that relevance to her readers.

The night she called me to babysit.
- my Mom said she wanted me to help out my cousin.

- plus, I figured her house would be quiet so I could study.

- the time she asked me to babysit—just about the only time she ever asked for help.

First everything went well
- played games

- colored

- stacking blocks

- building blocks

- read books

- Good Night, Gorilla

- Ten Little Ladybugs

- Caps for Sale

- Good Night, Moon

> Certainly, Maya understands that she needs details to make her essay stand out, but there doesn't seem much point to listing the names of the games and books unless they have a direct bearing on the central topic of the essay.

- she went to bed

Then, I messed up

> Maya will realize that, at some point, she'll have to reveal how she "messed up," so her reader will be able to appreciate the cousin's anger and the impact or influence it had on Maya.

- she was so angry
- I decided I would never babysit again.

> If Maya were to review this outline before writing her first draft, she might realize that her essay begins by promising to discuss how Cousin Becca helped her become independent and wise. By the end, however, the point seems to have changed to her decision never to babysit again. *One important function of an outline is to diagnose problems with the structure, organization, or content of an essay before you are committed to a full draft that can be several pages long and take several days to compose.*

STEP 5: Write your first draft

Although we have been aware of some fairly severe focus and organizational problems in Maya's plan, especially her outline, Maya believes she has followed every step of the process so far and is prepared to write an essay that completely addresses the prompt. Read this first draft and the commentary of a scorer who also read it. Consider the essay's strengths and weaknesses and what Maya can do to improve this attempt in her revision steps.

This sentence does approach an introduction to Maya's topic. The "significant person" is her cousin Becca. The influence, however, is less clear. Will it have something to do with Maya's decision never to babysit again, or will Maya focus on how her cousin taught her to be independent and sensible?

We can already see that Maya is overemphasizing the "indicate a person" part of the prompt. This paragraph is introducing a study of Becca, which is not what the prompt requests.

Even while talking about her cousin, Maya has slipped into a tangent.

Even though we are not very close, my cousin Becca has been one of the most influential people in my life. Her reaction to what happened the one night I ever babysat for her convinced me I'd never babysit again. But I also learned how important it is to think a problem through, and it taught me how to be independent and sensible. My cousin is ten years older than I am, and she has a four-year-old daughter. Becca is a very independent, very strong-willed, very determined young woman. When things get difficult for her, she does not give up and she very rarely asks for help. Her husband, Travis, is in the Air Force. He was deployed to Afghanistan a few weeks after their wedding. He was able to come home in time to see his daughter Gretchen be born. Then he was sent back to Afghanistan. Becca was left alone to raise daughter and run her house.

She was also, before she got married, her father's primary caretaker when he was sick and dying. During Uncle Dominic's last two months, she never complained even though Uncle Dominic was very mean to her, even sometimes yelling and cursing at her. I think this was mostly because he was in so much pain and probably angry and frightened because he knew he was dying. Watching how Becca took care of her father during his last months was a real inspiration to me. She and Travis only had a small wedding because U.J. was so sick. She had no bridesmaids, just a maid of honor, and he had only a best man, no groomsmen. The reception was only a dinner for the immediate families, but it was at a nice restaurant. They only took a weekend trip to Williamsburg for a honeymoon. Becca did not want to be too far away or be gone for too long in case something happened to Uncle Dominic.

Two years ago, when Becca's daughter was two, my cousin called me in a panic and asked if I could babysit for her that night. She said her daughter would be all ready for bed, and after I put her down, I'd have the rest of the evening to do whatever I wanted—watch TV, play with her Wii, study.

I did have a big test the next day, so a night of uninterrupted studying sounded like a good idea. My house tended to be a little rowdy with my three younger brothers. First everything went well. My little cousin wasn't really ready for bed, so we played a few games. We colored, made huge towers out of stacking blocks, and built a fairy castle out of building blocks. Then, my little cousin seemed to be getting tired, so I let her sit in my lap and I read her a few books—Good Night, Gorilla, Ten Little Ladybugs, Caps for Sale, and Good Night, Moon. Finally, she fell asleep, and I put her in her crib.

Then, I messed up. The doorbell rang. At first, I figured I knew better than to answer it, but it rang again, and I thought maybe Becca was back and had forgotten her key. When I answered the door, no one was there, and when I stepped out to the sidewalk to see if anyone was there, my cousin had climbed from her crib, and she shut the door behind me. I was locked outside, and she was locked inside.

Becca was only gone about three hours, so I was outside for less than an hour when she got

Maya's account is full of specific details and examples, but this is still a tangent, having virtually nothing to do with the directives in the prompt.

Maya seems to be bringing her essay around to the babysitting experience, and also to her cousin's influence on her, but there is no transition to ease and clarify the shift in topics between these two paragraphs.

Maya is certainly providing a lot of details, but they do not seem relevant to either of the introduced points.

In addition to this essay's content and organization problems, there are several language irregularities, especially the placement of modifiers like *only* and the use of incorrect verb tenses.

This does call to mind one of the points Maya hints at in her introduction, but if learning to be responsible is going to be the influence, it needs to be much more elaborated upon.

Finally, this is a pretty weak conclusion. The "influence" that Maya has written her college application about turns out to be her learning that she wasn't meant to be a babysitter.

back. When she let us into the house, my little cousin was curled up on the chair we sat in while I was reading to her sound asleep. Becca was very angry with me.

She kept telling me how irresponsible I was, how she thought she could trust me but really couldn't, and how she'd never be asking me to babysit again and she'd tell my mother that she shouldn't let me babysit either.

But I didn't need my cousin or my mother to tell me to never babysit again. I decided while sitting on the stoop of my cousin's house, thinking about everything that could be happening to my little cousin, and how it was all my fault.

I just knew that I was not meant to be a babysitter.

Analysis of First Draft

What is this writer's point? It is difficult to identify a single main idea or point to this essay. It is part character study and part narrative.

What is his/her angle? The truth is, this essay has severe enough problems in focus, organization, development, and language that it is premature to examine the essay for this level of control and planning.

What type or tone of voice has he/she created in his reader's mind? If there is an identifiable voice at all, it is conventional but informal.

What techniques has this writer used to create this voice? The main reason there is no distinct voice in this essay is that the writer does not seem to have done anything intentional to create a voice.

What specific details, facts, etc., make this experience real? The writer provides a wealth of details, facts about her cousin's wedding, the uncle's illness, and so on. These details do not develop one overall idea or point. Because the essay itself lacks focus, the details come across as tangential and irrelevant.

Now plan and write your own essay to the same prompt. You will probably find it helpful to follow the process outlined below. A discussion of how the student discussed above responded to each step's guiding questions should model the type of thinking you are doing at this point.

> Indicate a person who has had a significant influence on you, and describe that influence.

STEP 1: Select a Topic

About whom do you feel comfortable or excited about writing?

What significant influence has each of these persons had on your life?

What point would you want to make in sharing these influences with your reader?

> Think about how Maya's misinterpretation of the directives in the prompt leads to an essentially failed attempt at addressing the prompt. As you brainstorm potential topics and narrow the list to your final selection, remember that you are instructed only to "indicate" the person, but to "describe" the influence.

STEP 2: Develop a(n) slant/angle/hook

What will your angle be?

Where might you begin your essay?

What type or tone of voice do you want to create in your reader's mind?

STEP 3: Brainstorm, discuss, research

What specific details, facts, etc., will make this experience real and not merely hypothetical?

> Remember your focus. Remember your purpose and audience. Certainly, jot down every fact and detail that occurs to you, but do not make Maya's mistake of thinking you need to include every detail you think of in your outline and essay.

STEP 4: Outline

Remember there is a variety of outline forms available to you, and you should practice with as many as possible to find which one(s) work best for you.

STEP 5: Write your first draft

Go back and look at the scorer's notes and analysis of Maya's first draft and see if you can avoid some of the first-draft blunders Maya has committed, especially those concerning actually meeting the demands of the prompt.

STEP 6: Peer Edit

Again, here are some review questions you might find helpful.

What is this writer's point?

What is his/her angle?

What type or tone of voice has he/she created in his/her reader's mind?

What techniques has this writer used to create this voice?

What specific details, facts, etc., make this experience real?

STEP 7: Revised/Final Draft

Remember that the person editing your draft wants only for you to succeed with this essay. The final decision on all revisions is yours, but *you must have a valid reason that you can explain in your own words* for disregarding an observation or suggestion made by your editor.

Here are the comments Maya's editors noted while reading her essay and the analysis the editor drafted afterward.

- This sentence does approach an introduction to Maya's topic. The "significant person" is her cousin Becca. The influence, however, is less clear. Will it have something to do with Maya's decision never to babysit again, or will Maya focus on how her cousin taught her to be independent and sensible?

- We can already see that Maya is overemphasizing the "indicate a person" part of the prompt. This paragraph is introducing a study of Becca, which is not what the prompt requests.

- Even while talking about her cousin, Maya has slipped into a tangent.

- Maya's account is full of specific details and examples, but this is still a tangent, having virtually nothing to do with the directives in the prompt.

- Maya seems to be bringing her essay around to the babysitting experience, and also to her cousin's influence on her, but there is no transition to ease and clarify the shift in topics between these two paragraphs.

- Maya is certainly providing a lot of details, but they do not seem relevant to either of the introduced points.

- In addition to this essay's content and organization problems, there are several language irregularities, especially the placement of modifiers like *only* and the use of incorrect verb tenses.

- This does call to mind one of the points Maya hints at in her introduction, but if learning to be responsible is going to be the influence, it needs to be much more elaborated upon.

- Finally, this is a pretty weak conclusion. The "influence" that Maya has written her college application about turns out to be her learning that she wasn't meant to be a babysitter.

And here is Maya's response:

I think I understand the problem about my "influence" not being clear. By the end of the essay, I seem to have more to say about the babysitting experience and how that affected me, so I think that is what I will choose for my "influence."

If I don't talk about Becca's marriage and taking care of Uncle Dominic, that should take care of some of the irrelevant details. Maybe I also don't need to list all of the games we played and books we read.

I'll work on the language problems. I know "only" should go before the thing it is modifying—"I read only one book" ... NOT ... "I only read one book." I'll review verb tenses.

That last comment—about the weak conclusion. I need to say more about learning how to be more responsible.

Analysis of First Draft

What is this writer's point? It is difficult to identify a single main idea or point to this essay. It is part character study and part narrative.

> My point is going to be that the disaster babysitting taught me to be more responsible.

What is his angle? The truth is, this essay has severe enough problems in focus, organization, development, and language that it is premature to examine the essay for this level of control and planning.

> I think I could do something with Becca's anger. When someone is angry at you, it's usually a bad thing, but this turned into a positive experience. Or at least I learned a positive lesson.

What type or tone of voice has he created in his reader's mind? If there is an identifiable voice at all, it is conventional but informal.

> I don't see the need to be sarcastic, or funny or anything. As long as I'm not to formal or "stuffy" sounding, I should be okay.

What techniques has this writer used to create this voice? The main reason there is no distinct voice in this essay is that the writer does not seem to have done anything intentional to create a voice.

> Maybe I should avoid contractions because they tend to be too informal. I'll pay attention to my sentence structure because sentences that are too long or complex might make the whole thing too formal.

What specific details, facts, etc., make this experience real? The writer provides a wealth of details, facts about her cousin's wedding, the uncle's illness, and so on. These details do not develop one overall idea or point. Because the essay itself lacks focus, the details come across as tangential and irrelevant.

> I know I need to cut all that out about their marriage and Uncle Dominic. Maybe I need more details about being locked out and why it was irresponsible of me.

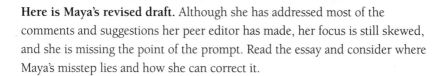

Here is Maya's revised draft. Although she has addressed most of the comments and suggestions her peer editor has made, her focus is still skewed, and she is missing the point of the prompt. Read the essay and consider where Maya's misstep lies and how she can correct it.

There are not all that many jobs available for teenagers. There is the "food service industry," which is basically flipping burgers at a fast food or busing tables at a diner that does not serve alcohol. There is cashiering at the Food Festival on Lambert Boulevard. And then there is babysitting.

I babysat once, and I will never babysit again.

My cousin is ten years older than I am, and she has a four-year-old daughter. Two years ago, when the daughter was two, my cousin called me in a panic and asked if I could babysit for her that night. She said her daughter would be all ready for bed, and after I put her down, I would have the rest of the evening to do whatever I wanted—watch TV, play with her Wii, study.

I did have a big test the next day, so a night of uninterrupted studying sounded like a good idea. My house tended to be a little rowdy with my three younger brothers.

I went to my cousin's house, and everything started out fine. My little cousin was in her pjs and nighttime diaper. We sat on the floor while we colored and played with blocks, and we snuggled in a "comfy chair" while I read her a couple of books. And then I put her in her crib and went back to the den to study. It was quiet for maybe 10 minutes, and then my little cousin, giggling and not at all sleepy, toddled into the den and climbed up into the chair with me.

Apparently she knew how to climb out of her crib.

I let her sit with me a few minutes, and then I put her back in her crib.

On the one hand, Maya has moved the revelation of the "influence" to earlier in her essay, but she seems not to appreciate that this simple decision is not necessarily a "significant influence."

This background might prove helpful. Still Maya needs to be careful not to let her essay slip into a retelling of the story.

We are five paragraphs into this second draft, and it seems as though Maya is, indeed, going to retell her story. A reader expects that she will remember to bring the essay around to a point about the significance of the experience and its impact.

So far, this essay is still nothing more than a retelling of the story. While the focus is clearer, this is still not what this prompt asks for.

Maya did say that she was going to avoid contractions in order to maintain a conventional tone, but some of the verb phrases she ends up with as a result are awkward and actually achieve the opposite effect, creating the "stuffy" tone she wanted to avoid.

This small digression does help to give the reader a glimpse of the writer's personality, but we still do not have a clear sense of the influence Maya wants to describe.

The reference to horror movies is entertaining and further develops a sense of Maya as a person.

Maya is still having problems with her choice of verb tense.

She climbed out and joined me in the den three more times before I finally had to get a little firm and tell her to stay in bed and go to sleep. I went back to the den and my studying. I was not disturbed again for at least a half hour. And then the doorbell rang.

Now, I am a big girl, and my mother has taught me right, so I know better than to answer the door when I am in someone else's house, and it is late at night, and I am alone in the house. But the doorbell rang a second time, and I was a little afraid my cousin would wake up. So I went to the door and peeked out the window on the side of the door. No one was there.

I still do not know why I did what I did next. I mean, I am not a stupid person, and even at the age of 13, I was pretty savvy. Firstly, you do not open the door when you are a woman alone in a house that is not yours, and it is late at night. Secondly, I have watched enough horror movies to know that you never open the door and look outside. And you never actually go outside when there is no one there.

But I opened the door and stepped outside to see who had rung the doorbell.

There was no one on the stoop or on the sidewalk. Yes, I walked down to the sidewalk and looked up and down. No one was there, and no one attacked me with an ax or knife or anything. When I turned around to walk back to the stoop, I saw a box by the door. The doorbell must have been a late mailman or UPS guy or someone dropping off the package.

My little cousin was also standing at the door, giggling. I guess the doorbell had woken her up. As I bent down to pick up the box, she giggled, and I heard the door click shut. The click made me feel especially uncomfortable. I knew, even before I tried the door, that I was locked out.

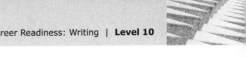

I was locked out, I did not have a key, and my little cousin was inside all alone.

I tried to talk to her through the door, reassure her that everything was going to be all right. I asked her to open the door, but I did not even know if she knew how. I am not even sure she could hear me through the door. I walked around the house to see if any windows were open, but they were all closed and locked. I thought about breaking one, but I did not want to scare my little cousin, and I knew coming home to a broken window would make my cousin really angry.

Not that she would be thrilled to come home to a daughter who could be hurt and bleeding—or worse—inside the house while the babysitter was locked outside the house.

Either way, I did not know what to do, so I sat on the front stoop with my back to the door. I kept up a nonstop train of meaningless blabber, talking to my little cousin just in case she was still on the other side of the door and could hear me. I told her that everything was going to be fine, that it was funny that she was inside all alone and I was outside all alone, that her mommy would be home soon. And every once in a while, I told her to try to open the door. I also stood up a couple of times and tried to peek into the window by the door, but I could not see anything. I could not tell where my little cousin was or what she was doing.

Finally, after what seemed like hours, my cousin came home. It turns out that she was gone for less than three hours, so I was on the porch for less than an hour. It seemed like so much longer!

My cousin was very angry with me. Even after she let us into the house, and we found my little cousin safe and asleep on the chair where I was studying. She kept telling me how irresponsible

Since the narrative is being told in the past tense and the cousin's being gone occurred before Maya realized it, the chronology requires the past perfect tense here.

Here, she repeats the same verb tense error. The child is asleep on the chair where Maya had been studying.

Again, unless the cousin still thinks she can trust Maya, the past perfect tense is needed here.

This is still, unfortunately, a low-scoring essay. Maya still does not address the directives of the prompt—to "indicate" the person and "describe" the influence. Her focus is clearer, but this draft is still not ready to be submitted.

This single, short sentence is definitely a stronger ending than Maya's previous draft, but it still does not end the essay on a point that addresses the directives of the prompt.

I was, how she thought she could trust me but really could not, and how she would never be asking me to babysit again and she would tell my mother that she should not let me babysit either.

But I did not need my cousin or my mother to tell me never to babysit again. I decided while sitting on the stoop of my cousin's house, thinking about all of the dangerous mischief my little cousin could be getting into, all the damage she could be causing, and how it was all my fault.

I just knew that I was not meant to be a babysitter.

My cousin did not even pay me.

Analysis of Revised Draft

What is this writer's point? The point is still unclear. The prompt instructs Maya to discuss the person's impact on her, and Maya focuses too heavily on the narrative.

What is his angle? The main idea is still too obscure. Might the reader infer that Maya wants to describe a positive outcome, a lesson learned, from her cousin's anger?

What type or tone of voice has he created in his reader's mind? Still a fairly nondescript, mildly formal tone.

What techniques has this writer used to create this voice? There is really no evidence that Maya has done anything intentional to achieve a consciously desired tone. There is some attempt at voice when Maya speaks directly to the reader to describe her thirteen-year-old self.

What specific details, facts, etc., make this experience real? The pre-bedtime routine and the "little cousin's" trick of climbing out of bed do a nice job setting up the crisis at the heart of this narrative.

POSSIBLE STEP 8: Rewrite Opportunity

Kyle's second draft was fully good enough to submit either for a grade or for review by his college admissions committee. A second revision might have helped him polish a good piece into a fine one, but there was really nothing more he needed to do to improve the fundamental focus, structure, or content of his essay.

Maya, on the other hand, still has a draft that fails to address the assigned prompt, focusing more on the experience than on the influence. It also still contains language errors that weaken its overall impact. Although most writing assessments and school assignments leave time for only a first and second draft, all professional writers know that their final, published work is often the product of three, four, even five or more drafts.

Some school and college writing programs also allow for a final rewrite after the work has been submitted and scored.

Although she was disappointed by the low score her essay received, Maya took the scorer's comments to heart and revised her essay a second time. Here is her third draft, along with the scorer's comments. Notice how Maya returns to some of her earliest material to provide her reader with a fuller understanding of her cousin. Notice how she also manages to approach the discussion of her cousin from its proper perspective, as a person who had an influence on her. Finally, notice how Maya succeeds in translating a narrative of her babysitting experience into a description of a valid, important influence.

> I'd like to think that I am a responsible person, level-headed, and cool in an emergency. Of course, I thought the same thing last year when my cousin Becca asked me to babysit for her. I found out that night that I wasn't as mature as I thought, but it took me placing my little cousin's life in danger and Becca getting very, very angry with me to learn how much I still needed to learn and to grow up. If Becca hadn't asked me to babysit, I might never have had the chance to face the consequences of my foolishness, so my messing up while babysitting and her getting angrier than I'd ever seen her had a very important influence on me.

Although there are some notable language problems and awkward sentence constructions in the opening paragraphs of Maya's previous two drafts. Her focus is clearly on her own developing sense of responsibility and the influence of her cousin Becca on that growth.

My cousin is ten years older than I am. We were not close when I was growing up, but when her father, my Uncle Dominic, became ill, we became a little closer, and I got to see what a truly remarkable person my cousin was. She moved home to care for her father. It could not have been easy for her because she left a good job and a nice apartment in Chicago.

But I never heard her complain. I never heard her say a harsh or angry word to Uncle Dominic, even when he was at his worst and would yell and curse at her. She took his abuse and cared for him patiently and lovingly right to the day he died.

When she and her husband, Travis, got married, she sacrificed a fancy wedding and big honeymoon because of my uncle. After Uncle Dominic died, and Travis was deployed to Afghanistan, Becca still was not a complainer, and I never heard her yell at her little daughter, Gretchen.

Two years ago, when Gretchen was two, my cousin called me in a panic and asked if I could babysit for her that night. She said Gretchen would be all ready for bed, and after I put her down, I would have the rest of the evening to do whatever I wanted—watch TV, play with her Wii, study.

I did have a big test the next day, so a night of uninterrupted studying sounded like a good idea. My house tended to be a little rowdy with my three younger brothers.

I went to Becca's house, and everything started out fine. My little cousin was in her pjs and nighttime diaper. We sat on the floor while we colored and played with blocks, and we snuggled in a "comfy chair" while I read her a couple of books. And then I put her in her crib and went back to the den to study. It was quiet for maybe 10 minutes, and then my little cousin, giggling and not at all sleepy, toddled into the den and climbed up into the chair with me.

Much of this information is developed from material Maya generated in the earliest steps of her process and tried to include in her first draft. Then, it was irrelevant because she had no clear focus, and there was no compelling reason to tell the reader all of this. Now, it provides important insight into Becca so that the reader will appreciate the cousin's reaction to the event and its impact on Maya.

Apparently she knew how to climb out of her crib.

I let her sit with me a few minutes, and then I put her back in her crib.

She climbed out and joined me in the den three more times before I finally had to get a little firm and tell her to stay in bed and go to sleep. I went back to the den and my studying. I was not disturbed again for at least a half hour. And then the doorbell rang.

Now, I am a big girl, and my mother has taught me right, so I know better than to answer the door when I am in someone else's house, and it is late at night, and I am alone in the house. But the doorbell rang a second time, and I was a little afraid my cousin would wake up. So I went to the door and peeked out the window on the side of the door. No one was there.

I still do not know why I did what I did next. I mean, I am not a stupid person, and even at the age of 13, I was pretty savvy. Firstly, you do not open the door when you are a woman alone in a house that is not yours, and it is late at night. Secondly, I have watched enough horror movies to know that you never open the door and look outside. And you never actually go outside when there is no one there.

So I opened the door and stepped outside to see who had rung the doorbell.

There was no one on the stoop or on the sidewalk. Yes, I walked down to the sidewalk and looked up and down. No one was there, and no one attacked me with an ax or knife or anything. When I turned around to walk back to the stoop, I saw a box by the door. The doorbell must have been a late mailman or UPS guy or someone dropping off the package.

We still have a lot of narrative here, but Maya will bring it around to at least a brief discussion of how this experience and her cousin's reaction influenced her.

In her earlier drafts, Maya predicted her cousin would be "very angry." She has most likely softened that description in order to emphasize the cousin's patience and to give her anger at the end of the essay more impact.

My little cousin was also standing at the door, giggling. I guess the doorbell had woken her up. As I bent down to pick up the box, she giggled, and I heard the door click shut. The click made me feel especially uncomfortable. I knew, even before I tried the door, that I was locked out.

I was locked out, I did not have a key, and my little cousin was inside all alone.

I tried to talk to her through the door, reassure her that everything was going to be all right. I asked her to open the door, but I did not even know if she knew how. I am not even sure she could hear me through the door. I walked around the house to see if any windows were open, but they were all closed and locked. I thought about breaking one, but I did not want to scare my little cousin, and I didn't think Becca would want to come home to a broken window.

Not that she would be thrilled to come home to a daughter who could be hurt and bleeding—or worse—inside the house while the babysitter was locked outside the house.

Either way, I did not know what to do, so I sat on the front stoop with my back to the door. I kept up a nonstop train of meaningless blabber, talking to my little cousin just in case she was still on the other side of the door and could hear me. I told her that everything was going to be fine, that it was funny that she was inside all alone and I was outside all alone, that her mommy would be home soon. And every once in a while, I told her to try to open the door. I also stood up a couple of times and tried to peek into the window by the door, but I couldn't see anything. I could not tell where Gretchen was or what she was doing.

Finally, after what seemed like hours, my cousin came home. It turns out that she was gone for less than three hours, so I was on the porch for less than an hour. It seemed like so much longer!

The cousin I had never seen lose her cool all the while she cared for her dying father, who'd never raised her voice to her daughter even though she must have been lonely and frightened with her husband overseas, was very angry with me. Even after she let us into the house, and we found Gretchen safe and asleep on the chair where I was studying, she kept yelling at me, telling me how irresponsible I was, how she'd thought she could trust me but really couldn't. She said she would never ask me to babysit again, and she would tell my mother that she shouldn't let me babysit either.

My cousin's anger surprised me and hurt me. But I knew I deserved it. She was only telling me what I had been thinking while sitting on the stoop of her house, thinking about all of the dangerous mischief Gretchen could be getting into, all the damage she could be causing, and how it was all my fault.

A responsible person would never have gotten into the position I was in. I knew that I was not meant to be a babysitter. I had too much growing up to do.

Although my cousin would not even pay me for the night, I ended up getting something far more important than money. When you are entrusted to care for something as precious as someone's child, you must be more careful and vigilant than you've probably ever been before. If your best instincts tell you not to do something, you should listen to them and not do it.

There is absolutely no room for error.

Contrasting the earlier picture of Becca with her current anger allows the reader to appreciate the impact. Maya finally understands the prompt and is transitioning from narrative to description of the influence.

Maya still has a problem with the placement of "only," but she does seem to have figured out the use of the past perfect tense.

Here is where Maya successfully brings her narrative around to a clear statement of the influence her cousin's anger had on her.

While not a perfect ending (the use of second person is a little amateurish and the reference to both "being vigilant" and "listening to [one's] instincts" confuses the focus a little), these final two paragraphs do establish an impact better than Maya's previous two attempts.

Analysis of Second Revision

What is this writer's point? Maya's point is that the anger her normally calm and compassionate cousin displayed motivated Maya to re-evaluate herself and decide that she was still rather immature in some areas of her life.

What is his angle? The angle is in the exposition about the cousin and narrative, the events that led to the cousin's anger. While Maya herself did nothing really "wrong," and the cousin is normally understanding and forgiving, the odd combination of events that night and the cousin's reaction provided the occasion for reflection and growth.

What type or tone of voice has he created in his reader's mind? It does seem as if Maya wants an informal, conversational tone.

What techniques has this writer used to create this voice? Maya frequently pauses in the narrative to comment briefly—telling the reader that she was not a stupid person, that she had watched enough horror movies to know better than to do what she did, that the cousin who became so angry had been unflappable while caring for her father.

What specific details, facts, etc., make this experience real? This is the first draft in which Maya had made it a point for the reader to know the cousin's and the "little cousin's" names. She also provides fairly specific paraphrase—some might say indirect dialogue—to recreate the cousin's reaction instead of simply referring to it, thus giving the reader a view of the cousin's anger.

ASSIGNMENT 3:

Fictional Narrative

While "creative writing" can provide students with rich psychological, emotional, and intellectual experiences, fiction writing is generally difficult to defend in a course of study intended to make its students "College and Career Ready."

Still one of the best statements of writing advice, which has been used as the title and/or subtitle of a number of writing texts, is that one should *read like a writer and write like a reader*. As you progress through tenth grade and into eleventh and twelfth, especially as you study both fiction and nonfiction literature, you will find yourself, not only paying attention to plot events and character relationships, but also examining how the story, poem, or play is put together; analyzing the structure of the piece, the writer's use of language, the craft of writing.

Working through the process of writing your own fictional narrative—actually doing what you are going to assume other writers have done—will make you a much sharper literary analyst.

The techniques and skills you practice in writing your own fictional narratives—even if you do not aspire to being a novelist, playwright, or memoirist—will serve you well in your other writing, the academic writing that will show you to be "college and career ready."

There are several reasons to study fiction writing, even if your entertaining and enlightening fictional narratives will never be read and evaluated by a college admissions officer or a potential employer.

Writing fiction might

- allow you to be completely creative, unfettered by prescribed content;

- allow you to experiment with form and convention;

- liberate your language, especially the use of literary and rhetorical devices in even your nonfiction, academic writing;

- expose you to different ways to plan and draft all of your writing.

There is also always the possibility that in a timed, on-demand writing setting like a state assessment or college or career entrance exam, you might not have a "real" experience appropriate to the prompt.

> While you do *not* want to lie in an essay that is specifically assigned to encourage you to reveal something about yourself, it is permissible to create events or facts in an essay that is assigned only to allow you to demonstrate your writing ability.

Thus, the assignment of a fictional narrative, or the permission to fictionalize in an essay, is much more than simply a "free-for-all," extra-credit throwaway. It has implications for a good deal of your future academic studies, possibly sharpening both your reading and your writing skills.

In fact, writing a series of fictional narratives can be excellent practice for the writing of your actual personal essays.

The development process of this narrative is, of course, essentially the same as the process for other, academic writing.

STEP 1: Select a Topic

Kyle understands this assignment to be, not a work of fiction like a short story, but a personal narrative that contains a substantial number of fictional elements and employs narrative techniques usually associated with fiction (dialogue, pacing, description, and so on). For his topic, then, he returned to the "significant experiences" he considered for his college application essay.

He immediately eliminates the topics that would likely result in a dull or clichéd essay. He also considered how this fictional *narrative* should be different from an *evaluation* of an experience and its impact.

- **grandfather's funeral**—it was kind of hard for me to be a pall-bearer. I was afraid I'd trip and fall or something. ~~Okay...am I different now because I did it? Maybe I'm more confident. How unique is that?~~ Maybe there's the possibility of some humor here.

- **finishing my first marathon**—~~same thing. What's unique?~~ Not everyone runs a marathon. I trained hard. ~~Learned the "benefit of dedication and hard work"?~~ But it was kind of dull. Nothing unexpected or funny or suspenseful. I trained and ran. Didn't win but didn't come in last either.

— **when I saw Maxie cheating**—this could be a good one. There's the whole friendship versus what's the right thing to do? ~~Maybe I could bring in a mention of Julius Caesar. But would they see me as a tattle-tale or something? What if they disagree with the decision I made? Do I even still believe I did the right thing?~~ But maybe I could talk about that...not knowing whether I did the right thing or not. I could do it like an interior monologue...a soliloquy?

STEP 2: Develop a(n) slant/angle/hook

WHAT CAN MY ANGLE BE?

— Funeral...I think I like the comic angle. Opa would have thought it was funny. Maybe I can make the character clumsy...and the grandfather had been clumsy...

— Cheating...(1) the disillusionment of seeing someone I liked and respected doing that
(2) wondering what's the right thing to do...can I turn in my friend...but
(3) if she were a "friend," would she really have put me in that position?

WHERE WOULD I BEGIN MY STORY

— I'm assuming a narrative should be in chronological order? Or maybe the cheating one could begin with "me" seeing Maxine in the cafeteria and having her and her friends snub me?

— The funeral one could begin with me already carrying the casket and thinking to myself, "Don't fall, don't trip..." something like that.

WHAT TYPE OR TONE OF VOICE DO I WANT TO CREATE IN MY READER'S MIND?

— The funeral one would be light...not flip or sarcastic, though.

— The cheating one would have to be regretful, sad...maybe bitter.

STEP 3: Brainstorm, discuss, research

Kyle is still undecided between his two story ideas, but this step will probably show him where he has the most and best ideas for full development of a narrative.

- The weight of the coffin...heavy steel...Opa was skinny as a feather...
- The ramp from the funeral home to parking lot...wood...uneven...
- Slippery new shoes—I didn't own good shoes and Mom wouldn't let me wear sneakers to the funeral.
- ...it had rained a little...so the ramp was slick
- ...fall on rear...seat of pants wet...other pall-bearers stumble
- How long the ramp seemed...how far away to the hearse...
- The cold steel of the handles...feeling as if my arms were being torn out of their socket
- The casket jostled with every step
- Everyone was a different height...so the casket was not level

(Remember that it is always easier to delete excess material than to run out while writing and have to come back to this step.)

STEP 4: Outline

With the help of his teacher, Kyle realized that the plot of his narrative should be more than just a series of events or occurrences. In a *narrative*, in order to keep the reader interested, the events should build to a climax. Each event that leads to the climax should be "bigger"—more intense—than the previous event. That is what the term "rising action" means.

So, instead of a traditional outline, Kyle has chosen to graph the plot of his fictional narrative the same way he might graph the plot of a story he was reading.

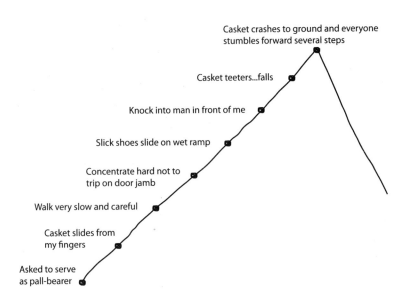

Casket crashes to ground and everyone
stumbles forward several steps

Casket teeters...falls

Knock into man in front of me

Slick shoes slide on wet ramp

Concentrate hard not to
trip on door jamb

Walk very slow and careful

Casket slides from
my fingers

Asked to serve
as pall-bearer

STEP 5: Write your first draft

Kyle seems to be having fun with this assignment, and his plot chart indicates that he does understand the idea of "rising action." He is definitely ready to write his first draft.

> Don't fall. Don't trip. And for God's sake, don't drop him.
>
> I didn't want to be a pall-bearer. I didn't ask to be a pall-bearer, and I didn't know I was going to be a pall-bearer until after the funeral was over and people were leaving. I was really frightened as I took my place among my other cousins. I was on the left-hand side of the casket, behind two of my cousins.
>
> Now, remember that I am not very strong, and I am not exactly graceful. In fact, clumsiness was the strongest trait I shared with this particular grandfather. The big joke in the family what that he would die one day by tripping over his shoelaces and falling, but actually he died peacefully in his

Kyle is using the opening he decided on in Step 2.

Language problem: Kyle needs the past perfect tense here, "I hadn't asked to be a pall-bearer."

Depending on who Kyle intends his audience to be, readers may need to be told that he is not very strong more than they need to be reminded.

A couple of things here: the way Kyle currently presents it, the way the grandfather died is irrelevant. Natural causes is probably the factual cause of death, but Kyle needs to remember that this is a fictional narrator, and he had planned on trying for some dark comedy. Perhaps, if the family joke was that the grandfather would die tripping over his shoelaces, Kyle should use this as his cause of death.

There are a few language problems here: verb tense and preposition use.

Kyle has eased nicely into his narrative. There are some language problems, especially the past-perfect tense, which he has not yet mastered.

sleep of natural causes. I was afraid I'd fall. Or drop the casket. Or both. And I'd turn my Opa's funeral into a spectacle.

My hands were drenched with sweat, and my fingers were stiff and trembling as I took hold of the handle that had been assigned to me. My one cousin counted three, and we all lifted my grandfather. The casket was a lot heavier than I expected, and the handle slipped from my fingers. My cousins must of all felt the weight shift, and the one on the other side of the rear of the coffin looked at me like he wanted to kill me.

We slowly began the slow march through the extra-wide door of the funeral home and down the ramp that ran from the porch to the sidewalk. The hearse was idling in the middle of the street, and there was already a line of cars lined up behind it, ready to follow my grandfather to the cemetery.

It was drizzling, and the cars had on their headlights and windshield wipers. I wanted to hold onto my handle with both hands, but none of my other cousins were, so I struggled and strained to carry it with just my one hand. Not only that, but the undertaker told us we were supposed to walk "in step." So I had to stay in step, carry my share of the coffin with one hand, and not trip or fall all at the same time.

I did almost trip on the doorstep as we passed from the funeral parlor onto the porch. My cousin glared at me again, and I was out of step, so I had to take a couple of little half-steps to get back into step again. Then we reached the ramp.

None of the cousins in front of me seemed to have any trouble. They just kept walking. I, however, was wearing brand new black shoes. My mother bought them for me because she

- 58 -

said I could not attend my grandfather's funeral in sneakers.

The soles of these new shoes were slick, and the wooden ramp was wet from the rain, so my first step onto the ramp I slipped a little. My second step, my rear foot slid. When I reached the actual incline, my feet slid forward. I scrambled my feet, trying to get back my footing, and I grabbed my handle with both hands.

But I couldn't stop myself from falling, and I ended up sitting on the wet ramp, still holding onto the coffin handle like a subway handrail. My other cousins were also struggling not to slide and fall or drop the coffin. The one in front of me fell on his rear end like me, and the one in front stumbled against the ramp's railing. I think that's what kept him from falling.

He was the only one on our side holding on, so the coffin started to fall toward us, but the undertaker ran and slid up the ramp, somehow ducking under the one cousin left standing and jumping over the two of us who fell. He fell to his knees. I don't know if this was on purpose or not, but he slid himself under the falling coffin and held it up with his shoulders until my cousin and I could stand and take a hold of our handles again.

We know this is only Kyle's first draft, and there is a great deal here he can work with. Remember, he said he wanted to make the narrative a little comedic, so turning a fairly flat account of events into something that might evoke a chuckle will have to be much of the focus of his revision process.

We made it the rest of the way to the hearse without incident, and from the hearse to the grave with no problem, but what surprised me most was, when we almost dropped Opa at the funeral home, no one laughed. I think Opa would have thought it was funny.

He probably would have enjoyed being part of something that was supposed to be serious but made everyone laugh.

This is not a bad way to end, but it depends on the reader's knowing the grandfather liked a good joke. Kyle does tell us the grandfather was clumsy, but he needs to provide this bit of information early in the narrative as well.

Analysis of First Draft

What is this writer's point? The clearest point the writer suggests is in the final paragraphs when he reflects that people should have laughed at the faux pas at the funeral because the grandfather himself liked a good laugh. The information about the grandfather's sense of humor, however, needs to be provided earlier.

What is his angle? The angle is an attempt at a comic approach to a story that could be disturbing.

What type or tone of voice has he created in his reader's mind? Right now, the tone is fairly nondescript.

What techniques has this writer used to create this voice? This writer has not yet taken control of style and voice. There are also some language problems that would prevent a desired voice from fully emerging.

What specific details, facts, etc., make this experience real? This narrative is full of useful details: the rain, the wooden ramp, the writer's new shoes, the facts of the writer's and the grandfather's clumsiness, and so on.

NOW you will plan your own fictional narrative, following the same process by which Kyle arrived at his first draft. Remember that Kyle thought about several possible topics and developed each of them to see which one would yield the best story.

STEP 1: Select a Topic

What experiences lend themselves to a successful evaluation?

What point would you want to make in evaluating each of these potential topics?

STEP 2: Develop a(n) slant/angle/hook

What will your angle be?

Where might you begin your evaluation?

What type or tone of voice do you want to create in your reader's mind?

STEP 3: Brainstorm, discuss, research

What specific details, facts, etc., will make this experience real and not merely hypothetical?

What specific details, facts, etc., will help you achieve your angle, tone, and mood (i.e., funny instead of somber, gentle instead of crude, etc.)?

STEP 4: Outline

Remember that Kyle actually used a graphic organizer instead of a traditional outline to plan and lay out his narrative.

STEP 5: Write your first draft

Certainly, the first draft is where you are "allowed" to make errors that might affect your reader's appreciation of your piece, but remember not to treat this as a "rough" draft. This step is not a "free-write," but an actual draft of your finished product.

STEP 6: Peer Edit

What is this writer's point?

What is his/her angle?

What type or tone of voice has he/she created in his/her reader's mind?

What techniques has this writer used to create this voice?

What specific details, facts, etc., make this experience real?

STEP 7: Revised/Final Draft

Kyle, of course, wanted to make sure he allowed his peer editor's comments to help shape his revision. Here are his partner's comments and analysis and his responses.

- Kyle is using the opening he decided on in Step 2.

- Language problem: Kyle needs the past perfect tense here, "I *hadn't asked* to be a pall-bearer."

- Depending on who Kyle intends his audience to be, readers may need to be *told* that he is not very strong more than they need to be *reminded*.

- A couple of things here: the way Kyle currently presents it, the way the grandfather died is irrelevant. Natural causes is probably the factual cause of death, but Kyle needs to remember that this is a fictional narrator, and he had planned on trying for some dark comedy. Perhaps, if the family joke was that the grandfather would die tripping over his shoelaces, Kyle should use this as his cause of death.

- There are a few language problems here: verb tense and preposition use.

- Kyle has eased nicely into his narrative. There are some language problems, especially the past-perfect tense, which he has not yet mastered.

- We know this is only Kyle's first draft, and there is a great deal here he can work with. Remember, he said he wanted to make the narrative a little comedic, so turning a fairly flat account of events into something that might evoke a chuckle will have to be much of the focus of his revision process.

- This is not a bad way to end, but it depends on the reader's knowing the grandfather liked a good joke. Kyle does tell us the grandfather was clumsy, but he needs to provide this bit of information early in the narrative as well.

And here are Kyle's responses:

> I agree that the tone is kind of flat. I was intending to work on that after I got the story down. That will be a big focus in this revision.
>
> Mentioning that Opa had a good sense of humor earlier in the essay is a good idea. Making the shoelaces the cause of death is good, too.
>
> Verb tenses...I will review the use of past-perfect.

Analysis of First Draft

What is this writer's point? The clearest point the writer suggests is in the final paragraphs when he reflects that people should have laughed at the faux pas at the funeral because the grandfather himself liked a good laugh. The information about the grandfather's sense of humor, however, needs to be provided earlier.

> The idea that Opa himself would have thought it was funny is my point. I think it will help if I mention his sense of humor early on.

What is his angle? The angle is an attempt at a comic approach to a story that could be disturbing.

> I do want this to be funny.

What type or tone of voice has he created in his reader's mind? Right now, the tone is fairly nondescript.

> That is one of the things I am working on in this revision.

What techniques has this writer used to create this voice? This writer has not yet taken control of style and voice. There are also some language problems that would prevent a desired voice from fully emerging.

> It seemed to work when I actually "quoted" Nick in my first essay, so maybe I'll use some dialogue here. Maybe try to make it sound more like a story than just a simple narrative.

What specific details, facts, etc., make this experience real? This narrative is full of useful details: the rain, the wooden ramp, the writer's new shoes, the facts of the writer's and the grandfather's clumsiness, and so on.

> But maybe I could do more with imagery...the rain shining on the ramp like ice?...the people standing in the rain, staring at us as we carry Opa from the funeral home?

And here is Kyle's second draft:

This is the same beginning as Kyle's first draft, but the addition of quotation marks give it more power. The reader instantly wonders who is speaking and to whom.

Kyle accomplishes two things here. First, he introduces the idea that the grandfather would have found the incident funny. Second, he builds suspense by referring to an embarrassing event without revealing what that event is.

Kyle is certainly making revisions that were recommended by his peer editor, but he is perhaps getting repetitive. The grandfather's finding it funny is part of the set-up, not a main focus.

Nice detail. Also, the word choice helps Kyle establish the comic tone. We are not to view the grandmother's grief with too much sympathy.

"Don't trip. Don't fall. For God's sake, don't drop him."

No one was saying that to me; I was silently commanding myself not to make a fool of myself and a spectacle of my grandfather's funeral. If I'd known what was about to happen, however, I might have just saved myself the bother. I'm still embarrassed when I think about it, and my cousin Zeke is still not speaking to me, but I can comfort myself with the thought that Opa wouldn't have minded.

He probably would have thought it was funny. After all, he was always pulling little pranks on people. My earliest memory of him is "stealing my nose," which meant he put his thumb between his index and middle fingers and pretended to pinch the nose off my face. As a kid, I cracked up every time he did it.

I also remember that once he got my Oma really angry with him. He'd mixed a lot of salt in with the sugar in Oma's canister, so when she tried to bake a cake, it came out really salty tasting. No one else thought it was very funny, but that was Opa. So, even though everyone else was really angry with me because of what happened, I think Opa would have laughed.

It all started when Oma, all puffy-eyed and tear-stained, asked me to be a pall-bearer. Even though she said all of her grandsons were helping, I didn't want to be a pall-bearer. This was after the funeral was over and people were leaving. If she'd asked earlier, maybe I would have had the time to come up with a good excuse why I couldn't.

Kyle is providing some nice small details that allow the reader to understand the experience a little more fully.

The job terrified me. So much could go wrong. I could really foul things up. I'm not strong, and I'm not exactly graceful. In fact, even more than the sense of humor, clumsiness was the strongest trait I shared with Opa. The big joke in the family was that he would die one day by tripping over his shoelaces and falling, and that's almost what actually happened. What happened was that his shoelace came untied while he was on an escalator at the mall. (I don't think I want to go into all of the details.)

This is another change recommended by the peer editor. Notice how Kyle avoids having to create an entire story and risk taking this narrative into a tangent.

But that why, when Oma asked me to be a pall-bearer, I was afraid I'd fall. Or drop the casket. Or both. And I'd turn my Opa's funeral into a spectacle. My hands were drenched with sweat, and my fingers were stiff and trembling as I tried to clutch the handle. My oldest cousin counted to three, and we all lifted my grandfather. The casket was a lot heavier than I had expected, and the handle slipped from my fingers. My cousins must have all felt the weight shift, and Dennis, who was right opposite me, looked at me as if he wanted to kill me.

Kyle has indeed fixed the most serious of his language problems: the use of past and present perfect tenses.

I grabbed at the handle and stared straight ahead of me, swallowing down the desire to cry.

We began the slow march through the extra-wide double doors of the funeral home. The hearse was idling in the middle of the street, and there was already a line of cars lined up behind it, ready to follow my grandfather to the cemetery. A few people were clustered under umbrellas around the bottom of the ramp, staring at us with such expectant expressions on their faces. Suddenly, I felt as if I was the center of attention.

It was drizzling, and the cars had on their headlights and windshield wipers. I wanted to hold onto my part of the handle with both hands, but none of my cousins were, so I struggled. To further enhance the experience, the funeral director told us we were supposed to walk "in step." So I had to stay in step, carry my share of the coffin with one hand, and not trip or fall—all at the same time.

How hard could it be?

Then, I <u>did</u> almost trip on the doorstep as we passed from the funeral parlor onto the porch. My cousin glared at me again, and I was out of step, so I had to shuffle and skip to get back into synch with the others.

Then we reached the ramp.

None of my cousins seemed to have any trouble. They just kept walking. I, however, was wearing brand new black shoes. My mother bought them for me because she said I could not attend my grandfather's funeral in sneakers.

The soles of these new shoes were slick, and the wooden ramp was wet from the rain, so on my first step onto the ramp I slipped a little. On my second step, my rear foot slid. When I reached the actual incline, my feet slid forward. I scrambled my feet, like a cartoon character trying to run, and I grabbed the handle with both hands.

But I couldn't stop myself from falling, and I ended up sitting on the wet ramp, still holding onto the coffin handle like a subway handrail. My other cousins were also struggling not to slide and fall or drop the coffin. The one in front of me fell on his rear end like me, and the one in front

Kyle used this same phrase in his first essay. It provides some nice suspense and foreshadowing here.

The shorter, one-sentence paragraphs help Kyle speed up the pace and build suspense.

stumbled against the ramp's railing. I think that's what kept him from failing. He was the only one on our side still really holding on, so the coffin started to list toward us.

Like the hero in an action movie, moving in slow motion with an explosion billowing behind him, the funeral director ran and slid up the ramp. He somehow ducked under the one cousin left standing and jumped over the two of us sitting on our butts on the wet ramp. In a single, dance-like motion, he fell to his knees and slid under the falling coffin, holding it up with his shoulders until my cousin and I could recover and resume our posts. We made it the rest of the way to the hearse without incident, and from the hearse to the grave with no problem. I was surprised, though, that no one laughed when we almost dropped Opa.

I think Opa would have thought it was funny.

Kyle has fixed most of the language problems and has worked to find more vivid words to replace some of the weaker phrases he used in his first draft.

Nice image.

More use of more powerful words.

Analysis of Final Draft

What is this writer's point? Kyle's point is that, even though this experience was embarrassing, at least some of the witnesses should have found it funny.

What is his angle? The angle is to tell the story of an embarrassing experience in a humorous way. Kyle invites the reader to laugh with him, rather than laugh at him.

What type or tone of voice has he created in his reader's mind? The tone is light, not flippant or glib, and not sarcastic, but not ponderous either.

What techniques has this writer used to create this voice? Kyle varies the length and structure of his sentences but often uses short sentences and paragraphs to keep up the pacing and tone. Images like the puffy-eyed grandmother and the funeral director's running up the ramp "like the hero in an action movie" also contribute to the tone.

What specific details, facts, etc., make this experience real? Kyle is quite good at identifying and using details to enhance the impact of his writing. Successful details in this draft include the puffy-eyed, tear-stained grandmother, the funeral director running like an action hero, the funeral attendees clustering under umbrellas, and so on.

POSSIBLE STEP 8: Rewrite Opportunity

PART II:

Informative Writing

[showing what students know about a subject]

Traditionally, when we talk about writing, we talk about the *purpose* of the writing—what motivated the writer to write?—and we typically consider there to be three main purposes: to express the self, to inform, and to persuade.

Of course, in actual writing, these purposes are rarely completely separate. You may need to provide some background information on a subject before you can hope to persuade your reader that your point is valid. You might find yourself trying to persuade your reader to see your point of view when you write a personal piece about a difficult person you once encountered. Still, there are things the writer needs to consider when he or she must step back from an argument or personal expression and simply provide some information.

There are times when it is convenient to talk about personal writing, informative writing, and persuasive writing as if they were different things.

As a writer, your key concerns in informative writing will always be:

- how much information do you need to share?

and

- how much does your reader already know?

The first concern is governed by your point or main idea. What knowledge or understanding do you want to leave your reader with? What information will be relevant to that point, and what information, no matter how interesting, is simply irrelevant?

For example, the central idea of an essay about Abraham Lincoln's Second Inaugural Address could be that it looks toward the future and suggests the tone Lincoln hoped the period of reconstruction after the Civil War would take. To establish this point, you might need to

- actually quote the relevant portions of the address;
- remind readers what Lincoln considered to be the reasons for and the goals of the War;
- inform readers that, by the time the speech was delivered, a Northern victory was all but guaranteed;

- inform readers that Lincoln and his advisors had already begun to map out a plan for the reconstruction of the South and the return of states that had seceded to the Union;
- inform readers that Lincoln had instructed his generals to conduct the rest of the War—to the final Southern surrender—with as little loss of life and destruction of Southern property as possible.

In this essay, however, some irrelevant information might include:

- the fact that Lincoln was the nation's sixteenth president;
- information about Lincoln's marriage or family;
- any mention of his first inaugural address or the Gettysburg Address or any other speech he may have delivered;

and so on.

The second concern is governed by your sense of audience. You don't, on the one hand, want to dive right into your main idea, but you don't want to bore your readers with a rehash of everything they already know or a parade of Civil War trivia that does not help to make the main point any clearer.

For example, in your essay on Lincoln's Second Inaugural Address, you could probably assume that your reader already knows

- who Abraham Lincoln was;
- the general issues that led to Southern states' secession and the beginning of the war;
- that presidents traditionally deliver a speech immediately following their taking the oath of office and that Lincoln had been elected to a second term as president;
- that Lincoln was assassinated not too long after this inauguration;

and so on.

To try to provide every background fact about Lincoln, his presidential campaigns, the Civil War, and so on, would mean that you were telling the reader a lot that he or she already knew *and* that you were filling the essay with information that was, ultimately, irrelevant to the point you wanted to make.

Informative writing, then, is more than simply writing a bunch of sentences that are crammed full of facts. It is involves sorting through and prioritizing the information you have and presenting only what is going to contribute meaningfully to your point, your central idea.

ASSIGNMENT 1:

Interview or Personal Profile

It might seem, at first glance, that a "personal profile" should be included in the "personal writing" section of this book, but once you realize that the purpose of this "interview" is to gather information about *someone else* and then to share that information with your reader, it makes more sense as an informative assignment.

Gathering information and then writing a personal profile is actually an excellent way to work through the issues of providing enough information without repeating what the reader probably already knows or slipping into a study of trivial facts. This assignment also provides you with a nice opportunity to practice thinking of a *point*, a reason for sharing the information beyond merely sharing it.

It's also important to note that, while choosing a personal friend or acquaintance for this assignment would certainly not be out of the question, it is not required.

Step 1: Select a Topic

Kyle begins by simply brainstorming a list of everyone he knows. He is smart enough to know not to reject or favor anyone of any age or relationship at this point. He just wants to list as many people as the can think of.

His second step…when he is running out of time or people…is to go back and jot a few notes about each person. In an interview, what would he want to know? In an article featuring each person, what would be the focus? Why would this person be at all interesting to someone other than Kyle?

He also constantly reminds himself that, while his essay about Nick was supposed to focus on the impact Nick had on his own development, this essay is supposed to be about the featured person.

(NOTE: In the interest of saving space, we're showing the results of Kyle's second step. After the first, he had simply the list of names.)

- **Coach Truesto**—Did he overcome any adversity? Work extra hard to get where he is?

- **Nick from work**—I don't really know anything factual about him. Not even sure of his last name. I guess there's not a lot here for an essay about him...I'd have to interview him and all.

- **Franco Giancarlo (Frank)**—I'll probably have to write about Marshall. He came to the United States when he was eight years old—I kind of remember his first day at school because he was a short, skinny kid, very scared-looking, and he spoke no English at all. Mrs. Heinstein sat him next to me, and I didn't know what I was supposed to do or say. Now...eight years later, he speaks English great. Is in all honors classes and even tutors most of us in algebra and geometry. He's definitely in the top 10 students in our class, and might actually be number 1 or 2.

While working on his second step, Kyle realized that most of the people he had chosen were not going to work. While he was able to discuss their relationship to him or their impact on him to some extent, once he reminded himself that this was supposed to be an essay featuring them, he realized that he simply did not know anything about most of the people he listed initially. Of course, the assignment allows for interviewing and research, but for some, like Coach Truesto and Nick, Kyle doesn't know enough about them to even begin research.

He very quickly went back to brainstorming names, this time being a little more selective and noting only those who could be the subject of an essay in their own right.

- **George Washington**—Great American leader. Relatively humble beginnings. Not classically educated. High standards of conduct and expected of others. Willing to serve but loved home most of all. To him, service was a sacrifice.

- **Aunt Stacy**—The family eccentric. Everyone teases her...they know the truth but ignore it ... something about a stroke after her third baby (Cousin Pia) was born. Not enough oxygen...Stacy was in coma for a week and had to learn everything over again: talk, walk, feed herself...She still is "not right," and has the sense of maybe a sixth grader, but she never gave up...and still continues to live every day to its fullest.

> These are only Kyle's preliminary thoughts and notes, so we can let him get away with clichés like this.

I need to talk to my mother and maybe Uncle Fred for more of the details and a more accurate timeline.

- **Maybe Uncle Fred!**—He stayed with Aunt Stacy and the kids through the whole stroke and recovery thing. I remember my mother and some other people taking turns—for a long time—taking over meals and babysitting so he could be with Aunt Stacy in the hospital and the rehabilitation place. I also remember something about them almost losing their house, but there was a big dinner at church...and Uncle Fred replaced all of our windows and siding outdoors...I think Dad paid him extra to help him out. Some men probably would have freaked out and left—maybe taking the kids, but not staying with a handicapped or disabled wife, but Uncle Fred has stuck it out.

- **The Last Lecture guy**—Randy Pausch. Pancreatic Cancer. Terminal diagnosis...apparently he initially fought with surgery and chemotherapy, but then stepped back...palliative care...Last Lecture was originally not about the cancer, but terminal prognosis was coincidence...Went against wishes of wife to deliver lecture...

Ultimately, Kyle listed some two dozen names of authors, politicians, historical figures, and people he has known. Every person in this new list had something interesting to tell about. This is much more in line with what this assignment is getting at.

STEP 2: Develop a(n) slant/angle/hook

WHAT CAN MY ANGLE BE?

Washington would be that he did not seek power or fame. All he wanted to do was go home...but he was willing to sacrifice his own desires to serve his country...and he is more famous than any other American ever. (That's pretty ironic.)

Aunt Stacy could be that she endures a lot of teasing, but she's still pleasant. But that's not the point. Does she even know people tease her? I think it's more that she didn't give up. She fought to get something of her life back, and she lives every day to its fullest. (When I say it like that, it doesn't sound all that unique.)

Uncle Fred is that he defies the stereotype. Society would expect a man in his position to just leave, and he didn't. I have no idea what he has actually given up because he never lets anyone see him complain or act depressed, but I know he's stayed with Aunt Stacy at a lot of sacrifice to himself.

STEP 3: Brainstorm, discuss, research

Still unable to choose between George Washington and Uncle Fred, Kyle hit the Internet and the school library for information on Washington's background and home life. He also emailed his Uncle Fred and asked if he could interview him, either in person, over the phone, or email him questions and have Fred email the answers back.

Washington:

- Christmas 1787, Washington hired a camel to entertain his guests at Mount Vernon with a recreation of the arrival of the Wise Men at the manger.

- The estate (Mount Vernon) always had more slaves than it needed because Washington refused to sell any or give any away if it meant breaking up a family. He hired skilled craftsmen from Europe to train the slaves so they were skilled at more than just the grunt labor associated with farming.

- During his eight years as president, Washington was home at Mount Vernon only 434 days.

- He liked to dance, watch plays, and play games like cards, backgammon, and billiards.

- Became famous in French and Indian War by accident and because of his family connections (brother Lawrence and the Fairfaxes)

- Became Commander in Chief of Continental Army (Revolutionary War) because he was there, and New England knew they needed a Virginia leader to get Southern support for cause of independence.

- The U.S. victory made Washington the national hero...first American celebrity...even though he did not seek it. He just did a job he didn't even ask for.

- After war, he only wanted to go home. Almost did not do Constitutional Convention but Madison persuaded him to...the work of the Convention would fail if it did not have the endorsement of a hero like Washington.

From his First Inaugural Address (1789):

- I was summoned by my country...from a retreat which I had chosen...as the asylum of my declining years—a retreat which was rendered every day more necessary as well as more dear to me by the addition of habit to inclination, and of frequent interruptions in my health to the gradual waste committed on it by time.

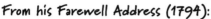

From his Farewell Address (1794):

- the office to which your suffrages have twice called me have been a uniform sacrifice...to the opinion of duty and to a deference for what appeared to be your desire. I...hoped that it would have been much earlier in my power...to return to that retirement from which I had been reluctantly drawn. The strength of my inclination to do this...had even led to the preparation of an address to declare it to you; but mature reflection...and the unanimous advice of persons entitled to my confidence, impelled me to abandon the idea.
- All he wanted to do was go home...and after the French and Indian War, the Revolutionary War, the Constitutional Convention, and as President of the United States...this is what his Farewell Address says.

Uncle Fred: was pretty unwilling to give many details. I don't know whether it's all painful to him, or he's afraid to let his real resentment show...But here's what I learned from some of my other family members:

- the stroke occurred while Aunt Stacy was giving birth...the baby (Pia) was actually being delivered.
- that's why they may have been a few seconds slow to pay attention to the trouble Aunt Stacy was in.
- In her coma for nine days. They did not expect her to live.
- No one knows the full extent of the brain damage because Uncle Fred won't tell anyone.
- Except for the job redoing our windows and siding, Uncle Fred never asked anyone for help.
- The kids take turns spending time with their grandparents (Uncle Fred's parents, not my grandparents) every summer.

STEP 4: Outline

Because he was able to find so much information on George Washington, and he liked the slant of writing about Washington's humility and desire to be home, Kyle chose Washington as the subject of his essay. He also did not want to feel as though he was exploiting his aunt and uncle by making their challenges so public for a simple grade on an essay.

Personal Study of George Washington

Purpose, Point, or End Result

George Washington is the United States' most well-known hero in history, but never wanted either fame or power. All he wanted was to stay home with his wife and family

Sequence of Events

First Event

FRENCH AND INDIAN WAR

Other Important Details

- First appointment was "inherited" from half-brother.
- First victory (de Jumonville) was sort of an accident

Second Event

REVOLUTIONARY WAR

Other Important Details

- Farmer on Mount Vernon Plantation
- Married Martha...2 step kids
- Said he was "not equal to" the appoint't but C. Cong needed a Virginian for Southern support.

Third Event

CONSTITUTIONAL CONVENTION

Other Important Details

- Was not going to go...tired...poor health...wanted to stay home...
- Madison persuaded him...Convention would fail without Washington's support.

Fourth Event

TWO TERMS AS PRESIDENT

Other Important Details

- Two quotations: first inaugural and Farewell Address, say it all.

STEP 5: First draft

George Washington was an interesting figure. In his own lifetime, he was the United States' biggest celebrity. Total strangers would knock on his front door at Mount Vernon, Virginia, to meet him, and he would let them into his home and offer them something to eat and drink. He is today probably the most famous American in American history. What's funny about Washington's fame, and the influence he had in shaping our nation, influence we still feel even today, is that he himself never really sought fame or power. He was not at all like today's politicians who spend their entire careers scraping and clawing for power; Washington wanted nothing more than to go home and be with his family. To Washington, the public service that he was called to was really a sacrifice, something that had to be done but something that, after it was done, he could return to his private life. It is ironic that the man who least wanted to be a bigger-than-life national hero is the one who ended up being one.

Today's leaders could take a lesson from this truly great American.

George Washington was born either February 11, 1731, or February 22, 1732, depending on whether you're using the Julian or the Gregorian calendar. I understand that the switch from the Julian to the Gregorian calendar caused an eleven-day jump in the date, but I don't understand how they could have calculated his birth to be a full year later than it really was. He was the first-born child of Augustine Washington and his second wife, Mary Ball Washington. It was from his half-brother Lawrence (his father's oldest son by his first wife) that George inherited the militia appointment that began his rise to fame, and also his beloved home, Mount Vernon. Lawrence was

As an introduction, this covers all the bases, but sentence structure and word choice are a little awkward and immature.

Once again, Kyle loses his focus quickly. He needs to pay attention to his outline/ graphic organizer and not include every bit of information simply because he has it.

The militia appointment is an important detail, but Kyle passes over it too quickly.

13 or 14 years older than George, so he filled in as a sort of father figure for George after their father Augustine died in 1743.

When Lawrence died, he was the son-in-law of one of Virginia's most rich and influential landowners, William Fairfax. His marriage to the fifteen-year-old Anne may have originally been a marriage of convenience because Lawrence had just returned home from military service in the Caribbean and was looking to establish himself in Virginia society, and Anne had recently been molested by the family's minister and needed to be married off in a hurry. In any event, Lawrence's friendship with the Fairfaxes seems to coincide with his appointment as an Adjutant General with the rank of Major in the Virginia militia (1742) and his election to the Virginia House of Burgesses (1744). All of Lawrence and Anne's children died in infancy.

When Lawrence died in 1752, George was only 20 (or 19). He was appointed District Adjutant of the Virginia militia and given the rank of major. This position was one of four created by the position that had been left open by Lawrence's death. It began Washington's military career and put him in a position to distinguish himself during the French and Indian War. But it was not a position he sought. In fact, he would never have gotten it if Lawrence hadn't died. The death of Joseph Coulon de Jumonville, leader of a French force in the area around Pittsburgh, Pennsylvania, almost caused the Seven Years War and catapulted George Washington to military fame.

After the war, Washington returned home to Mount Vernon, where he married the wealthy widow Martha Dandridge Custis and her two children. Washington now had a prosperous farm and a happy family. All he wanted to do was stay home.

Kyle has clearly done some research, but much of this information is tangential at best. What is the relationship of half-brother Lawrence's rise in society to the thesis about George Washington's never desiring power?

Kyle provides a hint of how this information about Lawrence contributes to his thesis, but it is not a strong enough hint to put this essay on the right track.

But then, in 1775, when the British fired on Americans in Massachusetts, George was unanimously appointed to be Commander-in-Chief of the Continental Army to fight the Revolutionary War. He did not seek the position, and his first answer to the call was that he was "not equal to it." But we won the war, and George Washington became a national hero. Wherever he went, people would shoot off cannons and ring church bells. He was constantly visited at home by both friends and total strangers who wanted to meet the man who had won American independence. Again, however, all George Washington wanted to do was be a Virginia farmer and enjoy his family.

> One detail that Kyle mentioned in his notes and on his graphic organizer is that part of Washington's appointment was political in order to gain Southern support of a "Northern" problem.

But it was not to be. In 1787, when it was time for the Constitutional Convention, Washington wasn't even going to go. James Madison came to Mount Vernon in September of 1786 to talk him into it. The Convention dragged on for four months before the Constitution was finally written and ratified. After the Constitution was ratified, George Washington was unanimously elected as the first president. I think it is interesting what he says in his inaugural address:

> In his haste to "tell the whole story" and not lose his focus, Kyle is oversimplifying some of the history and actually stating inaccuracies.

> This is historically inaccurate. The delegates did vote to accept the finished Constitution to then send to the states for ratification, but the Constitution was not ratified by the Constitutional Convention.

> I was summoned by my country...<u>from a retreat</u> which I had chosen...<u>as the asylum of my declining years</u>—<u>a retreat which was rendered every day more necessary as well as more dear to me</u> by the addition of habit to inclination, and of frequent interruptions in my health to the gradual waste committed on it by time.

The parts I've underlined prove that all Washington wanted was to stay home, but he was willing to give up his own comfort and peaceful life to serve his country. For Washington, being the Commander in Chief of the nation's army, the president of the Constitutional Convention, and the first President of the United States was not something he had spent his whole life desiring and working for. He did not

> In his rewrite, Kyle will have to eliminate this first person.

choose the "best schools" and make friends based on who would be able to help him achieve his dream of power and influence. What he wanted was to be at home with his wife and family, but he was willing to sacrifice for the sake of his country.

Toward the end of Washington's <u>second term</u> as president in 1797, he decided that he had given enough, and he wanted to go home. His Farewell Address, in which he announces once and for all that he is going home and will not be available for any more public service, is an important document in United States history:

> the office to which your suffrages have twice called me have been a uniform sacrifice...to the opinion of duty and to a deference for what appeared to be your desire. I...hoped that it would have been much earlier in my power... to return to that retirement from which I had been reluctantly drawn.

They had called him out of retirement to be president, and he was now going back into retirement. Unfortunately, George Washington's well-earned retirement was to be short-lived. He died in 1799 after barely two years of retirement.

Kyle has definitely overused the phrase "wanted to go home."

This essay ends on a poignant fact but does not satisfactorily conclude Kyle's thesis. He needs to end, as he suggests in the introduction, that Washington has been one of the most influential leaders this country has seen despite the ironic fact that he never sought such influence.

Analysis of First Draft

What is this writer's point? Kyle wants to emphasize Washington's humility, the fact that he attained his status as national icon at great personal expense, desiring only to return to his private life.

What is his angle? The author suggests that he would like his angle to be that self-interested modern politicians could take a lesson from Washington.

What type or tone of voice has he created in her reader's mind? Kyle's word choice tends to be imprecise and immature, so he has created a voice that is too informal, almost casual for the nature of this assignment.

What techniques has this writer used to create this voice? Word choice plays a big role in the creation of voice. Kyle also slips into the occasional first person with authorial or editorial intrusion.

What specific details, facts, etc., make this essay informative and powerful?
Historical facts about Washington's life: his relationship with his half-brother, the circumstances of his entering the Virginia militia, the direct quotations from Washington's inaugural address and Farewell Address are very helpful. He does, however, oversimplify some points and slip into at least one historical inaccuracy.

NOW plan your own essay, following the same process by which Kyle arrived at his first draft.

STEP 1: Select a Topic

What persons do you know (or know of) who have particularly interesting characters, have overcome some challenge or adversity, or have accomplished something noteworthy?

What point would you want to make in telling this person's story?

STEP 2: Develop a(n) slant/angle/hook

What will your angle be?

How close to—or detached from—your subject do you plan to be?

What type or tone of voice do you want to create in your reader's mind?

STEP 3: Brainstorm, discuss, research

What specific details, facts, etc., make this essay informative and powerful?

What specific details, facts, etc., will help you achieve your angle, tone, and mood (e.g., funny instead of somber, gentle instead of crude, etc.)?

STEP 4: Outline

Remember that Kyle used a graphic organizer instead of a traditional outline to plan and lay out his narrative.

STEP 5: Write your first draft

STEP 6: Peer Edit

What is this writer's point?

What is his/her angle?

What type or tone of voice has he/she created in his/her reader's mind?

What techniques has this writer used to create this voice?

What specific details, facts, etc., make this essay informative and powerful?

STEP 7: Revised/Final Draft

Here are the reader's comments and analysis and Kyle's responses.

- As an introduction, this covers all the bases, but sentence structure and word choice are a little awkward and immature.

- Once again, Kyle loses his focus quickly. He needs to pay attention to his outline/graphic organizer and not include every bit of information simply because he has it.

- The militia appointment is an important detail, but Kyle passes over it too quickly.

- Kyle has clearly done some research, but much of this information is tangential at best. What is the relationship of half-brother Lawrence's rise in society to the thesis about George Washington's never desiring power?

- Kyle provides a hint of how this information about Lawrence contributes to his thesis, but it is not a strong enough hint to put this essay on the right track.

- One detail that Kyle mentioned in his notes and on his graphic organizer is that part of Washington's appointment was political in order to gain Southern support of a "Northern" problem.

- In his haste to "tell the whole story" and not lose his focus, Kyle is oversimplifying some of the history and actually stating inaccuracies.

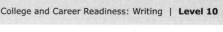

- This is historically inaccurate. The delegates did vote to accept the finished Constitution to then send to the states for ratification, but the Constitution was not ratified by the Constitutional Convention.

- In his rewrite, Kyle will have to eliminate this first person.

- Kyle has definitely overused the phrase "wanted to go home."

- This essay ends on a poignant fact but does not satisfactorily conclude Kyle's thesis. He needs to end, as he suggests in the introduction, that Washington has been one of the most influential leaders this country has seen despite the ironic fact that he never sought such influence.

> Still need to work on word choice and sentence structure.
>
> Focus! The only details I need are those that show Washington did not seek the positions he rose to. I also have to remember to tell my readers why the details are relevant.
>
> I can add a sentence or two about the Virginia/New England thing.
>
> Check my history facts.
>
> "Wanted to go home..." I'll fix it. Can replace with "retire," "go back to private life," I'll think of others, too.
>
> And I guess I need to rework my conclusion.

Analysis of First Draft

What is this writer's point? Kyle wants to emphasize Washington's humility, the fact that he attained his status as national icon at great personal expense, desiring only to return to his private life.

> They got my point. Good.

What is his angle? The author suggests that he would like his angle to be that self-interested modern politicians could take a lesson from Washington.

> If I'm only "suggesting" that I'd "like my angle to be,"
> then I guess I haven't fully achieved it.

What type or tone of voice has he created in the reader's mind? Kyle's word choice tends to be imprecise and immature, so he has created a voice that is too informal, almost casual for the nature of this assignment.

> I don't want a stuffy or too-formal tone, but I don't want to sound immature either.

What techniques has this writer used to create this voice? Word choice plays a big role in the creation of voice. Kyle also slips into the occasional first person with authorial or editorial intrusion.

> Need to pay attention to word choice. No first person.

What specific details, facts, etc., make this essay informative and powerful? Historical facts about Washington's life: his relationship with his half-brother, the circumstances of his entering the Virginia militia, the direct quotations from Washington's inaugural address and Farewell Address are very helpful. He does, however, oversimplify some points and slip into at least one historical inaccuracy.

> Yeah, I can fix this.

Here is Kyle's revised draft. Read the essay and consider how it is stronger and more to its purpose.

Kyle has made a good change here, "irony" instead of "what's funny about."

This is Kyle's first use of this phrase. He should remember not to overuse it.

George Washington was a fascinating figure. In his own lifetime, he was the United States' biggest celebrity. Total strangers would knock on his front door at Mount Vernon, Virginia, to meet him, and he would let them into his home and offer them something to eat and drink. He is today probably the most famous figure in American history. The irony of Washington's fame, a fact that most people do not often think about, is that he did not seek it. Washington's life story is that of a man who was willing to serve his country when called to do so—willing to serve at great sacrifice to his own health and happiness—but who only wanted to go home and live the life of a plantation farmer and family man. He was not at all like today's politicians who spend their entire careers pursuing power. As he himself publicly admitted in his two most famous speeches, he was almost unwilling to take on the offices being given to him. It is ironic that the man who least wanted to be a bigger-than-life national hero is the one who ended up being one.

Today's leaders could take a lesson from this truly great American.

This is a much better introduction. Kyle even mentions the two speeches he is going to quote later on as evidence. He also suggests that he is going to use the format of a biography to develop his thesis.

George Washington was the first-born child of Augustine Washington and his second wife, Mary Ball Washington. It was from his half-brother Lawrence (his father's oldest son by his first wife) that George inherited both the militia appointment that began his rise to fame, and also his beloved home, Mount Vernon. Lawrence himself had essentially married into the position of prominence that he then passed on to his brother. He'd married the fifteen-year-old daughter of William Fairfax, one of Virginia's wealthiest and most influential landowners. Whether he and Anne Fairfax were truly in love, it is well documented that Lawrence agreed to marry Anne <u>after</u> she told her parents that their family minister had molested her. Her parents may very well have wanted to marry their daughter off in a hurry and avoid a scandal. In any event, Lawrence's friendship with the Fairfaxes seems to coincide with his appointment as an Adjutant General with the rank of Major in the Virginia militia (1742) and his election to the Virginia House of Burgesses (1744). If Lawrence hadn't had his relationship with the Fairfaxes, brother George would not have had the start he had.

By cutting the irrelevant details about Washington's birth and the change of calendars, Kyle has been able to focus on what is pertinent: Washington's rise to fame began largely by accident of birth and inheritance.

It is possible that Kyle is, once again, losing his focus. He needs to make it clear to his reader how this information about Lawrence pertains to his thesis.

When Lawrence died in 1752, George was only 20. He was appointed District Adjutant of the Virginia militia and given the rank of major. This position was one of four created by the position that had been left open by Lawrence's death. It began Washington's military career and put him in a position to distinguish himself during the French and Indian War. But it was not a position he sought. In fact, he would never have gotten it if Lawrence hadn't died.

After the war, Washington returned home to Mount Vernon, where he married the wealthy widow Martha Dandridge Custis and her two children. Washington now had a prosperous farm and a happy family.

But then, in 1775, when the British fired on Americans in Massachusetts, Washington was unanimously appointed to be Commander-in-Chief of the Continental Army to fight the Revolutionary War. He did not seek the position, and his first answer to the call was that he was "not equal to it." Not only was Washington the most likely choice because of his record in the French and Indian War, he was also a prominent Virginia landowner, and Congress needed to secure Southern support for a military conflict that was focused primarily in New England. Politically, Washington was the best choice, whether he was "equal to it" or not.

The United States, of course, won the Revolution, and George Washington became a national hero. Wherever he went, people would shoot off cannons and ring church bells. He was constantly visited at home by both friends and total strangers who wanted to meet the man who had won American independence. Again, however, all George Washington wanted to do was return to his life as a Virginia farmer and enjoy his family.

But it was not to be. In 1787, when it was clear that the new Confederation of States was in trouble, Washington did not plan to attend the convention that was going to be held in Philadelphia. James Madison came to Mount Vernon in September of 1786 to talk him into

Kyle does establish the relevance of the Lawrence information, even if he is being a little repetitive.

Notice that Kyle has eliminated the second iteration of the "want[ing] to stay home" phrase.

This change is a good choice. Generally, writers refer to historical figures by their last names.

Kyle's peer editor recommended that Kyle include the information about the political aspect of Washington's appointment.

it. Madison was certain that whatever the Convention decided was doomed to failure unless the Great George Washington had played a role in its development. Once again, Washington was pressed to leave his home to serve his country. After the Constitution was ratified, Washington was unanimously elected as the first president. What he has to say in his Inaugural Address about his reluctance to serve is very telling:

> I was summoned by my country...from a retreat which I had chosen...as the asylum of my declining years—a retreat which was rendered every day more necessary as well as more dear to me by the addition of habit to inclination, and of frequent interruptions in my health to the gradual waste committed on it by time.

This is a clear and public declaration that, while Washington was willing to serve his country it was at the sacrifice of his own comfort and peaceful life. He was willing to serve in the office of President of the United States and accept whatever power and influence would accompany it, but he was not seeking it.

He had not spent his whole life desiring and working for power and fame. He did not choose the "best schools" and make friends based on who would be able to help him achieve his dream of power and influence. He was willing to serve in whatever role and do whatever work was necessary, but it was a sacrifice, not his desire.

Toward the end of Washington's second term as president in 1797, he decided that he had given enough. His Farewell Address is another important document in United States history. In this speech, Washington announces that he will not accept a third term as president; nor will he be available for any more public service:

Kyle does successfully eliminate the first person while also explaining to his reader the significance of the quotation.

the office to which your suffrages have twice called me have been a uniform sacrifice... to the opinion of duty and to a deference for what appeared to be your desire. I...hoped that it would have been much earlier in my power... to return to that retirement from which I had been reluctantly drawn.

Washington clearly states that service was a sacrifice, that even his second term as president was an imposition. Not many men or women today feel "imposed upon" when they accept public office, and none voluntarily remove themselves from power. They should take their example from George Washington, a man who served willingly but at great cost to himself. Unfortunately, George Washington's well-earned retirement was to be short-lived. He died in 1799 after barely two years of private life. His name and memory, however, remain in the United States as an American icon. The irony is, of course, that if he had been given the choice, George Washington would have remained a private citizen on his Virginia plantation. The man who least sought fame and power became the most famous American who ever lived.

Kyle manages to keep his poignant observation about Washington's untimely death, but he also manages to return to his thesis about the irony of Washington's fame.

Now write yours.

ASSIGNMENT 2:

Book or Article Report

As you progress through school and advance in your career, you'll more than likely find a number of occasions to write a report on a book or article you've read. Your high school might have a summer reading list with the requirement that you write a report on at least some of the material you read over the summer.

Your school might have an independent (or "outside") reading requirement, and again you might have to report on at least some of the material you've read on your own. Even if your *school* doesn't have an independent reading requirement, one or more of your individual teachers might, and they might require you to turn in reports on what you've read.

In college and graduate school, you might find yourself in a course with a particularly heavy reading load. Your study group might divide up the reading and require each member to report to the others the key information on his or her share of the reading.

Beyond school, most professions require their practitioners to stay abreast of current information or trends in the field. Doctors, lawyers and judges, legislators, and public administrators (to name only a few) all have assistants and interns working under them who read and write reports on countless books and articles to help their employers stay current. Early in their careers, these doctors, lawyers, etc., probably were the young assistants who did the reading and wrote the reports for their employers.

In the information age, the ability to read something and then produce an articulate, meaningful, *and concise* report on it for someone else is an indispensible skill.

As you should expect, the structure of a book (or article) report is not very different from any other academic essay you will write. It is important to follow a consistent pattern in the reports you write so that the people for whom you are writing the reports can predict what information they are going to find and where they will be able to find it.

Essentially, in a basic book or article report, the **introductory paragraph(s)** will reveal the essential information about the piece being reported on and make some statement about what the piece is about and how it goes about exploring its subject.

The **body paragraphs** follow through and expand on the topic and approach of the piece. The exploration of the approach might include some evaluation of the writing style, the overall readability of the piece, and a discussion of the author's bias, objectivity, fairness, or whatever might color a reader's appreciation of the piece.

Finally, the **concluding paragraph(s)** wrap up the presentation and explain the impression the piece left on you and what the person to whom you are reporting will likely think of it.

In addition to her tenth-grade English class, **Maya** is taking journalism. This teacher has a weekly "outside article" requirement for all of his journalism students. Here is the assignment template he distributed early in the school year and Maya's work for one of her article reports.

Notice how the teacher's assignment template follows the typical process for writing an academic essay.

STEP 1: Select a Topic

Title: "But What Do You Mean?"

Author: Deborah Tannen

Source Information (publication, publishing company, copyright date, etc.):
excerpted from: Talking from 9 to 5: Women and Men at Work. Harper Collins, 1994.

Genre: nonfiction

STEP 2: Develop a(n) slant/angle/hook

What is the general subject or topic of this piece? the 7 most common types of miscommunication between men and women in the workplace and how or why they occur

What is the author's angle, theme, or thesis? I think Tannen would say she is giving an objective account of how men and women miscommunicate, but I think she really favors women and makes the "differences" between how men and women communicate more about how women communicate all right, men communicate badly, and women are disadvantaged by being better communicators.

Who is the author? What are his or her qualifications to write on this subject? Deborah Tanner is a well-known linguist with a PhD in linguistics from U. C. Berkeley in California. She has taught linguistics at Georgetown University in Washington, D.C., for over 30 years, and is a New York Times bestselling writer on the topic of interpersonal communications, especially the relationship of gender and communication.

STEP 3: Brainstorm, discuss, research

Is there an obvious slant or bias? What evidence from the text can you provide to support your claim? There is a subtle bias in favor of the way women communicate. In her second paragraph: "Many of the conversational rituals common among women are designed to take the other person's feelings into account, while many of the conversational rituals common among men are designed to maintain the one-up position..."

"Because women are not trying to avoid the one-down position, that is unfortunately where they may end up."

In section about apologies...way to "share the blame" if both parties are partially at fault, but : "if one person, usually the woman, utters frequent apologies and the other doesn't, she ends up looking as if she's taking the blame for mishaps that aren't her fault."

Woman made gratuitous "thank you" when a man merely did his job. He said, "you're welcome": "Suddenly, rather than an equal exchange of pleasantries, she found herself positioned as the recipient of a favor."

Co-worker offered critique of presentation when asked "What did you think of...": "William may have <u>sincerely misunderstood</u> Deidre's intention—or <u>may have been unable to pass up a chance</u> to one-up her when given the opportunity." Either way, it's William's fault; either <u>he misunderstood</u>, or <u>he couldn't pass up the chance</u> to one-up her.

Is it well written?/What is the writing style?/Is there a notable tone?/ Generally, is the writing effective, powerful, difficult, beautiful?

Lots of second-person...is she talking only to other women?

- "What's important is to be aware of how often you say you're sorry (and why)..."
- "If you're not used to ritual fighting, you begin to hear criticism of your ideas as soon as they are formed...."it makes you doubt what you know..."

Lots of first person. Almost like a memoir or something:

- "A woman manager I know..."
- "A manager I'll call Lester..."
- "I heard a man call in to a talk show and say..." (talking about jokes).

Sections, paragraphs, examples slide from first person to second person to third person with no real transition and no sense of why:

- Apologies is in third person w/ first person example at end.
- Criticism is completely third person.
- Thank-yous begins w/ first-person example, then third-person example, and ends third person.
- Fighting begins in third person and then switches to second person: "But many women take this approach as a personal attack....If you're not used to social fighting..." Why does she switch to second person here? She could have done it still in third person.
- Praise begins first person. Continues in third person (William and Deidre).
- Complaints begins second person ("You complain about a problem..."), then switches to first person ("One woman told me..."), then switches to third person ("A man might take a woman's lighthearted griping literally...").
- Jokes begins w/ first person example ("I heard a man..."), then switches back and forth between first and third person ("For example, a teacher who went...")
- Concluding paragraph is second person ("If you want to get your message across...").

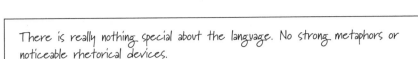

There is really nothing special about the language. No strong metaphors or noticeable rhetorical devices.

If there is a distinct mood or tone, discuss that as well. Mostly conversational. With the examples and the direct-address second person, there are times the tone sounds griping or complaining...men are wrong how they communicate. Woman are harmed by bad man-communication.

Generally, does the author achieve his or her purpose? Since her article is clearly directed toward a female audience, I think she does. She shows how men communicate wrong, and women are disadvantaged by it.

What are the strengths and weaknesses of the piece?

Strengths: Tannen does provide lots of examples from her own personal experience.

Weaknesses: Although she obviously does not want it to be, this article is biased. There is hardly a "difference" in communication styles that doesn't somehow show the woman to be a victim and the man is somehow wrong.

I don't like her use of second person, as if she's talking directly to her reader. First of all, she's not consistent. She should either talk directly to her reader all the time or never. Second, the second person/direct address means she is not talking to men, so they might as well not bother reading the article.

Do you agree with the author's arguments and conclusions? I'm not sure. I see her point about differences in how men and women communicate can lead to miscommunication in the workplace, but I don't agree that this puts the woman at a disadvantage or that the female way of communicating is better than the male.

Was the ending conclusion satisfying? Why or why not? Not really. First of all, it was hard to recognize that we'd reached the end of the article. All throughout, Tannen used numbered subtitles and spaces in the text to show she was changing topics, but there was no division between the end of her discussion of "Jokes" and her conclusion: "There is no 'right' way to talk." Her conclusion is also kind of wishy-washy, almost as if she's trying to make up for the bias she shows in the rest of the article. Her last sentence: "If you want to get your message across, it's not a question of being 'right'; it's a question of using language that's shared..." does not follow from the examples she's shown or the other points she's made. It just comes out of nowhere.

> **What is your overall response to the book or article? Did you find it interesting, moving, dull?** This one chapter was pretty interesting. I think I'd find a whole book written like this to become dull.
>
> **Ultimately, was the thesis supported by sufficient evidence?** For "evidence," she gives a lot of personal examples ("I knew a woman who..."), but there is no way to know if these examples are real or if she's telling them correctly. There might also be fifty examples opposite the ones she gives for every one she gives.
>
> **Would you recommend this book or article?** (To whom? Under what circumstances?) I think I would recommend it just because there are people who don't even know that men and women have different styles of communicating. That's an interesting point and could help in a lot of misunderstandings.

STEP 4: Outline

Maya approaches this step by dividing it into two sub-steps. First, she examines the questions her teacher assigned on the template and organized them into categories, ordering them in a way that she thought would help her communicate her ideas to her reader in an organized and meaningful manner.

I. Main idea:
  A. What is thesis?
  B. What is conclusion?
  C. Slant or angle? Intended audience?

II. Description of Article
  A. Quality of writing
  B. Notable language use
  C. Is article successful?/Does author achieve purpose?

III. Article's strengths:
  A. Qualifications of writer
  B. Quality of evidence
  C. Quantity of evidence

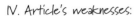

IV. Article's weaknesses:

    A. Bias

    B. Quality of evidence

    C. Quantity of evidence

V. Recommendation

Then she draws from the answers she provided on the assignment template to draft an outline specific to the article on which she is reporting.

I. Males and females by nature tend to have different styles of communication.

    A. Women in the workplace are at a disadvantage when communicating with men.

    B. There is no "right" way to communicate, but men and women need to understand each other.

    C. Intended audience is obviously women because of the disadvantaged-victim approach.

II. Nonfiction...informative...not really any attempt to persuade

    A. Writing is adequate, maybe some style problems

        1. No obvious rhetorical devices

        2. No obvious figurative language

    B. Second person/direct address to reader

    C. More confusing than successful

        1. Thesis and discussion do not really lead to conclusion

        2. Successful probably to those who already agree.

III. Article's strengths:

    A. Deborah Tannen is a linguist

        1. PhD in linguistics

        2. Professor of linguistics @ Georgetown University

    B. Evidence is mostly first-hand accounts

        1. Shows author as practitioner not just theorist

        2. Can't really argue with the eyewitness

    C. At least two examples for every point she makes

IV. Article's weaknesses:

    A. Bias: women are "disadvantaged" by their way of communicating.

> Some teachers and editors frown on lengthy or full-sentence outline entries. The outline, however, is merely a tool, not an end in itself, and as long as it helps Maya organize her ideas, it is serving its purpose.

    B. Quality of evidence: no objective or empirical evidence...only first-person accounts

        1. What if she witnessed only half of the situation?

        2. What if she misunderstood what she saw?

        3. What if her interpretation of the situation is colored by her bias?

    C. Quantity of evidence: How many situations that contradict her point did Tannen not see, or is she not reporting?

V. Recommended because the idea of different styles of communication is interesting. Not recommended if you're looking for a solution or answer to misunderstandings.

STEP 5: Write your first draft

Generally, we refer to writers by their last names, but since we know that Dr. Tannen has a Ph.D., it is appropriate to call her "Dr. Tannen."

Sentence structure problem here: subject and introductory phrase do not agree.

This is a nice introduction. There are a few word choice and sentence structure problems Maya will want to address in her revision, but this paragraph introduces the topic and predicts the nature of Maya's report/review.

"But What Do You Mean?," by Deborah Tannen, is an interesting article that raises an interesting question even if it doesn't offer any answers to that question. It was originally published as a chapter in Dr. Tannen's book Talking from 9 to 5: Women and Men at Work (Harper Collins, 1994). In this article, Dr. Tannen claims that men and women have different styles of communication and women are at a disadvantage in the workplace because their style of communication is different from men's. She concludes that there is no "right" way to communicate, but by really emphasizing the disadvantaged-woman angle, this article favors women and is most likely geared toward a female audience.

The article is essentially informative. Dr. Tannen doesn't seem to want to argue a point or make anyone agree with her except maybe to agree that the examples she gives prove that there are differences in styles of communication. And Dr. Tannen's writing is adequate for this purpose. There are no obvious attempts at rhetoric or figurative languages. There is one metaphor in the last paragraph, but this actually confuses the issue more than clarifies it. There are, in fact, a few style problems that don't necessarily cloud Dr. Tannen's point but make the reader less likely to agree with it. Several times through the course of her seven-part article (apologies, criticism, thank-yous, fighting, praise, complaints, and jokes), Dr. Tannen switches between her first-person narrative, third-person "expert-talk," and second-person direct address. The constant shifts sometimes make it hard to follow. And the second person makes it seem as if she is writing only for women.

> This detail is not in Maya's notes or outline. It may be useful to develop further, but this sole, brief mention of it does not add much to her point.

> Maya has a lot of information in her notes to illustrate her point about the language shifts and their impact on the essay. She needs to share at least some of that textual evidence with her reader in this section of her essay.

The article, then, is not too successful. It could have been more successful. Her thesis is that men and women have different styles of communication and that women are at a disadvantage. Her concluding paragraph says that neither side is right, and they all need to understand each other. The conclusion does not really follow from the thesis or from the examples she gives. Women being at a disadvantage in the workplace is a more important point than people who speak only French can't understand people who speak only English. If you already agree with Dr. Tannen's point, this article might convince you. But if you don't already agree, this article won't convince you.

> This is the metaphor Maya referred to earlier, but it makes no sense here without more elaboration when she first mentions it in paragraph two.

> Ironically, Maya uses direct address in much the same way that Tannen does. As she has already said the article is informative and not persuasive, she should not evaluate the article in terms of its ability to convince.

> A transition here would be nice.

This doesn't mean that the article doesn't have any strengths. It has many strengths. First, the author is clearly qualified to write about this subject. She has a Ph.D. in linguistics and have taught linguistics at Georgetown University for over forty years. And she does provide many examples of each of her points. All of these are from people she knows or situations she herself has witnessed. You can't argue with what she says she herself has seen and heard.

But some of these strengths are also its weaknesses. All of her evidence and examples come from her own personal observations. Is it not possible that she witnessed only a part of the miscommunication? What if two minutes after she stopped listening, the man clarified what he meant, and the woman clarified what she meant, and they both walked away happy? It's also possible that Dr. Tannen misunderstood what she saw and heard. Perhaps the woman really did want a suggestion on how to solve her problem. What if the complaining woman really can't handle her job? Also, since Dr. Tannen's view is clearly biased, it is probable that her interpretations of all of the situations she shows are colored by that bias. In order to really show that her point is valid, Dr. Tannen should provide some objective, empirical evidence, not just anecdotes. And because all of her examples come from her own experience and observation, you almost have to wonder if there might not be three or four situations to show the opposite for every story Tannen gives.

All in all, this article is worth reading because it introduces an idea that not many people may have thought about. Men and women have different styles of communicating, and sometimes these different styles can cause men and women to misunderstand each other. But I would not recommend this article to someone who already knows this and wants some advice on how to overcome these differences.

Overuse of rhetorical questions like this is really a lazy way of trying to establish a point. The main problem with the rhetorical question is that it assumes the reader already agrees with the writer—which is a point Maya criticizes in this article.

Maya is referring to specific examples provided in the article. Maya's reader, however, cannot possibly know that, and this section is confusing at best.

This type of statement is a logical fallacy called "begging the question." Maya has not shown this article to be "clearly biased." Before she makes this claim here, she needs to show the bias she sees.

Maya has written a review and not a report—and not a terribly successful review at that. While the points Maya makes are clearly grounded in a reading of the article, they are, at this point, little more than unsupported opinions. Maya's reader now knows what Maya thinks of this article without knowing much about the article itself. The report that Maya was to write, however, was to give her readers some basis for deciding whether the article would be worth reading and what to expect if they do decide to read it.

Analysis of First Draft

What is this writer's point? Maya's point is that, while interesting, Deborah Tannen's article "But What Do You Mean" is flawed enough to weaken its impact on readers who do not already understand and agree with her point.

What is his/her angle? First and foremost, Maya seems to want the reader to appreciate that Dr. Tannen's article is tinged with bias.

What type or tone of voice has he/she created in his/her reader's mind? Maya is not yet in enough control of her own language to talk about tone. There are times when Maya's writing is academic and objective but other times when she sounds angry. Control over her tone is something Maya needs to continue working on.

What techniques has this writer used to create this voice? Not applicable. One thing Maya can do is be very careful not to commit the same errors she criticizes in her essay.

What specific details, facts, etc., make this report a valid and valuable assessment of the book or article? This is probably this report's biggest failing. While there are a few points that call for additional discussion and, especially, examples and textual support, Maya offers none.

NOW plan your own article review, following a process similar to the one Maya followed.

STEP 1: Select a Topic

Choose a book or article and jot down the following information:

Title:

Author:

Source Information (publication, publishing company, copyright date, etc.):

Genre:

STEP 2: Develop a(n) slant/angle/hook

You may find it helpful to use the same template Maya used. If there is additional information or insight you think would be important to share with your reader, by all means, include it here and in Step 3.

What is the general subject or topic of this piece?

What is the author's angle, theme, or thesis?

Who is the author? What are his or her qualifications to write on this subject?

STEP 3: Brainstorm, discuss, research

Is there an obvious slant or bias? What evidence from the text can you provide to support your claim?

Is it well written?/What is the writing style?/Is there a notable tone?/ Generally, is the writing effective, powerful, difficult, beautiful?

If there is a distinct mood or tone, discuss that as well. Generally, does the author achieve his or her purpose?

What are the strengths and weaknesses of the piece?

Do you agree with the author's arguments and conclusions?

Was the ending conclusion satisfying? Why or why not?

What is your overall response to the book or article? Did you find it interesting, moving, dull? Ultimately, was the thesis supported by sufficient evidence?

Would you recommend this book or article? (To whom? Under what circumstances?)

STEP 4: Outline

STEP 5: Write your first draft

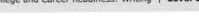
STEP 6: Peer Edit

You and your partner might find it helpful to use the same questions Maya and her partner used:

What is this writer's point?

What is his/her angle?

What type or tone of voice has he/she created in his/her reader's mind?

What techniques has this writer used to create this voice?

What specific details, facts, etc., make this report a valid and valuable assessment of the book or article?

STEP 7: Revised/Final Draft

Here are Maya's editor's comments and analysis as well as Maya's responses:

- Sentence structure problem here: subject and introductory phrase do not agree.

- This detail is not in Maya's notes or outline. It may be useful to develop further, but this sole, brief mention of it does not add much to her point.

- Maya has a lot of information in her notes to illustrate her point about the language shifts and their impact on the essay. She needs to share at least some of that textual evidence with her reader in this section of her essay.

- This is the metaphor Maya referred to earlier, but it makes no sense here without more elaboration when she first mentions it in paragraph two.

- Ironically, Maya uses direct address in much the same way that Tannen does. As she has already said the article is informative and not persuasive, she should not evaluate the article in terms of its ability to convince.

- A transition here would be nice.

- Overuse of rhetorical questions like this is really a lazy way of trying to establish a point. The main problem with the rhetorical question is that it assumes the reader already agrees with the writer—which is a point Maya criticizes in this article.

- Maya is referring to specific examples provided in the article. Maya's reader, however, cannot possibly know that, and this section is confusing at best.

- This type of statement is a logical fallacy called "begging the question." Maya has not shown this article to be "clearly biased." Before she makes this claim here, she needs to show the bias she sees.

- Maya has written a review and not a report—and not a terribly successful review at that. While the points Maya makes are clearly grounded in a reading of the article, they are, at this point, little more than unsupported opinions. Maya's reader now knows what Maya thinks of this article without knowing much about the article itself. The report that Maya was to write, however, was to give her readers some basis for deciding whether the article would be worth reading and what to expect if they do decide to read it.

And here is Maya's reaction:

I understand that a review is more opinion and evaluation, and a report is more information about the article. I think I can fix that by giving more support and examples right from the text.

I do think the article is biased, but I guess I need to support this. Maybe the "bias"-thing is my thesis, and I need to argue that thesis. I think I can do that.

I need to talk more about the comparison of male/female communication with talking two different languages. I need to give a lot more textual quotations all around—not just tell my readers what the article says and does but show them.

I need to stop using so much first and second person. "Direct address" to my reader is not allowed.

And no rhetorical questions!

Analysis of First Draft

What is this writer's point? Maya's point is that, while interesting, Deborah Tannen's article "But What Do You Mean?" is flawed enough to weaken its impact on readers who do not already understand and agree with her point.

> Okay...so at least my point is clear.

What is his/her angle? First and foremost, Maya seems to want the reader to appreciate that Dr. Tannen's article is tinged with bias.

> Good enough.

What type or tone of voice has he/she created in his/her reader's mind? Maya is not yet in enough control of her own language to talk about tone. There are times when Maya's writing is academic and objective but other times when she sounds angry. Control over her tone is something Maya needs to continue working on.

> Because this is a "report," I thought just a clear, objective, academic tone would be best. I'll look for where I sound angry and try to fix it. Maybe when I give examples of the point I'm making, the examples will help to even out the tone and make the report more objective. Right now, it's just me stating my opinion.

What techniques has this writer used to create this voice? Not applicable. One thing Maya can do is be very careful not to commit the same errors she criticizes in her essay.

> No first person. No direct address. Give examples to show that I'm not just spouting my opinion.

What specific details, facts, etc., make this report a valid and valuable assessment of the book or article? This is probably this report's biggest failing. While there are a few points that call for additional discussion and, especially, examples and textual support, Maya offers none.

> Yeah, I got that.

Here is Maya's revised draft.

By removing the "interesting article" evaluation, Maya has made this a more objective sentence. That it raises a questions but does not answer it is a fair observation for a report.

"But What Do You Mean?," by Deborah Tannen, raises an interesting question even if it doesn't offer any answers to that question. It was originally published as a chapter in Dr. Tannen's book Talking from 9 to 5: Women and Men at Work (Harper Collins, 1994). In this article, Dr. Tannen claims that men and women have different styles of communication and women are at a disadvantage in the workplace because their style of communication is different from men's. She concludes that there is no "right" way to communicate, but by really emphasizing the disadvantaged-woman angle, this article favors women and is most likely geared toward a female audience.

Another good change.

The article is essentially informative. Dr. Tannen doesn't seem to want to argue a point. The examples she gives simply illustrate the differences in styles of communication. Her writing is adequate for this purpose, but there are a few style problems that make the reader less likely to agree with her point. Several times through the course of her seven-part article (apologies, criticism, thank-yous, fighting, praise, complaints, and jokes), Dr. Tannen switches between her first-person narrative, third-person "expert-talk," and second-person direct address. The constant shifts sometimes make the article hard to follow. The second person makes it seem as if she is writing only for women.

Maya has done a nice job cleaning up her own language.

Her thesis is that men and women have different styles of communication, and these differences place women at a disadvantage. Her conclusion, that neither side is right, and men and women all need to understand each other, does not really follow from the thesis or from the examples she gives. Those who already agree with Dr. Tannen's point will probably find this article very convincing. Those who don't probably won't.

Notice how Maya successfully revises these sentences to eliminate the second person. Her second sentence is even, perhaps, a little rhetorically clever.

Dr. Tannen does provide a lot of examples of the phenomenon she is talking about. She divides her article into seven parts, "apologies," "criticism," "thank-yous," "fighting," "praise," "complaints," and "jokes," and gives at least one example for each category. For example, in "apologies," she mentions that women are likely to say "I'm sorry" in response to any mishap, even things that are no one's fault. Men tend not to. In "thank-yous," Tannen tells the story of a woman she knows who said "thank-you" to a male colleague who was simply obeying the terms of his contract. The co-worker said "you're welcome." In "praise," she tells of a woman who complimented a colleague on a presentation he had given. She then asked, "What did you think of mine?" His response was to offer a few points of constructive criticism. He, however, did not praise her talk, nor did he ask her for criticism. This, according to Tannen, put the woman at a disadvantage because there were some points she could have found to criticize in his presentation. But she never got to make them.

Dr. Tannen has a Ph.D. in linguistics and has taught linguistics at Georgetown University for over forty years. Her opinions and interpretations should certainly be believable. Also, all of these are from people she knows or situations she herself has witnessed.

But some of these strengths are also the article's biggest weaknesses. All of Dr. Tannen's evidence and examples come from her own personal observations. Her article is full of introductions like "I recently sat in on a meeting ...," "A woman manager I know...," and "I heard a man ..." It is possible that she witnessed only a part of the miscommunication. It is possible that two minutes after she stopped listening, the man clarified what he meant, and the woman clarified what she meant, and they both walked away happy. It's also

Maya has already listed Tannen's seven categories, but here is where the reader really needs to know them. In the earlier mention, she should simply mention the "seven-part article" and save the list for here.

These brief but pointed quotations work well to establish Maya's point. Her criticism that the examples are all personal is now an observed fact, not an unsubstantiated complaint.

Notice how Maya has changed her rhetorical questions into declarative statements.

This is a subtle change, but Maya has replaced a generic reference to a woman with a problem to a specific reference to the same woman mentioned earlier who's asked for feedback on her presentation.

possible that Dr. Tannen misunderstood what she saw and heard. Perhaps the woman really did want constructive criticism on her presentation. Tannen ends her "complaints" section by expressing her fear that "A man might take a woman's lighthearted griping literally ... [and] ... she may be seen as not up to solving the problems that arise on the job." It's possible, however, that the woman really isn't up to the job.

Dr. Tannen introduces her article with the seemingly objective thesis that men and women have different styles of communication. She ends by saying, "There is no 'right' way to talk." But all of her examples show women at the disadvantage in the miscommunication. In all of her examples, the woman comes across looking like a victim, while the man looks like the villain. She even says something like this in conclusion to a few of her points. In the case where the woman had complimented the man's presentation and then asked what he thought of hers, Tannen says, "[the man] may have been unable to pass up a chance to one-up her when given the opportunity." This is jab that reminds the reader of one of Tannen's points that she made earlier, "Because women are not trying to avoid the one-down position, that is unfortunately where they may end up." Along the same lines, in her section about apologies, she says, "if one person, usually the woman, utters frequent apologies and the other doesn't, she ends up looking as if she's taking the blame for mishaps that aren't her fault." In an example in "jokes" where she shows a woman earning her male coworkers' respect by railing on them, she also notes that the woman's female coworkers became less friendly toward her. She concludes, "Perhaps they were put off by her using joking to align herself with the bosses."

These are excellent uses of direct quotations. They establish the validity of Maya's criticism.

But Tannen's conclusions are guesses. Neither of them has anything to do with the fact of miscommunication, and both make the man (or the one who becomes man-like) look wrong. Dr. Tannen, in fact, actually almost says that the way women communicate is better. In her second paragraph: "Many of the conversational rituals common among women are designed to take the other person's feelings into account, while many of the conversational rituals common among men are designed to maintain the one-up position..." Then she accuses the man in the example above of <u>intentionally</u> trying to "one up" the woman who asked what he thought.

When she gives the example of the woman who "thanked" her coworker for doing his job, she concludes, "Suddenly, rather than an equal exchange of pleasantries, she found herself positioned as the recipient of a favor." This is not the only way to interpret what she herself admits was an "exchange of pleasantries."

Dr. Tannen's view is clearly biased, and it is probable that her interpretations of all of the situations she shows are colored by that bias. In order to really show that her point is valid, Dr. Tannen should provide some objective, empirical evidence, not just anecdotes. She should also have researched and found some anecdotes that were not things she saw and heard. As valid as her experience might be, there might be others, whose experience is different from hers but is also valid.

The problem caused by this bias is made even worse by some careless writing that sometimes makes Tannen's point hard to follow. There are times when Tannen writes in an objective, third-person "expert talk." Other times, however, she is writing in the first person, telling the reader about something she saw or heard. Then, there are times when she is speaking directly

This still might be a little more critical evaluation than a straight "report" would warrant, but at least Maya has led to it with actual support from the article she is criticizing.

to the reader. Usually, she switches from one to the other in the same paragraph or section. This makes the article confusing. The reader cannot know what Tannen's point is or who her intended audience is. The section on apologies is mostly in third person with a first-person example at the end.

"Criticism" is completely in the third person.

"Thank-yous" begins with a first-person example, but this is then followed by a third-person example. The section ends in the third person.

"Fighting" begins in third person and then switches to second person: "But many women take this approach as a personal attack....If you're not used to social fighting..." The second person makes it sound as if Tannen is writing only to women, and that she is giving advice more than information.

"Praise" begins in the first person and then continues in the third person with her example about William and Deidre and William's supposed inability not to "one up" Deidre.

"Complaints" begins in second person: ""You complain about a problem...", then switches to first person: "One woman told me...", then switches to third person: "A man might take a woman's lighthearted griping literally...." And the third person "expert talk" is only a speculation.

"Jokes" begins with a first person example: "I heard a man...", and then switches back and forth between first and third person: "For example, a teacher who went...."

And the concluding paragraph is in second person: "If you want to get your message across...."

Dr. Tannen's constant shifts in point of view, and especially her use of second person, are confusing and make it seem as if she is speaking only to women. That makes the article

Maya was advised to go back to her notes and provide some examples of the language problems, but all she is doing is rephrasing and repeating those notes, even to the point of naming "William" and "Deidre," whose names she did not include when she discussed their story. Maya's reader cannot help but wonder who William and Deidre are.

persuasive, not informative. She is giving advice, not being objective.

    All in all, this article is worth reading because it introduces an idea that not many people may have thought about. Men and women have different styles of communicating, and sometimes these different styles can cause men and women to misunderstand each other. But the article's usefulness ends there. Dr. Tannen's attempts to sway her reader to pitying the disadvantaged women hurts the article's objectivity and doesn't prove that point either.

> In terms of content, this section helps Maya establish her criticism. Because it is new material, however, it reads like a rough draft and could use some revision for style and sentence structure.

> This sentence is a nice reiteration of the point Maya began with, that Tannen raises an interesting question in her article.

> This is still a fairly weak conclusion, more because of simplistic word choice than its actual intent.

Analysis of Final Draft

What is this writer's point? Maya's point is that, while interesting, Dr. Tannen's article "But What Do You Mean?" could be written more clearly and supported with more objective data. The "informative" essay is somewhat biased.

Is his/her point clearer in this draft than in the previous one? The point is not necessarily clearer, but Maya does a better job supporting her comments and criticisms so they seem less like unsubstantiated opinions.

If so, how? If not, why not? Maya provides more solid, unarguable information in the form of direct quotations.

What language problems has the writer corrected, or attempted to correct? Maya has gotten rid of her own second person and eliminated all of her overused rhetorical questions.

What language problems persist, or what new problems appear? Maya has added a new section, the content of which strengthens her report, but the sentence structure and word choice in this new section tend to be repetitive and simplistic.

What new details, facts, etc., strengthen the validity and effectiveness of this draft? While Maya's previous draft came across as an expression of unsubstantiated criticism and opinion, Maya had provided more direct references to and direct quotations from the article. She also provides specific examples of the language problems she criticizes.

POSSIBLE STEP 8: Rewrite Opportunity

ASSIGNMENT 3:

Literary Analysis—Fiction

STEP 1: Select a Topic

Jonathan attended a private elementary school but now attends an academic high school in a large city. An early assignment in Jonathan's sophomore year was to read a story titled "Beware of the Dog" by Roald Dahl. After discussing the story in class, the students were given this prompt: "Discuss the use of character and point of view in 'Beware of the Dog,' and how Dahl's choices serve the story."

STEP 2: Brainstorm, discuss, research

The "research," means, first and foremost, reading and re-reading the story, mapping out its structure, and noting Dahl's use of language, imagery, irony, plot devices, and metaphor. Since the story is set during World War II, it may also involve doing some light historical research, to help Jonathan with the context of the period Dahl is writing about.

What is Dahl's major theme or the basic point of the story?

- The lead character is an RAF [Royal Air Force—Great Britain] pilot, whose plane has been hit by artillery and loses part of his leg. He seems oddly unconcerned with his physical condition, but this is probably denial and a coping mechanism. He manages to eject himself from the crashing plane before blacking out.

- He awakes in a hospital bed that appears to be in Brighton, England, but is distracted by what he thinks is the sound of German aircraft in the distance.

- While told by the nurse that there is nothing to worry about, the sound of the planes continues to distract him, and he manages to drag himself out of the bed to the window; he sees a sign that says "Beware of Dog" in French, and realizes he is not in Brighton, but in German-occupied France.

- One theme seems to be the need never to trust appearances.

- The story also seems to be a tribute to the bravery of English fighting men; the lead character never lets injury or pain detain him from doing what he feels he must as a soldier.

- 110 -

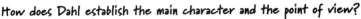

How does Dahl establish the main character and the point of view?

- The story opens with the pilot wounded in the plane, calmly assessing his situation even though part of his leg has been blown off.

- He does not feel any pain; he seems at first steadfast and strong, but he is probably in a state of shock.

- He imagines how he will get home, safely land the plane, and how he'll laugh off the reaction of his friends at the condition he's in.

- Even when he realizes he's sick and about to pass out, he calmly assesses the situation, positions the plane so he can evacuate, and pulls the cord of his parachute.

- He does this even though he's unsure whether he's over land or sea, but knows he has to make a choice in any case and take his chances.

- His character is established in the first few paragraphs as calm, professional, ironic, detached, and extremely brave; the reader is brought into his world and point of view.

What literary devices does Dahl employ, and how does that relate to the point of view?

- The story is told entirely from the point of view of the pilot.

- The reader sees only what the pilot sees and knows what he knows, experiencing the story as he experiences it.

- The twist of the ending is revealed to us only when it is revealed to him.

- Small details, such as the sound of the planes in the distance, the hardness of the water, etc., things someone else in his condition might not notice, are things he picks up on.

- Dahl creates suspense by strategically giving the reader information bit by bit.

- The main character's name is withheld from the reader until the last sentence.

What kind of voice is the story told in, and how does that serve the point of view?

- The detached, ironic voice established for the pilot both reveals his character and serves the story; plainly, he is not someone who would trust appearances or believe everything he is told, even in the most physically challenging circumstances.

STEP 3: Draft a Thesis

Jonathan considers both the story and his teacher's prompt very seriously, and thinks over several options for his thesis. Here are his ideas:

> Roald Dahl's "Beware of the Dog," shows the author's skill with character and point of view to build suspense and express a theme.
> — Too general, I'm all over the place with this. Doesn't every story show the writer's skill at doing what writers do?
>
> Roald Dahl employs a narrowed focus and specific character in "Beware of the Dog" that makes the story work as both a suspenseful and cautionary tale.
> — I'm not sure I'm addressing the prompt as directly as I should be.
>
> Establishing a single character's voice and point of view as the sole focus of "Beware of the Dog" helps Roald Dahl build his story to a climax that is not just a surprise for the reader, but a thematic point as well.
> — I think I can make this one work, it's specific and addresses the prompt.

> Jonathan has effectively brainstormed for his thesis, moving from something he knows is far too general to a much more specific, focused choice that will serve his essay well.

STEP 4: Outline

THESIS: Establishing a single character's voice and point of view as the sole focus of "Beware of the Dog" helps Roald Dahl build his story to a climax that is not just a surprise for the reader, but a thematic point as well.

   I. Plot summary

> Jonathan is committing a common error here. He assumes he must begin a discussion of a piece of literature with a plot summary. The choice of whether to summarize the plot, and how much summary to provide, must be governed by the same criteria as other information: what does the reader probably already know, and how much does the reader *need* to know in order to get the point?

     A. In plane

       1. calm

       2. maybe in shock

B. In hospital

    1. Nurse says he is in Brighton

    2. Hears planes

    3. Wonders about no air raid sirens

    4. Hears characters speak German

II. Character

A. Pilot

    1. Cool

    2. Unpanicked

    3. Analytical

    4. Sense of humor

III. Narrative point of view

A. We believe what the pilot believes

Ultimately, this is a pretty thin outline that will probably lead to a shallow and simplistic essay. Much of the problem originates with the fact that Kyle is not really paying attention to the information and structure demanded by his own thesis.

STEP 5: Write your first draft

Here is Jonathan's first draft:

Set during World War II, Roald Dahl's "Beware of the Dog," uses a narrowed focus, forcing the reader to experience the story through the eyes and viewpoint of its lead character, a seriously wounded RAF pilot who calmly assesses every situation he is in, no matter how dire. Establishing the character and voice of the pilot from the first paragraph, Dahl effectively brings the reader into his world, builds suspense by withholding information until the last possible moment, and ultimately concludes with a twist that expresses both narrative skill and a thematic point.

The story opens with the pilot, whose leg has been seriously wounded, calmly planning how he

The opening sentences meander here and don't express Jonathan's thesis succinctly enough.

- 113 -

This sentence is overlong and needs to be broken into two sentences.

will fly his Spitfire home and land safely, even thinking forward to how he will laugh off the concerns of his fellow soldiers at his condition. He is detached, cool and ironic, not feeling pain or not admitting to it—but as the story progresses, he has a reverie about returning to London and seeing his girlfriend, and it becomes apparent that he is probably in shock. As he begins to realize his condition is getting the better of him, he positions the plane so that he can bail, and manages to open his parachute before passing out. He regains consciousness some days later, finds himself in a hospital room, where a nurse greets him and tells him he's in Brighton. He realizes he has lost his leg, but she tells him not to worry about it and that he should get some sleep. Later the nurse returns with an Army doctor, who briefly examines him and mentions that his army buddies have been inquiring about his condition. The doctor leaves, and the pilot hears the sound of an airplane in the distance, but it sounds like a German bomber plane, a sound he knows all too well from combat. He hears the sound of more planes, but no air raid siren, no guns, and wonders why a German pilot would venture near Brighton in the daylight. When he questions the nurse about them, she dismisses him, saying they must be English fighters returning from France. Later that evening, he hears the noise of a plane again but begins to question his own perception, thinking he may be too ill to know one plane from another. The nurse returns to give him a bed bath, and he notices that the water is hard; this conflicts with his schoolboy memories of Brighton, and how soft the water was. He almost mentions this to the nurse, but stops himself. The next morning, after a sleepless night, he struggles to get out of the bed, crawls to the window, and looks outside. In the early morning light, he sees a sign next to a small house, but its message is in

A bit awkward here; again, Jonathan should consider breaking this into two sentences. He's also slipping into excessive plot summary, possibly losing sight of the analysis that this essay is supposed to be.

French, "Garde au chien,"—"Beware of the Dog." He realizes he is not in Brighton at all but a prisoner of war in occupied France. Later that morning, he is visited by someone posing as an RAF Wing Commander, who tries to debrief him, but he responds with the standard "name, rank, and serial number" response.

> This is a competent summary of the plot, but Jonathan might consider condensing it somewhat and get to the analysis portion of his essay sooner.

Dahl establishes the character of the pilot immediately; the coolness and detachment with which he regards his wounds and how he is going to navigate his plane safely—a situation that would completely distress most people—reveal not only his steely strength and courage, but a clear-eyed, realistic soldier's viewpoint. As he has a reverie about how he will calmly greet his fellow soldiers and laugh off their horror at his wounded leg, we also see his sense of irony: "I won't even bother to call up on the radio for the blood wagon, he thought. It isn't necessary. And when I land I'll sit there quite normally and say, some of you fellows come and help me out, will you, because I've lost one of my legs. That will be funny. I'll laugh a little while I'm saying it; I'll say it calmly and slowly, and they'll think I'm joking..." The reader is drawn into the view of the soldier, and begins to trust his perceptions, although Dahl leaves some room for doubt and suspense; as his reverie continues, and he thinks about visiting his girlfriend in London, we begin to see that perhaps the pilot is not as calm as he seems, but instead, in a state of shock. "...Bluey, I've got a surprise for you. I lost a leg today. But I don't mind so long as you don't. It doesn't even hurt. We'll go everywhere in cars. I always hated walking, except when I walked down the street of the coppersmiths in Bagdad, but I could go in a rickshaw..." Dahl thus makes the reader care about the pilot, whose name we are not even given at this point, while also raising some doubt about his mental state and how accurate his impressions might or might not be, and adds a significant element of suspense.

> The quotation nicely supports Jonathan's statement here, and will help him prove his thesis.

> This is an excellent point, and Jonathan is nicely addressing his teacher's prompt. He should, however, remove the reference to the reader not knowing the pilot's name here, and shorten the sentence in the process. The pilot being nameless should be saved for the section where he discusses how Dahl withholds information strategically in the story.

Jonathan makes a common error here that is easily fixed: the subject of the main clause must be the referent of the pronoun in the subordinate clause.

More pronoun confusion. Does "his" refer to the pilot or Dahl?

Once he ejects himself from the plane and opens his parachute, Dahl again makes the reader experience his blackout just as the pilot does, again narrowing the focus and bringing the reader into his world. "...The whole world was white, and there was nothing in it. It was so white that sometimes it looked black, and after a time it was either white or black, but mostly it was white. He watched it as it turned from white to black, and then back to white again, and the white stayed for a long time, but the black lasted only for a few seconds. He got into the habit of going to sleep during the white periods, and of waking up just in time to see the world when it was black. But the black was very quick. Sometimes it was only a flash, like someone switching off the light, and switching it on again at once, and so whenever it was white, he dozed off..." This reinforces the interesting ambiguity Dahl employs in manipulating the reader's attitude toward the pilot; we are unsure whether he is the clear-eyed, cool-headed soldier we have been presented with in the first paragraphs, or a severely traumatized man. As much as we want to trust his viewpoint, a small question lingers until the end of the story, which is the main thread of suspense.

While it's generally good to support the thesis of an essay with quotations, Jonathan should take care not to be excessive when doing so. This is a long quotation, and the third one, only halfway through the essay. Here he might consider paraphrasing, while commenting on Dahl's descriptive ability.

Really fine point here, and note how Jonathan is using his outline to structure the essay.

This thread of doubt feeds into the major theme of the story—the danger of trusting appearances, or believing what one is told. We are made to doubt the pilot just as he is doubting his situation in the "hospital"; interestingly, our trust in his veracity diminishes the more he questions and pushes past the surface of what he sees and is being told.

His strength and forbearance in the face of pain also compels the reader, and as the story moves to its conclusion, with the pilot forcing himself out of his bed and crawling to the window to view the outside world, his determination to find the truth brings us solidly to his side. Dahl is also making a statement here, about just how much strength, both of character and body, is needed in battle. The pilot becomes a symbol for the British ethic of "Keep Calm and Carry On," in the face of World War II. The story is almost a kind of anthem to England on that level.

> Good paragraph, but the last sentence is unnecessary.

Dahl's masterly handling of character and point of view, and his narrowed focus, only giving us the world through the pilot's eyes, finally builds to a solid payoff with an effective story twist, when the pilot realizes the truth of his situation. Nevertheless, he remains true to his character, crawls back into bed despite excruciating pain, and calmly continues with the hospital charade until the phony Wing Commander attempts to debrief him the next morning. "...He looked straight at the Wing Commander and he said, 'My name is Peter Williamson. My rank is Squadron Leader and my number is nine seven two four five seven.'" It is significant that Dahl has withheld the name of the pilot until the very last sentence of the story; it is at this point that we know precisely who this man is.

> This is a strong ending to this part of Jonathan's discussion, but he hasn't dealt much with Dahl's use of language and imagery and how those serve character and point of view. He also does not provide any type of conclusion that drives home the validity of his initial thesis. The next draft will have to address these problems.

Analysis of First Draft

What is this writer's purpose? The writer's purpose is to demonstrate how Roald Dahl uses character and point of view to effectively build to the climax of his short story "Beware of the Dog."

What is his/her thesis? His thesis is that Dahl's narrow focus, permitting the reader to experience the story only through the lead character's eyes, as well as Dahl's effective rendering of that character, are the chief tools the author uses to build to a revelation that is both a plot twist and a thematic statement.

What key points has the writer identified to *support* his/her thesis?

- The single point of view Dahl uses to tell the story.

- The characterization of the pilot from the very beginning of the story.

- The ambivalence Dahl plants in the reader's mind as to how stable the lead character actually is and how dependable his perceptions are.

- The resulting suspense.

- The reader becomes more invested in the pilot's plight and trusts his perceptions the more he probes and questions his situation.

What aspects of the story, in terms of language, imagery and voice, does the author cite to support his/her thesis? This writer quotes several passages from the story that illustrate Dahl's characterization, theme, and viewpoint, but does not delve substantially into imagery, language, or the voice of the author. The essay could benefit substantially by giving some attention to those elements.

Does the writer effectively prove his/her thesis? Overall, yes, the writer effectively proves his thesis about the short story. He could, however, strengthen his essay by tying in Dahl's use of language, imagery, and tone, and considering how they also contribute.

NOW you will plan your own fiction literary analysis, following the same process by which Jonathan arrived at his first draft.

STEP 1: Select a Topic

STEP 2: Brainstorm, discuss, research

What elements of the story will provide sufficient background, definitions, and evidence to support an argument?

What aspects of the story are the most key to proving your thesis?

How well does your analysis of the story address the prompt?

STEP 3: Draft a Thesis

Make sure your thesis is arguable—rooted in the text of the story, not pure opinion and not mere fact.

Make certain you have or know you can find sufficient evidence in the text of the story to explain and support your key points.

STEP 4: Outline

STEP 5: Write your first draft

STEP 6: Peer Edit

What is this writer's purpose?

What is his/her thesis?

What key points has the writer identified to support his/her thesis?

What aspects of the story, in terms of language, imagery, and voice, does the author cite to support his/her thesis?

Does the writer effectively prove his/her thesis?

STEP 7: Revised/Final Draft

Here are Jonathan's editor's comments and analysis as well as his responses

- The opening sentences meander here and don't express Jonathan's thesis succinctly enough.

- This sentence is overlong and needs to be broken into two sentences.

- A bit awkward here; again, Jonathan should consider breaking this into two sentences. He's also slipping into excessive plot summary, possibly losing sight of the analysis that this essay is supposed to be.

- This is a competent summary of the plot, but Jonathan might consider condensing it somewhat and get to the analysis portion of his essay sooner.

- The quotation nicely supports Jonathan's statement here, and will help him prove his thesis.

- This is an excellent point, and Jonathan is nicely addressing his teacher's prompt. He should, however, remove the reference to the reader not knowing the pilot's name here, and shorten the sentence in the process. The pilot being nameless should be saved for the section where he discusses how Dahl withholds information strategically in the story.

- Jonathan makes a common error here that is easily fixed: the subject of the main clause must be the referent of the pronoun in the subordinate clause.

- More pronoun confusion. Does "his" refer to the pilot or Dahl?

- While it's generally good to support the thesis of an essay with quotes, Jonathan should take care not to be excessive when doing so. This is a long quote, and the third one, only halfway through the essay. Here he might consider paraphrasing, while commenting on Dahl's descriptive ability.

- Really fine point here, and note how Jonathan is using his outline to structure the essay.

- Good paragraph, but the last sentence is unnecessary.

- This is a strong ending to this part of Jonathan's discussion, but he hasn't dealt much with Dahl's use of language and imagery and how those serve character and point of view. He also does not provide any type of conclusion that drives home the validity of his initial thesis. The next draft will have to address these problems.

And here are Jonathan's responses:

I'll work on the opening sentences; I was never really happy with them anyway.

Okay, that's just editing. An easy fix. I'm not sure about the "plot summary" comment. Maybe I should refer to plot events only as they become relevant to my analysis.

I'll just address it in editing it down to two sentences.

I'll try paraphrasing instead of the quote, and see if I can shorten that section.

> Good that they like the quote; I figured it supported what I was saying.
>
> I'll take out the part about not knowing the pilot's name and save it for the end.
>
> I think I understand the pronoun-referent problems and can fix them.
>
> Okay, another paraphrasing job, and I'll see if I can get into talking about Dahl's descriptions and imagery.
>
> Right, the outline really made this easier.
>
> I'll take out the last sentence. Another easy fix.
>
> Okay, I really didn't deal with language or voice or imagery, so I'll work to get that in the next draft.

Here is Jonathan's second draft:

Roald Dahl's "Beware of the Dog," narrows its focus to the viewpoint of its lead character, a seriously wounded RAF pilot during World War II. Establishing the character and voice of the pilot from the first paragraph, Dahl reveals to the reader only what is revealed to the pilot, building suspense by making both the character and the reader doubt his perceptions at strategic moments. Ending with a twist that expresses both narrative skill and a thematic point, the character and his point of view are intrinsic to both the structure and meaning of Dahl's allegory.

This paragraph may be a bit longer than the previous draft, but it makes its point much more effectively.

The story opens with the pilot, whose leg has been seriously wounded, calmly planning how he will fly his Spitfire home and land safely, even thinking forward to how he will laugh off the concerns of his fellow soldiers at his condition. He is detached, cool, and ironic, not feeling pain or, at least, not admitting to it. When he begins a reverie about returning to London and seeing his girlfriend, it becomes apparent that he is delusional, probably in shock. The reader begins to wonder about his condition. As he begins to realize his condition is getting the better of

The run-on sentence has been broken down, and Jonathan has added a nice touch on how Dahl plants some doubt in the reader's mind about the pilot early on.

- 121 -

him, he positions the plane so that he can bail, and manages to open his parachute before passing out. He regains consciousness some days later, finding himself in a hospital room, where a nurse tells him he's in Brighton. He realizes he has lost his leg, but retains his composure when the nurse and a doctor visit. Later the pilot hears the sound of an airplane in the distance, but it sounds like a German bomber plane, a sound he knows all too well from combat. He hears the sound of more planes, but no air raid siren, no guns, and wonders why a German pilot would venture near Brighton in the daylight. When he questions the nurse about them, she replies that they must be English fighters returning from France. Later that evening, he hears the noise of a plane again, but begins to question his own perception, thinking he may be too ill to know one plane from another. The nurse returns to give him a bed bath, and he notices that the water is hard. Having been a schoolboy in Brighton, he remembers the water being soft, so soft in fact that it was considered bad for a child's teeth, so soft in fact that children were given calcium tablets. He almost mentions this to the nurse, but stops himself. The next morning, after a sleepless night, he struggles to get out of the bed, crawls to the window, and looks outside. In the early morning light, he sees a sign next to a small house, but its message is in French, "Garde au chien,"—"Beware of the Dog." He realizes he is not in Brighton at all, but a prisoner of war in occupied France. Later that morning, he is visited by someone posing as an RAF Wing Commander, who tries to debrief him, but he responds with the standard "name, rank and serial number" response.

Dahl establishes the character of the pilot immediately; the coolness and detachment with which he regards his wounds and how he is going

---

Jonathan has broken the awkward sentence into two, and again added a nice detail from the story that clarifies the plot point. This section is still quite summary-laden, however.

Jonathan has edited down this section and cleaned up some grammatical issues, but he still provides much more blatant plot summary than his thesis requires. He is not, as he himself suggested, "refer[ing] to plot events only as they become relevant to [his] analysis." If he goes to a third draft, he must consider reducing this section even more.

to navigate his plane safely—a situation that would completely distress most people—reveal not only his steely strength and courage, but a clear-eyed, realistic soldier's viewpoint. As he has a reverie about how he will calmly greet his fellow soldiers and laugh off their horror at his wounded leg, we also see his sense of irony: "I won't even bother to call up on the radio for the blood wagon, he thought. It isn't necessary. And when I land I'll sit there quite normally and say, some of you fellows come and help me out, will you, because I've lost one of my legs. That will be funny. I'll laugh a little while I' m saying it; I'll say it calmly and slowly, and they'll think I'm joking..." The reader is drawn into the point of view of the soldier, wanting to trust his perceptions, although Dahl leaves some room for doubt and suspense. As his reverie continues, and he thinks about visiting his girlfriend in London, we begin to see that perhaps the pilot is not as calm as he seems, but instead, in a state of shock. "...Bluey, I've got a surprise for you. I lost a leg today. But I don't mind so long as you don't. It doesn't even hurt. We'll go everywhere in cars. I always hated walking, except when I walked down the street of the coppersmiths in Bagdad, but I could go in a rickshaw..." Dahl thus makes the reader care about the pilot, while also raising some doubt about his mental state and how accurate his impressions might or might not be, and adds a significant element of suspense.

Once the pilot ejects himself from the plane and opens his parachute, Dahl makes the reader experience the blackout just as the pilot does, again narrowing the focus and bringing the reader into the world of the short story. Focusing on first the whiteness of the clouds as they move across the sun, Dahl effectively describes the pilot's descent into unconsciousness as flashes of white followed by black, day followed by night,

Retaining the quotation, and this section in its entirety, was the right decision.

Jonathan has removed any mention of the pilot's being nameless, and made one other subtle but good change, from "beginning to trust his perceptions" to "wanting to trust his perceptions." This more effectively describes the reader's reaction to the pilot and his viewpoint.

Good fix.

Another good fix.

By paraphrasing instead of using a lengthy quotation here, Jonathan edits the section down to its essence while nicely commenting on Dahl's imagery and description.

Once again, Jonathan has kept what was working in the first draft, which is appropriate.

This is a good addition. Jonathan explains how the perception and trust issues work in more detail than he did in his first draft.

The exclusion of the previous last sentence in this paragraph, and the revision of the remaining sentence, strengthens Jonathan's essay. The allegorical aspect of the story is a fine choice to highlight here.

in dizzying succession, until all sense of reality is shattered. Finally, the next white the pilot sees turns out to be the white of the sheets on his hospital bed. This reinforces the interesting ambiguity Dahl employs in manipulating the reader's attitude toward the pilot; we are unsure whether he is the clear-eyed, cool-headed soldier we have been presented with in the first paragraphs, or a severely traumatized man. As much as we want to trust his viewpoint, a small question lingers until the end of the story, which is the main thread of suspense.

This thread of doubt feeds into the major theme of the story—the danger of trusting appearances, or believing what one is told. We have good reason to doubt the pilot just as he is doubting his situation in the "hospital"; interestingly, our trust in his veracity diminishes the more he questions and pushes past the surface of what he sees and is being told. After all, we've already been led to question the wounded pilot's perception, so it is easy for us to excuse away his distrust of his surroundings and, like the nurse, assure him that everything is all right.

As the story moves to its conclusion, with the pilot forcing himself out of his bed and crawling to the window to view the outside world, the reader is manipulated into a position of both admiring and dismissing the pilot. His determination to find the truth brings us solidly to his side, while we still suspect that he is not completely mentally fit. When the reader learns the truth, Dahl succeeds in making a statement about how much strength, both of character and body, is needed in battle. The now-justified pilot becomes a symbol for the British ethic of "Keep Calm and Carry On," in the face of World War II, and the story takes on an allegorical quality.

Dahl's masterful handling of character and point of view, and his narrowed focus—only giving us the world through the pilot's eyes—finally builds to a solid payoff with an effective story twist, when the pilot realizes the truth of his situation. It is only then that Dahl reveals the full extent of the pilot's character as he crawls back into bed despite excruciating pain, and calmly continues with the hospital charade until the phony Wing Commander attempts to debrief him the next morning. "...He looked straight at the Wing Commander and he said, 'My name is Peter Williamson. My rank is Squadron Leader and my number is nine seven two four five seven.'" It is significant that Dahl has withheld the name of the pilot until this very last sentence of the story; it is at this point that we know precisely who this man is and can admire his strength while we admit our own shortcomings in failing to accept his questioning.

"Beware of the Dog," then, is a short story that relies much less on plot than on narrative point of view and character revelation to build suspense, reveal a surprising twist, and drive home a theme about strength in trouble.

> Jonathan has retained his effective ending, which again is the appropriate choice. Overall, this is a strong essay, and he has given some more attention to Dahl's descriptive power, imagery, and language, although a bit more on those points would benefit here.

> While it is only half-hearted, Jonathan does provide an attempt at a conclusion here.

Analysis of Final Draft

What is this writer's purpose? The writer's purpose is to demonstrate how Roald Dahl uses character and point of view to effectively build to the climax of his short story, "Beware of the Dog."

Has the rewrite strengthened the case for his/her thesis? He has added some sections that address Dahl's imagery and language, showing how that contributes to the establishment of the character and his point of view. Some expansion on those points could still be inserted.

What new points has the writer identified to *support* his/her thesis?

- The description of the blackout section that substitutes for the previous long quote; he shows how this section plants a seed of doubt in the reader about the pilot's point of view.

- He has emphasized the ambivalence the reader has toward the pilot from the early point of the story, and how the reader becomes increasingly invested in the pilot and trusting of his point of view as the story progresses.

- He has delayed any mention of the timing of the revelation of the pilot's name until the end of the essay, underlining Dahl's technique of withholding information from the reader until the strategically correct moment.

Is there additional consideration of any aspects of the story, in terms of language, imagery, and voice, that the writer cites? While giving additional mention to imagery, language, and voice, the essay is still somewhat lacking in any substantial treatment of those elements.

Does the writer effectively prove his/her thesis to any greater degree than in the previous draft? For the most part, yes; he had made a strong case for his thesis in the first draft, and finds additional points to strengthen his point. Again, a deeper analysis of imagery and language, as well as Dahl's unique voice as a writer, would make this essay stronger yet.

POSSIBLE STEP 8: Rewrite Opportunity

MINI LESSON 1:

The Reading Check Essay: Summary

Strange as it might seem, much of what you learn "in school" you are likely to learn outside of the classroom in assigned homework and independent reading. The "Reading Check" is a common assignment that does exactly what its name suggests: checks whether you have completed an assigned or independent reading and evaluates what you have learned from it.

The summary is a condensation, a shortened retelling, in your own words, of the reading material. A supervisor might ask you to prepare a summary to save him/her the time of having to read the original or to help him or her to decide whether to read it.

Instructors often assign summaries to make certain their students have understood the key points of something they've read.

Because a summary is essentially a retelling, it is not appropriate to interject analysis, interpretation, opinion, or evaluation. The summary is about what the source says, not what you thought of the source. It is actually not as easy as it sounds.

"**Danae**" is in Kyle's English and social studies classes. She is an avid reader and prefers nonfiction, especially biography and autobiography, to fiction. Here is her work when she was assigned to read and then summarize the full text of Dr. Martin Luther King, Junior's "Letter from Birmingham Jail."

Reading Check Essay: Summary

Title: "Letter from Birmingham Jail" (1963)

Author: Martin Luther King, Jr.

Source Information (publication, publishing company, copyright date, etc.): The Martin Luther King Jr. Research and Education Institute: http://mlk-kpp01.stanford.edu/index.php/resources/article/annotated_letter_from_birmingham/

Genre: Nonfiction, letter to the editor

What is the general subject or topic of this piece? The subject is, generally, the Civil Rights Movement in the United States and the role of Southern clergy in fighting equal rights. Specifically, the subject is Dr. King's presence in Birmingham, Alabama, and the organized protest that resulted in the arrests of Dr. King and several other African-American protestors.

What is the author's approach to that topic? Dr. King's tone is straightforward and sincere. His immediate audience is a group of Selma, Alabama, clergymen so he uses a number of biblical allusions and references to Judeo-Christian tradition and theologies to support and illustrate his claims.

If there is a distinct mood or tone, discuss that as well: The tone is serious and earnest.

Does the author achieve his or her purpose? I don't know whether the letter had an impact on the ministers and rabbis Dr. King was writing to, but the letter has a long republication history, and it did have an impact on the Civil Rights movement in general, so the answer is probably yes.

How? People's attitudes did begin to change. Churches began to support Civil Rights, and many ministers participated in, and were also arrested for, Civil Rights protests.

Brief summary of reading:

For the most part, a summary should be written in your own words, but there will be the occasional time when the words of the original cannot be paraphrased clearly or accurately.

Dr. King addresses his letter to "fellow clergymen," and he outlines the reason he is writing this letter; while in jail in Birmingham, he happened to read a letter-to-the-editor from this group of clergymen criticizing the recent protest in Birmingham and suggesting that Dr. King was nothing more than an outside agitator, stirring up the minority population of a peaceful city.

He then lists his various ties to Birmingham that justify his being there. He is a clergyman and president of the Southern Christian Leadership Conference. He compares himself to the Apostle Paul in traveling to places where he is called and to places where there is injustice to be addressed.

- 128 -

He then criticizes the clergymen for condemning the recent protests without also condemning the conditions that made the protests necessary. He explains that there are four steps that are always accomplished before a protest is held in a city. Those steps are to collect facts to decide whether there is injustice; to negotiate to try to end the injustice without protests; to perform a self-examination and purification to make certain the protestors are acting for the right reasons; and then direct action, the protest itself.

The facts, as King explains them, are that Birmingham was infamous as the most completely and brutally segregated city in the United States, and more African-American homes and churches had been bombed there than anywhere else in the United States. Those bombings remained unsolved.

Negotiations were attempted but Birmingham's leaders time and again refused to talk. Finally, however, they promised to take down the signs in stores indicating whether African-Americans were allowed to shop there. Based on that promise, plans for a demonstration were delayed. But the signs were never taken down.

Then, Dr. King explains, they postponed the protest until after the city's mayoral election.

He explains that "direct action," protests and demonstrations, are necessary because they create the non-violent crises that motivate people to act. If the oppressed African-American citizens of Birmingham simply kept quiet, there would be no reason for the white citizens to work to improve conditions for the African-Americans.

He address the clergymen's letter point by point.

First, the clergymen say the action in Birmingham is untimely. Dr. King and the protestors should have given the city's officials time to take care of the situation. His response is that he did wait, and the

There is an element of evaluation or interpretation in "criticize."

city refused to act. In the recent elections, staunch segregationists were elected to office, not offering much optimism that segregation would end.

By the same token, American blacks had already waited for centuries to have their rights protected. While underdeveloped nations all over the world are creating democracies for their citizens, blacks in the United States still shop in segregated stores and eat at segregated lunch counters. African-Americans were routinely beaten, lynched, and publicly humiliated. King insists that there is no more time to wait.

Second, the clergymen expressed concern that the activists in the Civil Rights movement broke laws during their protests, but Dr. King counters that, since the 1954 Brown v. Board of Education Supreme Court Decision, integrated schools have been the law, but Southern segregationists have freely disregarded this law. King draws the distinction between a just law and an unjust law and says that just people have no choice but to disobey unjust laws. He says just and unjust laws can be told apart by the types of relationships they create between people. Just laws create relationships in which both parties are treated like humans, but unjust laws turn one of the parties into inhuman things. Segregation laws are unjust laws because they treat African-Americans like things.

He further explains that Alabama's segregation laws are unjust because they impact a class of people who was not able to participate in the creation of the law. To disobey an unjust law is, according to Dr. King, the only just thing to do. He then cites several examples: Shadrach, Meshach, and Abednego (who were thrown into a fiery furnace for refusing to pray to the god commanded by Nebuchadnezzar), the early Christians who were fed to the lions by the Romans, Socrates, the men of the Boston Tea

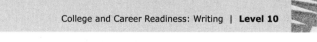

Party, and the Hungarian freedom fighters who resisted the Nazis in World War II.

Dr. King then expresses "bewilderment" and sadness about the white moderate who prefers peace and stability over justice and who would rather see an entire portion of United States citizens continue to suffer segregation than experience social unrest and turmoil in the process of making the situation better.

Another point in the clergymen's letter is that the Civil Rights protests are wrong because they cause violence. Dr. King's rebuttal is that this is like blaming the robbed man for having something worth robbing.

. . .

King notes that the clergymen's original letter commends the Birmingham police force for not responding to the protest with force, but he adds that he wished the clergymen would also praise the patience of the black community and the courage of the protestors who risked physical confrontation and allowed themselves to be arrested for their cause.

He also comments on the brutal way the Birmingham police treat the protestors now that they are in jail, and he questions whether the clergymen would praise them then. He says the prisoners, who included a seventy-two-year-old woman, were even denied food because they wanted to say grace together.

He suggests that the reason his letter is so long is that he is in jail where he has a lot of time with nothing to do but to think and to write.

He ends politely, wishing the clergymen good faith and expressing a desire to someday meet them. He expresses hope that the days of racial prejudice will end soon, and he ends on the optimistic note that "love and brotherhood will shine over our great nation."

"Politely" and "optimistic" also provide more interpretation and commentary than are generally appropriate for a summary.

Reading Check Essay: Summary

Title:

Author:

Source Information (publication, publishing company, copyright date, etc.):

Genre:

What is the general subject or topic of this piece?

What is the author's approach to that topic?

If there is a distinct mood or tone, discuss that as well: The tone is serious and earnest.

Does the author achieve his or her purpose?
How?

Brief summary of reading:

ASSIGNMENT 4:

Literary Analysis—Nonfiction

The analysis of nonfiction will not be too different from your analysis of a piece of fiction. Writers use words and combinations of words to convey information and to create effects like laughter, anger, bewilderment, and many other emotions. Except perhaps for the most dry, academic, purely informative pieces, writers will want their writing to be interesting, inspiring, funny, thought provoking, and so on.

The purpose of analysis is simply to examine how the writer conveyed the information he wanted to convey or created the response she wanted to create. Just like other literary analysis, it's an examination of organizational patters, structures, word choice, and the other tools available to the writer.

It is an examination of the writer's craft.

The development process of a literary analysis is, of course, essentially the same as the process for other academic writing.

STEP 1: Select a Topic

"Jacob" and Maya are friends and rivals. Both participate on their school's forensics team, and Jacob also competes in his school's poetry and dramatic reading competitions. He hopes these activities will win him some scholarship money for college.

Jacob and Maya's social studies teacher, who is also the forensics coach, assigned the entire class to analyze the structure and language of John F. Kennedy's "Ich bin ein Berliner" speech, which the president made during a state visit to West Berlin in June of 1963.

STEP 2: Brainstorm, discuss, research

The "research," of course, includes reading the speech, mapping out the sequence of ideas, and noting significant features of the language. It also involves researching the historical context of the speech, what Kennedy's intended impact was, and how effective the speech was in achieving that impact.

What was Kennedy's intent in delivering the speech?

— It was the height of the Cold War. The Berlin Wall had just been erected, and the U.S. had been criticized for not taking strong action against it. Kennedy needed to be perceived as strongly anti-Communist.

— The relationship between East and West was extremely tense, and Kennedy wanted to reassure West Germans that the U.S. was committed to defending their freedom.

— West Berlin felt especially vulnerable, being a divided city in the middle of the Eastern sector, surrounded by barbed wire and concrete.

— At home, Kennedy had been criticized by conservatives as being "soft" on Communism, and he needed to counter that perception.

— Kennedy was up for re-election the following year.

How does Kennedy begin his speech? What idea? What appeal?

Kennedy begins with a rhetorical appeal directly to the people of West Berlin: "Two thousand years ago the proudest boast was 'civis Romanus sum.' Today, in the world of freedom, the proudest boast is 'Ich bin ein Berliner.'"

Kennedy essentially states that every free citizen of the West has a bond with every West Berliner. He speaks the line "I am a Berliner" in German, which he pronounced with the help of cue cards written phonetically. He then goes on to indict Communism and, implicitly, the Soviet Union, for dividing the people of Germany.

His intended appeal is not just to the people of West Berlin, but to the citizens of the world, and especially of the U.S., to paint himself and his country as crusaders for freedom and justice. (Do some research on the politics in '63.)

What's in the middle? What's the transition?

The second part begins, "I want to say, on behalf of my countrymen, who live many miles away on the other side of the Atlantic, who are far distant from you, that they take the greatest pride that they have been able to share with you, even from a distance, the story of the last 18 years."

Here he directly addresses Germany's recent history, from the end of the war to 1963, expressing admiration for their "vitality and the force, and the hope and the determination" in the face of living as a "defended island of freedom" in the midst of the Eastern Bloc. He then returns to attacking the "failures" of Communism, which he makes the Wall an effective symbol of.

How does he end? What idea or sentiment?

The final part begins with "So let me ask you as I close, to lift your eyes beyond the dangers of today, to the hopes of tomorrow..."

It is an appeal to idealism; he is asking the citizens of Germany to look toward the advance of freedom and Democracy not just in their own country, but everywhere in the world. He links the citizens of West Berlin to all citizens who hope for freedom by repeating the phrase, "Ich bin ein Berliner." (Kennedy went off book on this speech, improvising a large part of it; check on how that played out.)

Repetition of words or structures?

Two key phrases are repeated: "Ich bin ein Berliner," which he uses to open and close the speech, and "Let them come to Berlin," which he repeats four times in the opening.

freedom six times, out of 588 words

first paragraph—"...Today, in the world of freedom..."

third paragraph—"Freedom has many difficulties..."

fourth paragraph—"You live in a defended island of freedom..."

—"...beyond the freedom merely of this city..."

—"...to the advance of freedom everywhere..."

fifth paragraph—"Freedom is indivisible..."

"free" eight times out of 588 words

second paragraph—"...what is the great issue between the free world..."

fourth paragraph—"...denied the elementary right of free men..."

—"...that is to make a free choice."

—"...has earned the right to be free."

fifth paragraph—"...and when one man is enslaved, all are not free..."

—"...when we are all free

last paragraph—"All free men...are citizens of Berlin..."

—and, therefore, as a free man, I take pride in the words 'Ich bin ein Berliner.'"

"**peace**" four times out of 588 words

　　fourth paragraph—"...real, lasting peace in Europe can never be assured..."

　　　　—"In 18 years of peace and good faith..."

　　　　—"...and their nation in lasting peace..."

　　　　—"...beyond the wall to the day of peace..."

Words that relate to the meaning of free or freedom

third paragraph—democracy

fourth paragraph—justice

final sentence—repeated sentence, underlining message: "All free men, wherever they may live, are citizens of Berlin, and, therefore, as a free man, I take pride in the words 'Ich bin ein Berliner'."

> Jacob has done a fairly thorough first pass at analyzing the speech for structure and repeated words and phrases to support a thesis on how effective the speech was when Kennedy made it.

STEP 3: Draft a Thesis

Although Jacob's essay will not be strictly persuasive, he knows that he's not being asked simply to list facts about the structure and language of Kennedy's speech. His essay must develop and support a thesis, an original idea that can be defended by facts. Here are several attempts at a thesis with some of his thoughts about what might work, what might not, and why.

John Kennedy's "Ich bin ein Berliner" speech is a prime example of rhetoric that is not just a foreign policy statement, but a political maneuver at home.

　　—I could back this up, but is it too pointed and narrow an interpretation? It's a part of what Kennedy was up to in the speech, but not really all. Maybe it's actually closer to a statement of fact than a thesis.

John Kennedy's "Ich bin ein Berliner" speech was an inspirational, poetic, yet politically pointed statement that drew an emphatic line against Communist expansionism.

　　—This is also kind of limited; it's true, and I could point to plenty of material in the speech to support it, but it's only part of what makes the speech important.

John Kennedy's "Ich bin ein Berliner" speech was a multi-pronged effort to inspire both the West and the people of the U.S. with his commitment to democracy, while underlining his opposition to Communism and its adherents.

—I need to work on the sentence, it's a little awkward, but I think this is closer to what I want to say about the speech. I still need to get the politics at home aspect in there.

> So far, all of Jacob's attempts at a thesis deal more with the history and purpose of the speech rather than its impact and how the impact was achieved. The closest to an analytical thesis Jacob has drafted so far is his first.

John Kennedy's "Ich bin ein Berliner" speech was a dual-edged effort...

John Kennedy's "Ich bin ein Berliner" speech was both an international and domestic political statement...

Using the international stage as a bully pulpit, John Kennedy's "Ich bin ein Berliner" speech was intended both as a rallying cry for freedom among all nations, and a political gesture embracing anti-Communist sentiment at home in the U.S.

> This is a good example of brainstorming a thesis statement, but Jacob has lost sight of the original assignment, to "analyz[e] the structure and language of ...". Clear, pointed, and accurate as this thesis is, it is not the thesis to the essay Jacob has been assigned to write.

STEP 4: Outline

This is an academic essay, essentially a thesis-proof piece. Jacob decides, therefore, to follow a traditional, academic outline format.

Thesis: Using the international stage as a bully pulpit, John Kennedy's "Ich bin ein Berliner" speech was intended both as a rallying cry for freedom among all nations, and a political gesture embracing anti-Communist sentiment at home in the U.S.

I. Structure

    A. Statement of solidarity with West Germany

        1. First paragraph

            a. "... Today, in the world of freedom, the proudest boast is 'Ich bin ein Berliner'".

    2. Second paragraph

        a. "... what is the great issue between the free world and the Communist world."

        b. "Let them come to Berlin."

        c. "There are some who say that Communism is the wave of the future...."

        d. "Let them come to Berlin."

        e. "And there are some who say in Europe and elsewhere we can work with the Communists."

        f. "Let them come to Berlin."

B. Call for democracy

    1. Third paragraph (difference between democracy and Communism)

        a. "Freedom has many difficulties and democracy is not perfect..."

        b. "...but we have never had to put a wall up to keep our people in, to prevent them from leaving us."

        c. "I want to say, on behalf of my countrymen..."

        d. "that they take the greatest pride that they have been able to share with you, even from a distance, the story of the last 18 years."

        e. "While the wall is the most obvious and vivid demonstration of the failures of the Communist system"

        f. "...the vitality and the force, and the hope and the determination of the city of West Berlin."

    2. Fourth paragraph

        a. "...real, lasting peace in Europe can never be assured as long as one German out of four is denied the elementary right of free men..."

        b. "...this generation of Germans has earned the right to be free..."

C. Call to action

    1. Fifth paragraph

        a. "Freedom is indivisible, and when one man is enslaved, all are not free."

    b. "When all are free, then we can look forward to that day when this city will be joined as one..."

    c. "So let me ask you, as I close, to lift your eyes beyond the dangers of today, to the hopes of tomorrow..."

  2. Sixth paragraph

    a. "All free men, wherever they may live, are citizens of Berlin, and, therefore, as a free man, I take pride in the words 'Ich bin ein Berliner!'"

So far, this outline reads like more an explication of the speech than an analysis.

  D. Unified by language

The use of language to unify a "dual-edged" or "multi-pronged" speech would made a good thesis to examine.

---

  1. "Let them come to Berlin."—repeated four times in the second paragraph:

    (1) Berlin as symbol of the fragile balance of power between East and West

    (2) Berlin as an example of the price of Communist totalitarianism

    (3) Berlin as proof that Communism does not work, nor can it collaborate with the West

    (4) Berlin as an example of the corruption of the Communist model

II. Idealistic Language

Jacob is indeed having trouble pinpointing exactly what this assignment wants him to do with Kennedy's speech. This is reflected in his confusion about how to indicate a discussion about "language" and the role such a discussion will have in the overall essay.

  A. References to West Berlin

  1. "I know of no town, no city, that has been besieged for 18 years that still lives with the vitality and the force, and the hope and the determination of the city of West Berlin."

  2. "You live in a defended island of freedom, but your life is part of the main."

  3. "When all are free, then we can look forward to that day when this city will be joined as one..."

B. References to freedom and democracy

    1. "Freedom has many difficulties and democracy is not perfect, but we have never had to put a wall up to keep our people in, to prevent them from leaving us."

    2. "real, lasting peace in Europe can never be assured as long as one German out of four is denied the elementary right of free men, and that is to make a free choice."

    3. "You live in a defended island of freedom, but your life is part of the main."

    4. "So let me ask you, as I close, to lift your eyes beyond the dangers of today, to the hopes of tomorrow, beyond the freedom merely of this city of Berlin, or your country of Germany, to the advance of freedom everywhere, beyond the wall to the day of peace with justice, beyond yourselves and ourselves to all mankind..."

    5. "Freedom is indivisible, and when one man is enslaved, all are not free..."

C. Words that express the virtues of democracy and freedom

    1. "...we have never had to put a wall up to keep our people in, to prevent them from leaving us."

    2. "...I know of no town, no city, that has been besieged for 18 years that still lives with the vitality and the force, and the hope and the determination of the city of West Berlin."

    3. "...the wall is the most obvious and vivid demonstration of the failures of the Communist system..."

    4. "...this generation of Germans has earned the right to be free..."

    5. "to the day of peace with justice, beyond yourselves and ourselves to all mankind."

    6. "When all are free, then we can look forward to that day when this city will be joined as one and this country and this great Continent of Europe in a peaceful and hopeful globe."

Jacob should carefully examine his outline before he writes his first draft in order to avoid some problems that may actually result in his having to take this essay into a *third* draft.

STEP 5: Write your first draft

Despite warnings from his teacher and his peer editor, Jacob decides he is ready to write his first draft.

From the early days of his presidency, John Kennedy was confronted with the seemingly intractable Cold War between East and West, specifically between the U.S.S.R and the U.S.A. The post-war division of Germany had been a flash point of contention for eighteen years, culminating in the division of East and West Germany, first by barbed wire, then by the Berlin Wall. Having grappled with Nikita Khrushchev over issues from Germany to Cuba to nuclear disarmament, and knowing he was perceived in some sectors both at home and abroad as being weaker than the Soviet premier, Kennedy no doubt felt the necessity, both as a statesman and as a politician, to make a bold, inspirational, and definitive statement, outlining the U.S. commitment to protecting West Germany from Communist expansionism, and promoting democracy as an ideal for the rest of the world to aspire to.

> Jacob is right to include historical background of the speech, but he is presenting this information a bit too simplistically. He has also misstated history. The issue in 1962 was the isolation of the Western sectors of the city of Berlin, which was geographically surrounded by East Germany.

The "Ich bin ein Berliner" speech, as it came to be known, was partly based on an earlier speech Kennedy had given in New Orleans in 1962. In this speech to a civic reception in 1962, he also used the phrase civis Romanus sum by saying "Two thousand years ago the proudest boast was to say, 'I am a citizen of Rome.' Today, I believe, in 1962 the proudest boast is to say, 'I am a citizen of the United States.'" Seizing on this sentence as a possibly potent opening, Kennedy began to consider the phrases "I am a citizen of Berlin" and "I am proud to be in Berlin" as key statements in the speech he was composing. Although he did not have a natural gift for languages, he made the decision to have "I am a citizen of Berlin" translated into German,

> Great information, but this is an impossibly long, complicated sentence that needs to be broken down into more manageable and comprehensible sentences in the next draft. It is also important to note that we are at the end of the second full paragraph, and Jacob has still not revealed his thesis—the argument at the backbone of this essay.

> Jacob refers to the speech as if he has already introduced it. A reader who has not had the benefit of seeing all of Jacob's preliminary work would not know what speech he is talking about—or why he is talking about it.

> This is an interesting historical footnote, but it does little to advance Jacob's thesis. It may also confuse the reader who knows that what Kennedy "actually" said in his Berliner speech was "I am a citizen of Berlin."

While feasible, Jacob's statements here seem to be largely assumptions and need supporting info to back them up. His reference to a "potent opening" is the first suggestion in this essay that he is going to discuss impact and how that impact was achieved.

Although it's good that Jacob is moving on from background to actual analysis of the speech, this is an awkward jump, with no transition.

Again, a reader who has not had the benefit of seeing Jacob's preliminaries has no idea where "Let them come to Berlin" comes from and what it has to do with anything Jacob is talking about.

Jacob uses phrases like "beautifully worded" and "strikingly confrontational," which are valuable in an analysis of language and impact, but he does not discuss the beauty or the striking power of the language.

Evoking symbols is another idea that needs further exploration in an analysis of the power of the speech. Jacob gives it a mere mention.

which he learned phonetically, wanting to express a deep bond between America and West Berlin.

Structurally, the Berlin speech, only 688 words long, can be divided into three parts. It opens with an impassioned statement of solidarity between the United States and West Germany, most specifically West Berlin, while making an implicit and powerful indictment of the oppressive policies of the Soviets, who have divided not just a city, but families and loved ones. Kennedy effectively repeats the phrase "Let them come to Berlin," as a rallying cry against Communism's abuse of individual freedom, or anyone who would excuse or apologize for it.

The second section enumerates the differences between East and West, between the U.S.S.R and the U.S.A., between democracy and communism. It opens with this beautifully worded and strikingly confrontational sentence: "Freedom has many difficulties and democracy is not perfect, but we have never had to put a wall up to keep our people in, to prevent them from leaving us." Kennedy continues to emphasize the closeness between West Berlin and the U.S., and pays the city itself homage for its fortitude in the face of adversity: "I know of no town, no city, that has been besieged for 18 years that still lives with the vitality and the force, and the hope and the determination of the city of West Berlin..." He goes on to effectively make the Berlin Wall a symbol of the oppression of Communism, "...the most obvious and vivid demonstration of the failures of the Communist system..."

The third and final section is an idealistic call to action, asking the citizens of West Berlin and the free world to remain steadfast in their opposition to Communist expansionism and its threat to individual freedom. He makes this statement in terms larger than just encompassing the issue of a divided Germany, but as more of a rallying point for the cause of worldwide freedom: "So let me ask you, as I close, to lift your eyes beyond the dangers of today, to the hopes of tomorrow, beyond the freedom merely of this city of Berlin, or your country of Germany, to the advance of freedom everywhere, beyond the wall to the day of peace with justice, beyond yourselves and ourselves to all mankind." Kennedy effectively casts himself in the role of a crusader for freedom in this final portion of the speech, which must have resonated at home in the US as much as it did for those gathered at the Berlin Wall, with statements like "...when one man is enslaved, all are not free..." He again praises the people of West Berlin, saying that when unification is achieved, when Europe is peaceful again, they can "...take sober satisfaction in the fact that they were in the front lines for almost two decades."

The very last words of the speech echo the memorable phrase of the opening, that expressed Kennedy's empathy and commitment, and underlined the role he was embracing internationally and domestically, as the world's most visible freedom fighter:

"Ich bin ein Berliner!"

> Idealism is another aspect that needs to be further explored. At this point, really all Jacob has done is walk his reader through the speech, summarizing, paraphrasing, and mentioning what the president said and meant.

> Here, Jacob isn't really digging deep enough; he's just restating Kennedy's words. He's at the end of his essay, but hasn't really examined the structure, language or political impact of Kennedy's speech.

> This is a disappointing conclusion; Jacob has remained on the surface of the speech he is analyzing. Instead of searching for the deeper meaning and intent of Kennedy's words, he has taken them mostly at face value. Moreover, he has not explored the historical impact of the speech, the fact that Kennedy went "off book" for much of it, making it far more confrontational than the original draft.

Analysis of First Draft

What is this writer's purpose? The writer was instructed to analyze John Kennedy's renowned "Ich bin ein Berliner" speech and show the reader why it is still such a powerful, resonant speech. It is difficult to infer from this essay, however, what exactly the purpose was other than perhaps to recap the speech.

What is his/her thesis? The thesis, as stated, is that the speech was intended both to rally the West to continue support of besieged West Berlin and to publicly state the United States' commitment to containing Communist expansion.

What key points has the writer identified to clarify his/her thesis? This is a weak point for this draft of the essay. Jacob himself seems uncertain of the purpose and point of his essay, whether it is supposed to be a description, historical commentary, or evaluation of the speech.

What key points has the writer identified to support his/her thesis?
- The writer asserts that the speech has three sections: first, it is a statement of solidarity with West Germany, especially West Berlin; second, it makes a dramatic contrast between Communism and the free world; third, it makes an idealistic call to action, asking the citizens of West Berlin and the free world to look beyond the current conflicts toward the possibility of a freer tomorrow, and to take steps to work toward that goal.
- The language of the speech helps to unify it.
- Much of Kennedy's word choice suggests a high level of idealism.

What verifiable facts does the writer provide to illustrate and support his/ her key points? While this writer does provides a number of direct quotations, he usually offers only the quotation and then moves on. It is never clear to the reader exactly what we are to make of the quotation or why it is relevant to the topic.

Among the quotations he provides to support his key points are:

- Three key sections of the speech, moving from statement of solidarity, to indictment of Communism, to idealistic call for action:
  "Let them come to Berlin,"
  "… but we have never had to put a wall up to keep our people in, to prevent them from leaving us."
  "I know of no town, no city, that has been besieged for 18 years …"
  "…the most obvious and vivid demonstration of the failures of the Communist system…"
  "So let me ask you, as I close, to lift your eyes beyond the dangers of today, to the hopes of tomorrow…."

- Idealistic language … establishes the United States as unique and worth preserving.
  "a new nation, conceived in liberty, and dedicated to the proposition that all men are created equal"
  "this nation, under God" "that Government of the people, by the people and for the people"

- Idealistic references to freedom and democracy ...
  "Let them come to Berlin..."
  "Freedom has many difficulties and democracy is not perfect...."
  "nobly"
  "...the vitality and force, and the hope and the determination of the city of West Berlin..."
  "lift your eyes beyond the dangers of today, to the hopes of tomorrow, beyond the freedom merely of this city of Berlin, or your country of Germany, to the advance of freedom everywhere..."

- Indictments of Communism
  "...we have never had to put a wall up to keep our people in, to prevent them from leaving us."
  "I know of no town, no city, that has been besieged for 18 years..."
  "...the most obvious and vivid demonstration of the failures of the Communist system..."

NOW you will plan your own nonfiction literary analysis, following the same process by which Jacob arrived at his first draft.

STEP 1: Select a Topic

STEP 2: Brainstorm, discuss, research

What specific details, facts, etc., will provide sufficient background, definitions, and evidence to support an argument?

What specific details, facts, etc., will help you achieve your purpose (i.e., inform, persuade)?

What specific details, facts, etc., will help you achieve a desired tone (i.e., academic, authoritative, humorous, etc.)?

STEP 3: Draft a Thesis

Make sure your thesis is arguable—neither simple fact nor pure opinion.

Make certain you have or know you can find sufficient evidence and examples to explain and support your key points.

STEP 4: Outline

STEP 5: Write your first draft

STEP 6: Peer Edit

What is this writer's purpose?

What is his/her thesis?

What key points has the writer identified to clarify his/her thesis?

What key points has the writer identified to support his/her thesis?

What verifiable facts does the writer provide to illustrate and support his/her key points?

STEP 7: Revised/Final Draft

Here are Jacob's editor's comments and analysis as well as his responses:

- Jacob is right to include historical background to the speech, but he is presenting this information a bit too simplistically. He has also misstated history. The issue in 1962 was the isolation of the Western sectors of the city of Berlin, which was geographically surrounded by East Germany.

- Great information, but this is an impossibly long, complicated sentence that needs to be broken down into more manageable and comprehensible sentences in the next draft. It is also important to note that we are at the end of the second full paragraph, and Jacob has still not revealed his thesis—the argument at the backbone of this essay.

- Jacob refers to the speech as if he has already introduced it. A reader who has not had the benefit of seeing all of Jacob's preliminary work would not know what speech he is talking about—or why he is talking about it.

- This is an interesting historical footnote, but it does little to advance Jacob's thesis. It may also confuse the reader who knows that what Kennedy "actually" said in his Berliner speech was "I am a citizen of Berlin."

- While feasible, Jacob's statements here seem to be largely assumptions and need supporting info to back them up. His reference to a "potent opening" is the first suggestion in this essay that he is going to discuss impact and how that impact was achieved.

- Although it's good that Jacob is moving on from background to actual analysis of the speech, this is an awkward jump, with no transition.

- Again, a reader who has not had the benefit of seeing Jacob's preliminaries has no idea where "Let them come to Berlin" comes from and what it has to do with anything Jacob is talking about.

- Jacob uses phrases like "beautifully worded" and "strikingly confrontational," which are valuable in an analysis of language and impact, but he does not discuss the beauty or the striking power of the language.

- Evoking symbols is another idea that needs further exploration in an analysis of the power of the speech. Jacob gives it a mere mention.

- Idealism is another aspect that needs to be further explored. At this point, really all Jacob has done is walk his reader through the speech, summarizing, paraphrasing, and mentioning what the president said and meant.

- Here, Jacob isn't really digging deep enough; he's just restating Kennedy's words. He's at the end of his essay, but hasn't really examined the structure, language or political impact of Kennedy's speech.

- This is a disappointing conclusion; Jacob has remained on the surface of the speech he is analyzing. Instead of searching for the deeper meaning and intent of Kennedy's words, he has taken them mostly at face value. Moreover, he has not explored the historical impact of the speech, the fact that Kennedy went "off book" for much of it, making it far more confrontational than the original draft.

And here are Jacob's responses:

> I guess I have to dig a little deeper into the research.
>
> I need to make my thesis clearer sooner. Is it possible I need a new thesis?
>
> I know I'm supposed to discuss "language," but I guess I need to pull more from my original notes and outline. I leave too much for the reader to infer?
>
> How do I "discuss" the beauty and confrontation? Am I supposed to actually point out the words and phrases to my reader?

What is this writer's purpose? The writer was instructed to analyze John Kennedy's renowned "Ich bin ein Berliner" speech and show the reader why it is still such a powerful, resonant speech. It is difficult to infer from this essay, however, what exactly the purpose was other than perhaps to recap the speech.

> I need to clarify my thesis. I want to show that Kennedy had two purposes for the speech, and the repetition of key phrases and certain words and concepts allowed him to achieve both purposes without a long, rambling speech.

What is his/her thesis? The thesis, as stated, is that the speech was intended both to rally the West to continue their support of besieged West Berlin and to publicly state the United States' commitment to containing Communist expansion.

> Okay, I understand that the assignment was to write an essay about structure and language, not just purpose.

What key points has the writer identified to *clarify* his/her thesis? This is a weak point for this draft of the essay. Jacob himself seems uncertain of the purpose and point of his essay—whether it is supposed to be a description, historical commentary, or evaluation of the speech.

> I get the impression the "unified by language" is important. Also the "confrontational" and "beautifully worded" aspects I mention.

What key points has the writer identified to *support* his/her thesis?

- The writer asserts that the speech has three sections: first, it is a statement of solidarity with West Germany, especially West Berlin; second, it makes a dramatic contrast between Communism and the free world; third, it makes an idealistic call to action, asking the citizens of West Berlin and the free world to look beyond the current conflicts toward the possibility of a freer tomorrow, and to take steps to work toward that goal.
- The language of the speech helps to unify it.
- Much of Kennedy's word choice suggests a high level of idealism.

> Okay ... that's what I said above.

What verifiable facts does the writer provide to illustrate and support his/ her key points? While this writer does provides a number of direct quotations, he usually merely offers the quotation and then moves on. It is never clear to the reader exactly what we are to make of the quotation or why it is relevant to the topic.

> I think I understand. I need to put the quotations into some kind of context, either the context of my essay—why am I quoting that quotation—or the context of the speech—why did Kennedy say it in that way?

Among the quotations he provides to support his key points are:

- Three key sections of the speech, moving from statement of solidarity, to indictment of Communism, to idealistic call for action:
  "Let them come to Berlin,"
  "... but we have never had to put a wall up to keep our people in, to prevent them from leaving us."
  "I know of no town, no city, that has been besieged for 18 years ..."
  "...the most obvious and vivid demonstration of the failures of the Communist system..."
  "So let me ask you, as I close, to lift your eyes beyond the dangers of today, to the hopes of tomorrow...."
- Idealistic language ... establishes the United States as unique and worth preserving.
  "a new nation, conceived in liberty, and dedicated to the proposition that all men are created equal"
  "this nation, under God" "that Government of the people, by the people and for the people"

- Idealistic references to freedom and democracy ...
  "Let them come to Berlin..."
  "Freedom has many difficulties and democracy is not perfect...."
  "nobly"
  "...the vitality and force, and the hope and the determination of the city of West Berlin..."
  "lift your eyes beyond the dangers of today, to the hopes of tomorrow, beyond the freedom merely of this city of Berlin, or your country of Germany, to the advance of freedom everywhere..."
- Indictments of Communism
  "...we have never had to put a wall up to keep our people in, to prevent them from leaving us."
  "I know of no town, no city, that has been besieged for 18 years..."
  "...the most obvious and vivid demonstration of the failures of the Communist system..."

Because much of Jacob's trouble started when his thesis started to move away from the assignment, he played around with a few versions of his first attempt at a thesis.

John Kennedy's "Ich bin ein Berliner" speech is a prime example of rhetoric that is not just a foreign policy statement, but a political maneuver at home.

Needing to "kill two birds with one stone," John Kennedy wrote his "Ich bin ein Berliner" speech to be rhetorically strong, so that it was not just a foreign policy statement, but a political maneuver at home.

> —I can't say "kill two birds with one stone." This is a long and clumsy sentence, and still too general about the rhetoric and policy, etc.

Kennedy needed to inspire the people of West Berlin and also make it clear that he hated Communism, so he ...

John Kennedy had one speech in which to inspire the people of West Berlin and prove to the world that he was fiercely anti-Communist ...

Needing to inspire the besieged people of West Berlin while proving to the world that he was a fierce anti-Communist, John Kennedy used the only weapon available to him to ...

The Cold War between the West and East was a war of words, and John Kennedy used his "Ich bin ein Berliner" speech to prove ...

In his famous "Ich bin ein Berliner" speech, John Kennedy wielded the chief weapon of the Cold War, language, to inspire the besieged people of West Berlin and prove to the world that he was a fierce anti-Communist.

He also revised his outline, keeping in mind that his thesis should govern the organization of his essay, not Kennedy's speech.

Thesis: In his famous "Ich bin ein Berliner" speech, John Kennedy wielded the chief weapon of the Cold War, language, to inspire the besieged people of West Berlin and prove to the world that he was a fierce anti-Communist.

I. Two purposes

  A. Inspire Berlin

    1. Idealistic language

      a. "Freedom is indivisible, and when one man is enslaved, all are not free."

      b. "When all are free, then we can look forward to that day when this city will be joined as one..."

      c. "So let me ask you, as I close, to lift your eyes beyond the dangers of today, to the hopes of tomorrow..."

      d. "I know of no town, no city, that has been besieged for 18 years that still lives with the vitality and the force, and the hope and the determination of the city of West Berlin."

      e. "You live in a defended island of freedom, but your life is part of the main."

  B. Anti-Communist

      a. "...the wall is the most obvious and vivid demonstration of the failures of the Communist system"

      b. "Freedom has many difficulties and democracy is not perfect but we have never had to put a wall up to keep our people in, to prevent them from leaving us."

II. Single speech unified by language

   A. Begins and ends with "Ich bin ein Berliner."

   B. Challenge to Communism: "Let them come to Berlin."

      a. "... what is the great issue between the free world and the Communist world."

      b. "Let them come to Berlin."

      c. "There are some who say that Communism is the wave of the future...."

      d. "Let them come to Berlin."

      e. "And there are some who say in Europe and elsewhere we can work with the Communists."

      f. "Let them come to Berlin."

III. A speech for its day and also for posterity

   A. Comparison of Berliners w/ ancient Romans

   B. "So let me ask you, as I close, to lift your eyes beyond the dangers of today, to the hopes of tomorrow, beyond the freedom merely of this city of Berlin, or your country of Germany, to the advance of freedom everywhere, beyond the wall to the day of peace with justice, beyond yourselves and ourselves to all mankind..."

   C. "Freedom is indivisible, and when one man is enslaved, all are not free..."

   D. "When all are free, then we can look forward to that day when this city will be joined as one and this country and this great Continent of Europe in a peaceful and hopeful globe."

Here is Jacob's second draft:

From the early days of his presidency, John Kennedy was confronted with the seemingly intractable Cold War between East and West, specifically between the U.S.S.R. and the U.S.A. The post-war division of Germany had been a flash point of contention for eighteen years, culminating in the division of East and West Berlin, first by barbed wire, then by a concrete wall. President Kennedy was already perceived to be a weak opponent of Soviet Premier Nikita Khrushchev, and the United States had been harshly criticized for failing to respond to the 1961 construction of the barrier between West Berlin and the Soviet-controlled portion of Germany. Given the opportunity to visit West Germany and West Berlin in 1962, Kennedy no doubt felt the necessity to make a bold, inspirational, and definitive statement, asserting the U.S. commitment to protecting West Germany from Communist expansionism, and promoting democracy as an ideal for the rest of the world to aspire to. In his famous June 26, 1963 speech, delivered at Berlin's historic Rathaus Schoneberg, John Kennedy wielded the chief weapon of the Cold War—language—to inspire the besieged people of West Berlin and prove to the world that he was a fierce anti-Communist. Much of the powerful impact of this speech came, of course, from the message itself, that the United States was committed to defending West Germany and protecting the West's democratic principles from Communist influence, as well as from the way the speechwriters phrased and organized that message to convey both clarity and strength.

> This is a much stronger introduction. Jacob not only specifies his thesis but he makes it clear that at least part of his intent in the essay is to examine the phrasing and organization of the speech and how they contribute to the speech's impact.

The "Ich bin ein Berliner" speech, as it came to be known, was partly based on an earlier speech Kennedy had given in New Orleans. In this earlier speech, he compared the ancient "proudest boast, "civis Romanus sum" (I am a citizen of Rome), with the modern boast, "I am a citizen of the United States." Seizing on this sentiment as a possible potent opening, Kennedy began to consider the phrases "I am a citizen of Berlin" and "I am proud to be in Berlin" as key statements in the speech he was composing. Although he did not have a natural gift for languages, he made the decision to have "I am a citizen of Berlin" translated into German, which he learned phonetically, wanting to express a deep bond between America and West Berlin. To bolster the emotional impact of

> Jacob presents this information better here than in his first draft, but its relevance to the thesis is still not apparent.

> These statements are still largely unsupported assertions, and the issue's relevance is still not clear.

this identification with the people of Berlin, and to emphasize the strength of his anti-Communist stance, Kennedy drafted a second refrain, which he also says once in German: "Let them come to Berlin" (Lass' sie nach Berlin kommen). These two famous and often-quoted lines, as well as a heavy use of idealistic language and anti-Communist rhetoric, give the speech its power and lasting appeal.

Jacob has misused the word "rhetoric" and may have forgotten his outline.

The historical fact is that, while the West Germans were thrilled with the speech, the Communists were, indeed, a little put off by the confrontational tone of "Let them come to Berlin," which Kennedy repeats four times in English and once in German. He uses this refrain as a response to those who say they don't understand why there is a problem, who say that Communism is inevitable, that there can be compromises between the free world and the Communist world, and that the Communist system works and allows for economic progress. To all of these arguments, Kennedy responds, "Let them come to Berlin" and see how freedom has <u>not</u> succumbed, how the Communists have <u>not</u> kept their promises, and how the Communist sectors of Germany and Berlin are economically <u>far behind</u> the free, Western sectors. He is especially confrontational when he mocks the Communists by saying, "Freedom has many difficulties and democracy is not perfect. But we have never had to put a wall up to keep our people in—to prevent them from leaving us."

This section is fairly rhetorically sophisticated, and Jacob raises an interesting point about the single repeated sentence taking on four different meanings, but he makes this point almost accidentally and in passing. Much of this paragraph does little more than summarize and paraphrase the speech.

Not only does Kennedy issue a challenge to the supporters of Communism, he also inspires the West Berliners and the free world in general to look beyond the present crisis to a brighter future. As he enters the concluding paragraphs of his speech, he asks his audience to "lift [their] eyes beyond the dangers of today, to the hopes of tomorrow, beyond the freedom merely of this city of Berlin, or your country of Germany, to

- 154 -

the advance of freedom everywhere, beyond the wall to the day of peace with justice, beyond yourselves and ourselves to all mankind." He asks them to look toward a day "when all are free," and he talks of "when" that day will come, not "if," and he promises, "When that day comes, as it will..."

> Nothing Jacob says here is wrong, and he raises a good point about Kennedy's word choice— *when* versus *if*—that need more exploration and discussion. He still cites the speech while essentially summarizing it.

The very last words of the speech echo the memorable phrase of the opening, which expressed Kennedy's empathy and commitment, and underlined the role he was embracing internationally and domestically, as the world's most visible freedom fighter.

"Ich bin ein Berliner!"

> Surprisingly, Jacob does nothing to his conclusion, which was weak in his original draft.

Analysis of Revised Draft

What is this writer's purpose? The writer was instructed to analyze John Kennedy's renowned "Ich bin ein Berliner" speech and show the reader why it is still such a powerful, resonant speech. This draft does provide evidence of an attempt to analyze language and structure, but there is still a strong tendency merely to recap and discuss the speech.

What is his/her thesis? The thesis is that Kennedy had essentially two goals in delivering this speech and that the structure and language of the speech helped him attain those goals.

Has the writer's new draft strengthened his/her point? Jacob has obviously done additional research, adding greater historical background and context, which greatly supports his point. He has cleaned up some grammatical issues, and the result is clearer, more concise, and a better read overall. He also seems clearer on the analytical purpose of the essay.

Has the rewrite strengthened the case for his/her thesis? Jacob has developed a new thesis for this draft, and he does provide support when he discusses repeated lines like "Ich bin ein Berliner" and "Let them come to Berlin." Still, there are times when he suggests points that might be worth discussing, but he does not follow through. A closer examination of Kennedy's use of *when* rather than *if* and the way each repetition of "Let them come to Berlin" takes on a slightly different meaning warrant further exploration.

What new details, facts, etc., have been included to make this a more potent assessment of the book or article?

- the use of "Let them come to Berlin" as a second refrain and the various false claims it responds to

- the assurance (neither conditional nor subjunctive) that the West *will* prevail and the brighter future *will* be realized

- allusions to the Soviet Union's considerable displeasure with the confrontational tone of the speech

Does the writer effectively prove his/her thesis to any greater degree than in the previous draft? Again, Jacob has abandoned his first draft thesis for a better, more pertinent one. He does support this one better, but there are still sufficient problems with purpose and focus that would make another revision desirable.

POSSIBLE STEP 8: Rewrite Opportunity

Jacob thinks he understands his editor's comments and concerns, so he decides he will take his essay into a third draft. Since he didn't really follow his revised outline, he is using his previous draft as the basis of the revision.

Here is Jacob's third and final draft:

> From the early days of his presidency, John Kennedy was confronted with the seemingly intractable Cold War between East and West, specifically between the U.S.S.R. and the U.S.A. With a failed invasion of Communist Cuba and a public admission that the United States could, at best, defend the already-free West Germany and West Berlin but could not successfully liberate Communist-controlled East Germany on his record, Kennedy was already perceived as a weak opponent of Soviet Premier Nikita Khrushchev. The United States had also been harshly criticized for failing to respond to the 1961 construction of the Berlin Wall, a physical barrier between free West Berlin and Communist East Germany. Given the opportunity to visit West Germany and West Berlin

in 1962, Kennedy no doubt felt the necessity to define himself and the United States as both strong and on the side of freedom everywhere. He needed to make a bold, inspirational, and definitive statement, asserting the U.S. commitment to protecting West Germany from Communist expansionism, and promoting democracy as an ideal for the rest of the world to aspire to. In his famous June 26, 1963 speech, delivered at Berlin's historic Rathaus Schoneberg, Kennedy successfully wielded the chief weapon of the Cold War—language—to inspire the besieged people of West Berlin and prove to the world that he was a fierce anti-Communist. Much of the powerful impact of this speech came, of course, from the message itself. The way the speechwriters phrased and organized that message , however, also conveyed both clarity and strength. On all fronts, the speech was a success.

The "Ich bin ein Berliner" speech, as it came to be known, was partly based on an earlier speech Kennedy had given in New Orleans. In this earlier speech, he compared the ancient "proudest boast," civis Romanus sum (I am a citizen of Rome), with the modern boast, "I am a citizen of the United States." Kennedy recognized this sentiment as a possibly potent opening. Working with his advisors and speech writers, including Ted Sorenson and State Department translator Margaret Pliscke, he began to consider the phrases "I am a citizen of Berlin" and "I am proud to be in Berlin" as key statements in the speech he was composing. He decided to deliver the chosen "I am a citizen of Berlin" in German order to demonstrate the deep bond between the United States and West Berlin. To bolster the emotional impact of this identification with the people of Berlin, and to emphasize the strength of Kennedy's anti-Communist stance, the writers drafted a second

While there was nothing terribly wrong with his earlier introduction, Jacob has clarified some of the reasons for Kennedy's early weak appearance.

Notice that Jacob has changed the focus away from the process of translation to the reason for the delivery. This clarifies the relevance of this historical information.

refrain, which would also be delivered in German: "Let them come to Berlin" (Lass' sie nach Berlin kommen). These two famous and often quoted lines provide most of the speech's unity and allow Kennedy to achieve both of his goals: inspire the people of West Berlin and challenge the supporters of Communism.

Jacob is now talking about the crafting of the speech, which is a focus very different from a simple description of what Kennedy said.

The speech did indeed achieve both goals for the president: the West Germans were thrilled and, the Communists were put off by the confrontational tone of "Let them come to Berlin." Kennedy repeated this sentence four times in English and once in German, and every repetition takes a slightly different tone as he uses it to refute a slightly different argument.

To those who claim they don't see what the problem is between the free West and the Communist East, Kennedy says, "Let them come to Berlin" and see how the political and economic differences play out in people's lives. Let them see the atrocities committed by the Communists toward the citizens of West Berlin.

To those who claim that Communism is the inevitable next step, the way the entire world will eventually go, Kennedy says, "Let them come to Berlin," and see firsthand how freedom has not succumbed, that freedom can thrive even when surrounded and threatened by forces that would change it.

To those who insist that there can be compromise between the free world and the Communist world, Kennedy says, "Let them come to Berlin" and see that the Communists have not kept their promises. The Communists have tried to starve and freeze the people of West Berlin into submission. The Communists have broken treaties and agreements in blocking free travel between the two sectors of Berlin and between Berlin and East Germany.

To those who say that Communism may indeed be evil, but it at least allows for economic growth, Kennedy replies, "Let them come to Berlin" and see firsthand that the Communist sectors of Germany and Berlin are economically <u>far behind</u> the free, Western sectors, that the residents of West Berlin, despite Eastern attempts to defeat them, enjoy a far higher standard of living than their East Berlin counterparts.

By discussing the meaning of the response right with the argument being responded to, Jacob has really tightened up this section. He is speaking about the structure and language of the speech and their contribution to the speech's overall success.

The strongest challenge to Communism, however, is probably in Kennedy's blatant observation that, "Freedom has many difficulties and democracy is not perfect but we have never had to put a wall up to keep our people in, to prevent them from leaving us." Here he gets directly at the crux of the issue of the partition of Berlin and the construction of the wall. Hundreds of thousands of East Germans were using their access to West Berlin as means to defect to the West. The very fact of the Berlin Wall proved the failure of the Communist ideal.

And Kennedy proclaimed that to all the world in this speech. Even Nikita Khrushchev commented on the stronger tone of this speech, claiming that Kennedy actually sounded like a different president.

Not only does Kennedy issue a challenge to the supporters of Communism, however, he also inspires the West Berliners and the free world in general to look beyond the present crisis to a brighter future. As he enters the concluding paragraphs of his speech, he asks his audience to "lift [their] eyes beyond the dangers of today, to the hopes of tomorrow, beyond the freedom merely of this city of Berlin, or your country of Germany, to the advance of freedom everywhere..." The key word here is clearly "beyond." He asks his audience to look beyond the present to the future day of the reunification of Berlin, of Germany, of all of Europe, of the entire world into a peaceful entity.

And he speaks of this day in certain terms. He does not ask his audience to imagine what it <u>would</u> be like if such a day came; he says <u>when</u>:

> When all are free, then we can look forward to that day ...

> When that day finally comes...

And he reinforces his certainty with the assurance, "as it will." Kennedy does not fill his audience with empty notions of what <u>might</u> come to pass, but what <u>will</u> be. The language, Kennedy's very careful word choice, contribute as much inspiration as do the ideals being expressed.

This is a much better, more focused, and developed treatment of this aspect of language.

One final goal Kennedy probably had in mind when he wrote this speech was to deliver an address that would become a historical document rather than a temporarily popular item. He achieves this goal at the beginning and the end of the speech by assuring the citizens of West Berlin that theirs is a timeless struggle that will be long remembered. His early quotation of the Roman boast, "civis Romanus sum" and the fact that he equates that with the modern boast, "Ich bin ein Berliner" connect the people of 1962 Berlin with the ancient world and emphasizes the timelessness of people's desire to be free. In his closing, when he asks his audience to look "beyond," he ends by encouraging them to see "beyond yourselves and ourselves to all mankind."

He clearly hoped to strike a timeless and universal chord with this speech, and it is apparent fifty years later, that he has.

This is still a relatively weak conclusion, given the other improvements Jacob has made. Overall, however, Jacob has finally achieved an essay that does more than describe the content and intent of Kennedy's speech; he now describes its historical context and significance. This essay does address how the structure and language of the speech helped Kennedy achieve the goals he set out to achieve in writing and delivering it.

The very last words of the speech, "<u>Ich bin ein Berliner!</u>" echo the memorable phrase of the opening. They expressing Kennedy's empathy and commitment to a particular embattled people, while underlining the role he was embracing internationally and domestically, as the world's most visible freedom fighter.

MINI LESSON 2:

The Reading Check Essay: Interpretation

Because the purpose of a summary is simply to retell the contents of something you've read, summary allows for no interpretation or commentary. As a Reading Check exercise, the summary is a means for your teacher to test the extent to which you understood the surface information of the original. At other times, however, in addition to repeating what the source has said, you may actually be asked to make a statement of what it means.

This is interpretation. Think of what a sign language interpreter does when he or she listens to a speaker and then translates the spoken language into hand signs that the hearing impaired can comprehend. Conversely, the interpreter might observe someone's hand signals and tell a hearing audience what the signs mean.

Having information or data is an important part of learning, but it is only a part. Another important part is being able to interpret that information or data. What does it mean? What is the speaker, or writer, or signer suggesting? What can be inferred from the specific word choice, tone of voice, structure, and so on?

In addition to the Reading Check: Summary, a common independent reading assignment is a brief interpretive essay. While studying United States Romantic and Anti-Romantic literature, Kyle's class was assigned to read several works by poets represented in their anthology and submit essays interpreting these works.

Here is Kyle's essay interpreting Edgar Allan Poe's *The Raven*.

Title: The Raven

Author: Edgar Allan Poe

Source Information (publication, publishing company, copyright date, etc.): Retrieved from poets.org, the site of the Academy of American Poets. Originally published 29 January 1845 in the New York Evening Mirror.

Genre: (narrative) poem

What is the general subject or topic of this piece? The poem involves grief and then either damnation or madness. There are strong suggestions of witchcraft and necromancy, which is a physical or romantic love of the dead.

> There is nothing wrong with the possibility that Kyle might have done a little research while reading this poem, as long as he does not allow information and information from his sources to excessively influence his own reading and interpretation.

What is the author's approach to that topic? The author, Poe, tells the story of a man who has lost his girlfriend. The poem has long lines with a rhythm pattern and rhyme scheme that are impossible to miss. There is a lot of imagery and a lot of repetition in the poem. It's dark, mysterious, maybe even frightening. The raven itself might be a symbol.

If there is a distinct mood or tone, discuss that as well: The mood is dark and mysterious. Frightening.

Does the author achieve his or her purpose? Yes.

How? Poe creates a lot of imagery—reading by firelight, the room and its furnishings. The lines of poetry are long, and the internal rhyme (dreary/weary; napping/tapping/rapping, etc.) makes you read them fast and always look ahead to what's still coming, what's going to happen.

Brief interpretation of reading:

In essays like this, it is customary to discuss plot events in the present tense.

The Raven is probably Edgar Allan Poe's most famous poem. Everyone agrees that it is a spooky poem that has to do with the speaker's grief over the death of a woman we know only as "Lenore." Most people think the poem tells the story of the speaker's fall into insanity because his grief is so deep. The raven is a hallucination, and the message at the end of the poem is that he will never ever get over the sharpness of his grief. There is nothing much wrong with this interpretation, but I think there is a lot of evidence in the text to support an interpretation that the speaker is trying to use witchcraft to conjure Lenore, and the raven arrives as a messenger to tell him that he is now condemned to an eternity in Hell for dabbling in the dark arts.

Kyle has an interesting thesis, certainly one that is worth considering, but he needs to learn to state a "contrary to common belief" thesis without using the first person. Still, as this is a relatively informal essay, written in a short period of time, the scorer would most likely be instructed to ignore minor infractions like this.

This is a very awkward sentence that Kyle would want to revise if he were to take this essay into a second draft.

That there is a Lenore who is dead and missed by the speaker cannot be argued. References to

Lenore in the second stanza can be read only a certain number of ways:

> ... vainly I had sought to borrow
>
> From my books surcease of sorrow—
> <u>sorrow for the lost Lenore—</u>
>
> For the rare and radiant maiden <u>whom</u>
> <u>the angels name Lenore</u>
>
> <u>Nameless here for evermore.</u>

There is sorrow. Lenore is lost. The angels name her, but she no longer has a name "here." Clearly she is dead. That Lenore is dead and in Heaven is reinforced toward the end of the poem:

> Tell this soul with sorrow laden if, within
> the distant Aidenn,
>
> It shall clasp a sainted maiden whom the
> angels name Lenore—
>
> Clasp a rare and radiant maiden whom
> the angels name Lenore.

No one really questions the basic facts of dead Lenore and grieving speaker. What no one seems to notice is that, early in the poem, the speaker says he has been trying to conjure Lenore. Instead, the raven comes to tell him of his eternal damnation. The most important clues to this interpretation are the books the speaker is reading at the beginning of the poem combined with the "bust of Pallas," the speaker's reaction to the arrival of the raven, and specific questions the speaker asks that the raven answers "nevermore."

The speaker says in the first stanza that he is reading—not only reading but "ponder[ing] weak and weary over many a <u>quaint and curious</u> volume of <u>forgotten lore</u>." He's not reading the newspaper. He's not reading a gothic romance or techno-spy thriller. He is reading closely ("ponder[ing]") large books ("volumes") of ancient, mystical wisdom ("forgotten lore"). He continues to tell the reader, not that he

Kyle seems to be setting himself up for a five-paragraph essay format, always a safe choice for an informal and/or timed essay.

Near-vulgar slang is never appropriate, even in a quick homework essay like this.

was simply passing the time reading, hoping to feel less crappy about Lenore. He says he had "sought to borrow <u>from [his] books surcease</u> of sorrow..." Whatever he was looking for in those books was not a temporary relief; it was supposed to <u>end his sorrow</u>. Finally, too many readers simply overlook the bust of Pallas on which the raven perches and where it stays. On the one hand, it is true that a lot of Victorian homes had elaborate woodwork with statues and things over the doors. But Poe makes it a point for the statue over this door to be a bust of Pallas. In Greek mythology, Pallas is closely associated with the goddess Athena. As often as not, Pallas and Athena are the same person. As a goddess, Athena governed all sorts of knowledge, wisdom, and arts and crafts, so it is not too big a stretch to connect the raven's perching on the bust of the pagan goddess of knowledge and craft with the speaker's trying to use this ancient, pagan knowledge and craft to conjure up his dead girlfriend.

The speaker's reaction to the arrival of the raven supports this. When he hears the tapping, "as of someone gently rapping" on his chamber door, his response is not simply to call "come in" or "who is it?" Instead, he tries to convince himself that it is only a visitor:

'Tis some visitor,' I muttered, 'tapping at my chamber door—

Only this and nothing more.'

You're tempted to ask, <u>What else could it be? What were you expecting?</u> I think the answer would be that he was maybe expecting Lenore. The next stanza intensifies the idea that he is expecting something terrifying when he hears the knock on his door. Every little sound terrifies him, as he's never been terrified before. His heart is pounding, and he <u>stands up</u>, saying over and over to himself that it is <u>only a visitor</u>.

His reaction must make the reader wonder why he is so frightened. What else could it be? Who or what was he expecting that a simple knock at the door would terrify him so much? This terror continues into the fourth and especially the fifth stanzas:

> Deep into that darkness peering, long I stood there wondering, fearing,
>
> Doubting, dreaming dreams no mortal ever dared to dream before;

Remember that the literal situation is a man who has been reading and dozing in his chair. He is startled awake by a knock on his door, but his reaction is far more intense than simply being startled awake. It is even more intense than someone who is afraid of a late-night phone call because he's afraid it must be bad news. This man is "dreaming dreams no mortal ever dared to dream before." The most intriguing piece of evidence that those dreams "no mortal ever dared to dream before" involve bringing Lenore back from the dead comes in the next couple of lines:

> But the silence was unbroken, and the stillness gave no token,
>
> And the only word there spoken was the whispered word, 'Lenore?'
>
> This I whispered, and an echo murmured back the word, 'Lenore!'—
>
> Merely this and nothing more.

When he says her name, he is asking it, not stating it. The text depicts him as standing at his open door, peering into the darkness asking Lenore if she's there. He knows she's dead; why would he ask for her?

Clearly, at the beginning of the poem, he is studying books of ancient magic. Just as he feels he has not succeeded in ending his grief

Again, if this were a more formal essay, Kyle would want to eliminate these rhetorical questions in revision.

Kyle is getting a little melodramatic here, but he does put forth a compelling point.

by bringing Lenore back, he hears a knock at his door and is <u>terrified</u> of the possibility: it's not just any ordinary visitor; it is Lenore Come Back from the Grave.

For the speaker, whether literally or in his guilt-and-grief-baffled mind, his attempt to restore Lenore to life has resulted in his being separated from her forever. The raven's one-word vocabulary is well-known. Everything the speaker says, and every question the speaker asks is answered with "Nevermore." Most people, I think, take "nevermore" to mean "no." It actually means "not anymore" or "never again." What is possible "nevermore" was probably once possible, but something has made it now impossible. What will happen "nevermore" probably happened once or more in the past, but for some reason it will never happen again.

Here are the statements the speaker makes and questions he asks that are all answered, "not anymore, never again":

- What is your name? ("Tell me what thy lordly name is...")

- He will abandon me just as everyone else in my life has. ("Other friends have flown before—On the morrow he will leave me, as my hopes have flown before.")

- You fool (speaking to himself), this bird has come to ease your sorrow. Take advantage of the distraction and forget Lenore. ("Wretch," I cried, "thy God hath lent thee—by these angels he hath sent thee/ Respite—respite and nepenthe, from thy memories of Lenore;/Quaff, oh quaff this kind nepenthe and forget this lost Lenore!")

- Is there hope and healing for the bereaved? ("...tell me truly, I implore—Is there—is there balm in Gilead?—tell me—tell me, I implore!")

- Will I (will my soul) ever be reunited with Lenore('s soul)? ("Tell this soul with sorrow laden if, within the distant Aidenn,/It shall clasp a sainted maiden whom the angels name Lenore.")

- Go away, leave me alone, stop tormenting me, and leave no sign of your ever having been here. ("Get thee back into the tempest and the Night's Plutonian shore!/ Leave no black plume as a token of that lie thy soul hath spoken!/Leave my loneliness unbroken!—quit the bust above my door!/ Take thy beak from out my heart, and take thy form from off my door!")

> In a more formal essay, this section would need to be formatted better. As it is, however, Kyle is demonstrating and supporting his understanding of the text.

There may have been a time when the raven would leave the speaker alone to his grief. There may have been a time when the speaker would have forgotten Lenore, and the pain of her loss would have healed. There may have been a time when he and Lenore would be reunited in Heaven. But something has happened so that those situations exist and those occurrences are possible "not anymore" or "never again." What has happened is open to speculation, but I think the answer is clear in the beginning of the poem. The speaker is so filled with grief that he tries to meddle with things he has no business meddling with. He tries to resurrect or conjure Lenore, to bring her back from the dead, and instead he encounters the raven who tells him that never again will he know peace or healing or the loving presence of Lenore.

> These few sections are important. Notice that Kyle does not simply offer his reader a quotation and require the reader to arrive at his or her own conclusion; after the quotations, Kyle discusses what the text means and what point he is illustrating with the quotation.

The Raven is truly more than just a spooky and puzzling poem. The raven itself is more than just a symbol of death or grief. The poem tells the story of a man so filled with grief, he sacrifices his soul, his salvation, for the chance to bring his dead love back to life.

> All in all, this is a good first-draft-quality essay of interpretation. Kyle has a clear and reasonable thesis. He keeps his interpretation close to the text, and he provides plenty of evidence to support his claims.

Template for the Reading Check Essay: Interpretation

Title:

Author:

Source Information (publication, publishing company, copyright date, etc.):

Genre:

What is the general subject or topic of this piece?

What is the author's approach to that topic?

If there is a distinct mood or tone, discuss that as well:

Does the author achieve his or her purpose?

How?

Brief interpretation of reading:

PART III:

Persuasive Writing

[asserting and defending claims]

You learned last year that the basis of a persuasive essay is the **claim**, the central point or argument that you want to establish. Claims are similar to theses in other essays: they cannot be mere fact because, while a fact might need to be verified, it cannot be reasonably argued. Likewise, claims cannot be mere opinion; even an informed and reasonable opinion cannot be argued beyond stating the opinion and your reasons for holding it.

While some claims are specific enough that they can be argued directly, most claims will be too broad to throw evidence at them and expect the reader to be convinced. Instead, the central argument will be broken down into smaller claims that can be proven directly.

Stephen Toulmin, the philosopher whose model for argument has become the standard for persuasive writing and speaking, based his system of practical argument on the type of argument found in courts of law. In a criminal trial in the United States, because the defendant is *presumed innocent until proven guilty*, the burden of proof is on the prosecution. Theirs is the initial argument—the claim.

The prosecution's **central claim** is that X is guilty of the crime. For the sake of argument, let's say it's a juicy murder.

The prosecuting attorney will open his or her case by laying out the **supporting claims**:

1. X was in possession of the murder weapon on the night of the murder.

2. X was physically present at the murder scene on the night of the murder.

3. X had a motive for wanting the victim dead.

During the trial itself, the prosecutor will present to the jury evidence and testimony—*not to prove the central claim, but that each of the supporting claims is true.*

X's fingerprints were on the gun.

X had the gun in her purse at the time she was arrested.

X was arrested on the same night as the murder.

Therefore, X was in possession of the gun on the night of the murder. (1)

X's fingerprints are everywhere inside the house and the room where the murder took place.

DNA tests on hairs found near the body show the hair to be X's.

Several eyewitnesses saw X entering the house and then leaving it again roughly around the time of the murder.

Therefore, X was physically present at the murder scene on the night of the murder. (2)

X was deeply in debt and hounded by organized criminals who wanted their money.

The victim was insured for $1 million, and X was the sole beneficiary.

X had wanted to move into the victim's apartment building, but there were no available apartments.

Therefore, X had a motive for wanting the victim dead. (3)

Having established each of the supporting claims, the prosecutor can close the case like this: Since (1) has been established as true, and (2) has been proven, and the truth of (3) has been demonstrated, **the only likely conclusion is that X is guilty of the crime (*central claim*).**

For Jacob and his classmates, then, this step does not only require them to formulate a central claim but also means they must establish two or more supporting claims. Like many of his classmates, Jacob took a few of his possible topics into the next step. He realized that the process of generating claims and sub-claims would help him exclude topics that wouldn't work and identify the argument he was most interested in pursuing.

Between the claims, supporting claims, and evidence are the **warrants**, the reasons or rationale that explain *how* the evidence points to a certain claim. Take, for example, our second supporting claim, that **X was physically present at the murder scene on the night of the murder**. The claim is based on fingerprints,

DNA, and eyewitness accounts. If we did not have the eyewitness accounts, however, it could be argued that X left her fingerprints and DNA at the scene when she returned a library book several hours before the murder. Without the eyewitness testimony, the supporting claim is *warrantless*.

Your warrant might be a new connection you have realized and must explain to your readers. It might be an idea that is obvious to some but needs to be pointed out or verified to others, or it might be a thought or value that most everyone generally accepts. In any case, it is crucial for you to make sure that your readers understand not only your claims and evidence, but that they also accept your warrants. Even the most talented and persuasive prosecutor will be unable to win a warrantless argument.

ASSIGNMENT 1:

The Initial Argument

In terms of our criminal trial analogy, the initial argument is the charge brought by the prosecution against the defendant. The burden of proof lies with the prosecution. When you are assigned to develop and argue a point, you are the prosecution.

Just as the prosecution will not pursue a case until it feels it has enough evidence to win, you should not assert a claim or begin to write your essay until you know you will be able to make a strong case.

Just as the prosecution will lay out its case in terms of its general claim (defendant is guilty) and several supporting claims (defendant had the weapon; defendant was present at scene; defendant had motive), you will develop a number of supporting claims, each of which backs the general claim.

And just as the prosecution will present evidence for each of its supporting claims, you will organize your essay around your supporting claims and use them to establish the credibility of your general claim.

Jacob's social studies class has a "Contemporary Issues" component. Every marking period, students are to select a current issue they've been following and write an essay in which they take a position on the issue and write an essay supporting that position.

Here is Jacob's work for one of his essays.

STEP 1: Select a Topic

Jacob has been following these issues and is considering each for this marking period's persuasive essay topic:

teaching "intelligent design" in school—too controversial?

whether or not phys ed and/or drivers ed should be removed from the school schedule—I wonder if I could find real, factual evidence about costs and instruction time, etc.

> Jacob almost decided on this topic and was prepared to argue to drop the high school drivers education requirement as a means to save money. In his preliminary research, however, he learned that most states already had abolished in-school driver's ed and that the current trend was for such courses to be reinstated. He also found that he agreed with the reasons for the return of mandatory drivers ed. He, therefore, dropped his plans for this topic. It's always a good idea to consider more than one possible topic at this step.

New York City's anti-soda law—this could be really pretty clear-cut

mandatory foreign language study—I can start with the information I got last year for debate class. I was amazed at some of the statistics, and I think I can present a different angle from what most people argue about.

ratings labels on CDs and music products—yawn. Does anyone even buy CDs anymore?

mandatory "volunteer" programs—maybe another yawn, but there are some things I could say that might be a little original. But will I be able to find facts, or will all of my support be opinion?

STEP 2: Develop an argument

Topics are essentially neutral. Those that Jacob is considering, for example:

- teaching "intelligent design" in school
- whether or not phys ed and/or drivers ed should be removed from the school schedule
- New York City's anti-soda law
- mandatory foreign language study
- ratings labels on CDs and music products
- mandatory "volunteer" programs

neither state nor imply whether Jacob favors the "pro" or the "con." *Should* "intelligent design" be taught or not? *What about* New York's anti-soda law?

This step is when you "take sides," as it were and state the point you are going to argue. The argument you develop *should* be one that you can actually support (unless, of course, you are required to argue *both sides* of an issue). Here are the various arguments Jacob considered based on his chosen potential topics.

New York City's anti-soda law is a necessary part of our fight for better health for all citizens.

Drinking soda, especially sugared soda, contributes to poor nutrition.

High-sugar foods and beverages, like soda, are leading causes of juvenile obesity and adult-onset diabetes.

Stores, restaurants, and soda manufacturers will not willingly curb the supply of soda to the public.

> Jacob has laid out a nice argument here. The third supporting claim is especially important because it will address why a law banning the sale of soda is important.

In order to receive a high school diploma in our state, every student should be required to be fluent, in at least two languages, English and some other.

> Right now, it's awkwardly written, and Jacob will soon learn that "fluency" is an extremely high goal, so he will be rewording this central claim as he works on his essay.

Most students in other countries are required to study their own language and some other.

Many of them learn English.

> This second supporting claim is not independent of the first. Jacob will fix this in his writing and revising process.

Knowing a second language makes a person smarter more than just knowing a second language.

> This is another very awkwardly worded sentence, but Jacob knows what he means, and he has enough clarity to do some research to learn what he needs to learn—and learn how to communicate it.

The process of learning a second language helps students learn English better.

Students whose first language is not English will learn English but will not have to give up their native language.

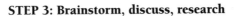

STEP 3: Brainstorm, discuss, research

Jacob got excited about his language topic; he'd never heard anyone argue either side, and he was certain he could find enough factual information to support the benefits of learning a second language. His research takes him mostly to the Internet. This is not a formal research paper, so he knows a few journal or news articles will be sufficient as long as he can verify that his information is accurate and authoritative.

STEP 4: Outline

Given his central claim and his supporting claims, Jacob found drafting his outline fairly easy. His biggest mistake, however, was confusing this preliminary outline—intended to guide his research—with the final outline from which he would write his first draft.

Central Claim: In order to receive a high school diploma in our state, every student should be required to be fluent, in at least two languages, English and some other.

I. Most students in other countries are required to study their own language and some other.

    A. What can I find about foreign language requirements in other countries?

        1. reasons for requiring a foreign language

        2. What and how many languages are required?

    B. What can I find especially about learning English?

        1. How many students worldwide study English in school? (not counting in English-speaking countries!)

        2. Is English required anywhere?

            a. Why is it required where it is required?

            b. What are the requirements where E is not required, but a f.l. is?

        3. Maybe something about exchange students and summer workers who come to America to improve their English.

    C. Why two languages, though? Why not just switch to English?

    D. How about England and Canada? Do they require a foreign language?

II. Knowing a second language makes a person smarter more than just knowing a second language does.

   A. Brain information—exercise the part of the brain that does language

   B. Cultural stuff—learning about the people and their culture and seeing things from their point of view

   C. Reasoning and "thinking about thinking" ... talking about how you think and learn things. When you have more than one language to think about things, that does something to how you think.

III. The process of learning a second language helps students learn English better.

   A. Grammar, mechanics, sentence structure, syntax, etc.

   B. Vocabulary

IV. Students whose first language is not English will learn English but will not have to give up their native language.

   A. "English only" and "English first" are really hot topics in America

      1. Whatever happened to that English-as-official-language amendment?

      2. This would make sure that everyone in America can speak and read English

   B. All of the benefits of learning a second language probably apply to non-English-speakers learning English.

This outline indicates a strong structure, but its content would work better as an element in STEP 3—a preliminary outline to lay out the information Jacob intends to search for. This outline should be Jacob's final preparation for a solid first draft.

STEP 5: First Draft

Although Jacob's teacher advised him that he is not yet ready to write his first draft, Jacob insisted that he "knew what he wanted to say" and that he "didn't want to fall behind."

Here, then, is Jacob's first draft. Read it and consider its strengths and weaknesses. How successfully does Jacob develop and support his supporting claims and, thus, establish his argument?

There's a lot of controversy right now in the United States about whether or not the people who live and work here and who receive public services and apply for things like drivers' licenses, etc., should be required to speak only English. People are actually offended when they hear some people speaking some other language than English. On the other hand, everyone else in the world speaks at least two languages fluently. Americans are looked down upon and considered self-centered for not bothering to learn another language. There are also many benefits to being able to speak, read, and write in more than one language. Knowing a second language makes a person smarter more than just knowing a second language. The process of learning a second language helps students learn English better. Therefore, in order to receive a high school diploma in our state, every student should be required to be fluent, in at least two languages, English and some other. One final benefit of this would be that students whose first language is not English will learn English but will not have to give up their native language.

One reason American students should be required to know two languages is because most students in other countries are required to study their own language and some other. In 1995, the European Commission published a paper in which they stressed how important it is for children to learn at least two foreign languages before they enter "upper secondary" school. The European Commission is to the European Union what the White House staff is to the United States. They are an executive body whose responsibilities include proposing legislation and making sure that decisions are implemented and laws are enforced. The issue discussed in the 1995 paper isn't only about learning two languages but also beginning the instruction at an early age. Both are important.

Jacob does manage to state his claims, but the structure of this paragraph reveals a lack of parallelism among the supporting theses. Three of the four support a student's learning a second language, but the fourth directly supports the central claim. This oddly-structured paragraph might foreshadow an oddly-structured essay.

This is not exactly the same wording as Jacob's central claim, and it does not mean exactly the same thing. Jacob will need to examine both and decide which it is that he means.

A little explanation is called for but not a lengthy definition. The second sentence begins to shift the focus away from the actual topic of the essay.

Jacob has twisted the sense of his sentence around an awkward passive construction.

This paragraph does little to advance Jacob's argument. It confuses the point—is the issue the need to learn a second language or to begin language instruction at a young age? It also presents additional claims instead of actual evidence.

There may be a certain just logic to Jacob's reasoning here, but it really has nothing to do with his argument. He also needs to eliminate the rhetorical questions in order to strengthen whatever points he is trying to make.

So far, this is the first bit of hard data Jacob has provided. Ironically, these statistics more weaken Jacob's claim than strengthen it.

Jacob's attempt at a transition is good, but he has not discussed a "benefit," so it is not logical to claim to be offering "another" benefit.

Almost all students in Europe study at least one foreign language as a mandatory part of their education. They study foreign language three to four hours a week. And all of these languages are started being learned while the student is very young, sometimes as young as six years old.

In order to study at Central European University in Budapest, for example, you have to demonstrate "proficiency in English by submitting standardized English language test scores, e.g., the Test of English as a Foreign Language (TOEFL) or other ... tests." Central European University is in Hungary, where the main language is Hungarian. Most students come from other countries where the mail language is not English. Why, then, should the school require its students to be proficient in English? Why doesn't a school in Hungary require its students to learn Hungarian?

Beginning in 2010, every school child in the United Kingdom learns a foreign language beginning at the age of seven. Canada is an officially bilingual country, its two official languages being English and French. They highly value their two languages and have made it a goal to increase the number of bilingual graduates. In 2003, the Canadian government announced a ten-year plan to fund programs in each Canadian province to increase bilingualism among all Canadian graduates. Then, the bilingual students were 24% of the overall population. Their goal is to make it 50% by 2013.

Another benefit of knowing a second language is that it makes a person smarter more than just knowing a second language. When you learn a foreign language, things happen in your brain.

A study done at the University College of London in 2004 showed that the brains of people who studied their second language at a young age had denser "grey matter" than those who learned one later. Grey matter is the part of the brain that processes information. Other studies show that learning a second language at an early age helps the child develop divergent thinking. This kind of thinking doesn't only involve learning languages but things like math. The second language gives children another way of expressing themselves. This helps them learn that there is more than one way to look at a problem, and there is probably more than one way to solve it. All of these benefits come from studying a second language.

> Jacob's conclusion does not follow the evidence. The benefits he claims are the result of early study of language, not just the study of a second language.

Students who study a foreign language also don't study just the language. Usually foreign language classes also teach the culture of the country that speaks the language. They teach the food, clothing, and the music and dancing and other entertainment of the country. Where a country has different words to mean the same thing, we learn how those synonyms tell us something about what those people think and value. So learning a language is not just learning the language but learning the culture, too.

> Jacob relies quite heavily on unsupported generalizations like this one.

Learning a language also has an effect on how the student's brain works. This is called metacognition, and it has to do with how we see the world, take in information, and solve problems. It also has to do with how we express what we know. Knowing a second language allows a person to see things from different points of view and to find more than one way to solve problems.

> The paragraph is unclear and vague. For the most part, it simply repeats what Jacob has already said.

The process of learning a second language helps students learn English better. Most schools' English courses don't teach English as a language. Because the majority of students can already speak and understand some English, they aren't taught a lot of structure and grammar. They are taught to use the language in writing and skills like that. When you begin to study a foreign language, you

> Here is another unsupported generalization.

There are many problems with this paragraph. Word choice and point of view are confusing. While speaking about the same group of students, Jacob uses third person, second person, and then third person again. He limits his content to loose summary with no specifics and no detail.

start at the very beginning, and you are taught aspects of the language that you didn't even know existed in English. When they learn these things, and if they apply them to what they know about English, they actually become better in English. There are also benefits to helping learn vocabulary words if the words in English are similar to or come from the word in the foreign language. Learning the foreign language helps the student see English in a whole new light.

Jacob provides no transition to this "final benefit," and the reader may actually have forgotten what Jacob started out arguing.

A final benefit of my plan is that students who do not speak English as a first language will be able to get taught in both their own language and in English. By the time they graduate from high school, they will be fluent in English, which is what those English-only people want, so this is a win-win.

This is why it would be a really good idea for every school student in our state to have to be fluent in two languages by the time he graduates, and one of those languages should be English.

STEP 6: Peer Edit

What is this writer's point? Jacob's point is that the benefits of studying a second language, especially when that study begins early in the child's education, provides so many benefits that every student should be required to study a foreign language to the point of proficiency (Jacob writes "fluency," but this is a completely unrealistic requirement). A second and somewhat related point is that all students should be required to demonstrate proficiency in English as well. Thus, all students, whether or not they be native speakers of English, should be required to demonstrate proficiency in two languages, one of them being English.

What is his/her angle? His angle is suggested in the two-language requirement. Such a requirement would give native English-speakers the benefits of foreign language study while satisfying the demands of those who advocate "English only" or "Official English" legislation. One key problem with Jacob's essay, however, is that this angle, which is stated as a key part of his argument, is never allowed to shape the essay beyond mentioning it at the beginning and again at the end.

How strong is this writer's support? How authoritative is his or her overall argument? This is the most severe flaw with Jacob's essay. He provides assertions, but no real support. The one bit of actual data he does provide actually weakens his argument.

What techniques has this writer used to establish this authority? This is what Jacob needs to focus on in his rewrite. Without factual evidence, and without the ability to cite authoritative sources for that evidence, Jacob hasn't done anything to establish a sense of authority.

What specific details, facts, etc., make this argument convincing? Again, this is the fundamental flaw in Jacob's essay. He makes claims; he offers no specific development or support for those claims.

NOW plan your own argumentative essay. Remember that Jacob brainstormed and took notes on several possible topics, developing each of them to see which would yield the best essay.

STEP 1: Select a Topic

What topics or issues have you read about or discussed in school that might make for an interesting argument?

What issues or controversies in your school, community, state, or nation have attracted your interest?

What trends or movements might have a direct impact of you or those you love?

STEP 2: Develop an argument

What aspects of your indicated issues are most important? Why?

What aspects of your indicated issues are most interesting? Why?

What ideas or insights do you have that others seem not to have noticed or seem to undervalue?

STEP 3: Brainstorm, discuss, research

What sources are likely to provide the most accurate and authoritative support for your argument?

What specific details, facts, etc., are likely to make your argument convincing?

STEP 4: Outline

STEP 5: Write your first draft

STEP 6: Peer Edit

What is this writer's point?

What is his/her angle?

How strong is this writer's support? How authoritative is his or her overall argument?

What techniques has this writer used to establish this authority?

What specific details, facts, etc., make this argument convincing?

STEP 7: Revised/Final Draft

Here are Jacob's editor's comments and analysis as well as Jacob's responses.

- Jacob does manage to state his claims, but the structure of this paragraph reveals a lack of parallelism among the supporting theses. Three of the four support a student's learning a second language, but the fourth directly supports the central claim. This oddly-structured paragraph might foreshadow an oddly-structured essay.

- This is not exactly the same wording as Jacob's central claim, and it does not mean exactly the same thing. Jacob will need to examine both and decide which it is that he means.

- A little explanation is called for but not a lengthy definition. The second sentence begins to shift the focus away from the actual topic of the essay.

- Jacob has twisted the sense of his sentence around an awkward passive construction.

- This paragraph does little to advance Jacob's argument. It confuses the point—is the issue the need to learn a second language or to begin language instruction at a young age? It also presents additional claims instead of actual evidence.

- There may be a certain just logic to Jacob's reasoning here, but it really has nothing to do with his argument. He also needs to eliminate the rhetorical questions in order to strengthen whatever points he is trying to make.

- So far, this is the first bit of hard data Jacob has provided. Ironically, these statistics more weaken Jacob's claim than strengthen it.

- Jacob's attempt at a transition is good, but he has not discussed a "benefit," so it is not logical to claim to be offering "another" benefit.

- Jacob's conclusion does not follow the evidence. The benefits he claims are the result of *early study* of language, not just the study of a second language.

- Jacob relies quite heavily on unsupported generalizations like this one.

- The paragraph is unclear and vague. For the most part, it simply repeats what Jacob has already said.

- Here is another unsupported generalization.

- There are many problems with this paragraph. Word choice and point of view are confusing. While speaking about the same group of students, Jacob uses third person, second person, and then third person again. He limits his content to loose summary with no specifics and no detail.

- Jacob provides no transition to this "final benefit," and the reader may actually have forgotten what Jacob started out arguing.

And here is Jacob's reaction:

> Okay, there are some writing problems: parallelism, passive, awkward sentence structure, and so on; but this was supposed to be my rough draft, right? I can fix those language problems now.
>
> They seem to think I don't have enough actual material, but I didn't think this was supposed to be a research paper. It's an essay. Everything I say is true, and I have the evidence to prove it.

> Jacob is making two very dangerous presumptions here. First, no draft that is going to be read and evaluated by someone else can be "rough." That other person cannot evaluate how well you are making your case if language and structure get in the way. Second, even though this is not a formal research paper, it is still an argument. Jacob's goal is to convince his reader that his view is correct, and that will take more than his insisting that he "has evidence."

Analysis of First Draft

What is this writer's point? Jacob's point is that the benefits of studying a second language, especially when that study begins early in the child's education, provides so many benefits that every student should be required to study a foreign language to the point of proficiency (Jacob writes "fluency," but this is a completely unrealistic requirement). A second and somewhat related point is that all students should be required to demonstrate proficiency in English as well. Thus, all students, whether or not they be native speakers of English, should be required to demonstrate proficiency in two languages, one of them being English.

> My point is that students should be required to know two languages because of both the benefits to the kid learning the language and the political benefit of ending this language controversy.

What is his/her angle? His angle is suggested in the two-language requirement. Such a requirement would give native English-speakers the benefits of foreign language study while satisfying the demands of those who advocate "English only" or "Official English" legislation. One key problem with Jacob's essay, however, is that this angle, which is stated as a key part of his argument, is never allowed to shape the essay beyond mentioning it at the beginning and again at the end.

> *I don't think they understood my essay. I don't care about the benefits of studying a second language. That's only part of my reasons for supporting my plan to require two languages.*

Jacob insists his point has to do with the two-language plan and not the benefits of language. If this is really the case, he must spend much more time and energy in his essay explaining it and then tying his claims about the benefits of language in to that point.

How strong is this writer's support? How authoritative is his or her overall argument? This is the most severe flaw with Jacob's essay. He provides assertions, but no real support. The one bit of actual data he does provide actually weakens his argument.

> *So what am I supposed to do? Quote, and paraphrase as if this were a research paper? Actually name my sources and have a works cited page?*

Actually, yes, that is exactly what Jacob is supposed to do.

What techniques has this writer used to establish this authority? This is what Jacob needs to focus on in his rewrite. Without factual evidence, and without the ability to cite authoritative sources for that evidence, Jacob hasn't done anything to establish a sense of authority.

> *I'm still not sure I understand how to do this without making my essay read like a research paper.*

What specific details, facts, etc., make this argument convincing?

> *Okay. this part I get. More hard facts. More statistics. Things like that.*

Here is Jacob's revised draft. Notice the editorial criticisms he addressed and the ones he simply ignored. Overall, how much has his essay improved from his first draft to this one?

This sentence is a bit better, but it is still weakened by thoughtless word choice like "centers around."

This use of second person is still unnecessary and inappropriate.

Jacob is still being careless with language. In this sentence, he inappropriately uses first person, and the phrase "another foreign language" is illogical since English would not be, for English speakers, a "foreign" language.

The last sentence improves this paragraph a little, but we wonder whether Jacob realizes what his argument really is.

A major issue in the United States right now centers around whether or not the people who live and work here, who receive public services, and take advantage of whatever benefits our society provides, should be required to speak English. People are actually offended when they hear some people speaking some other language than English, and in many states there have been attempts at passing legislation to require that public employees speak only English when dealing with the public. If you can't speak English, then you shouldn't be able to receive the service. On the other hand, in other parts of the world, Americans are looked down on because most of us speak <u>only</u> English and cannot speak another foreign language. There are many benefits to being able to speak, read, and write in more than one language. For one, knowing a second language makes a person smarter more than just knowing a second language. The process of learning a second language also helps students learn English better. Therefore, in order to receive a high school diploma in our state, every student should be required to be fluent, in at least two languages, English and some other. One final benefit of this policy would be that students whose first language is not English will learn English but will not have to give up their native language. Everyone wins.

One reason American students should be required to learn a second language is because most students in other countries are required to study their own language and some other. In 1995, the European Commission, the executive body of the European Union, published a paper in which they stressed how important it is for children to learn at least two foreign languages before they enter "upper secondary" school. The issue discussed in the 1995 paper isn't only about learning two languages but also beginning the instruction at an early age. Both are important. Almost all students in Europe study at least one foreign language as a mandatory part of their education. In Europe, 44% of citizens are at least proficient in two or more languages compared to only 9% of Americans. For example, in Finland, they devote 16 hours a week to foreign language instruction.

Jacob makes good use of this fact from his second round of research, but he needs to cite his source.

For another example, to get accepted into Central European University in Budapest, students have to demonstrate "proficiency in English by submitting standardized English language test scores, e.g., the Test of English as a Foreign Language (TOEFL) or other ... tests." Central European University is in Hungary, where the main language is Hungarian. Most students come from other countries where the main language is not English. It would make more sense for a school in Hungary to require its students to speak Hungarian. To require everyone to speak English is the same as requiring a foreign language for everyone.

Jacob has indeed revised his word and sentence choice, but the point to which this information is leading is still unclear.

Since 2010, every school child in the United Kingdom studies a foreign language beginning at the age of seven.

But Americans have always resisted learning another language. Even Benjamin Franklin expressed fear that, since there were so many Germans living in Pennsylvania, German would replace English as the main language of the state. Later on, President Theodore Roosevelt said, "We have room for but one language here, and that is the English language." Doesn't this put American students at a disadvantage compared to students in other nations? Some important Americans seem to think so. During the 2008 presidential campaign, Barack Obama said he believed American students should all be required to learn a second language. A lot of people criticized him, saying he wanted to change American culture, and weaken

Jacob would still be wise to avoid asking rhetorical questions.

American unity. Many thought he was making a case for immigrants not learning English. To which he replied, "... absolutely immigrants need to learn English, but we also need to learn foreign languages ... we should want children with more knowledge. We should want our children to have more skills. There's nothing wrong with that! It's a good thing."

As Mr. Obama points out, having knowledge and skills is a good thing. Learning and knowing a second language have many benefits beyond knowing that second language. When you learn a foreign language, things happen in your brain. Learning language affects how the student's brain works. A study done at the University College of London in 2004 showed that the brains of people who studied their second language at a young age had denser "grey matter" than those who learned one later. Grey matter is the part of the brain that processes information. Other studies show that learning a second language at an early age helps the child develop divergent thinking enabling him to see things from different points of view and to find more than one way to solve a problem.

As student proficiency in the language grows, the second language gives children another way of expressing themselves. This helps them learn that there is more than one way to look at a problem, and there is probably more than one way to solve it. While many of these studies focus on beginning the language instruction at an early age, even if the student begins to study the language as late as middle or high school, he will experience these same benefits.

Experts believe that learning a foreign language is a thinking and problem-solving activity more than simply a language activity. This is probably why students who study a foreign language

This is a better transition, but "learning and knowing" are not necessarily the same thing. Jacob needs to clarify which one he is writing about.

This sentence reflects a very nice revision. Jacob has managed to bring in a benefit of knowing in addition to the benefits of learning.

do better academically in school than students who don't. Foreign language learners generally score higher in the verbal and math sections of standardized tests than students who have not studied a foreign language. Even if the foreign language study takes time away from mathematics, mathematics test scores of foreign language learners are higher than the scores of students who do not study a foreign language. Increasing the amount of time spent on mathematics has not been shown to improve test scores as much as using that additional time on foreign language learning. Consider Finland where they devote 16 hours a week to foreign language. Despite this amount of time "lost" to other academic subjects, Finland students scored second in reading and math in the world and first in science. By comparison, the United States scored fourteenth in reading, twenty-fifth in math, and seventeenth in science.

Just as Barack Obama explained in 2008, he was not wanting to eliminate any requirements to learn English. He even said that he agreed it was important for immigrants to learn English. But he believed it was important for Americans to learn other languages as well. That is why my plan is so perfect. If every student were required to be proficient in at least two languages—and one of them had to be English—the immigration-language problem would be solved, and all students would get the benefits of studying a foreign language.

> This is all very good information, but Jacob must find some way to cite his sources. We need to be assured that Jacob is not just making this date up.

> Overall, this is a much better draft. The conclusion, however, could be stronger.

Analysis of Revised Draft

What is this writer's point? The point has not changed from the first draft. Because of the strong benefits to be gained in the process of studying a foreign language and to meet the demands of those who desire to maintain the primacy of the English language in the United States, all students, whether or not they be native speakers of English, should be required to demonstrate proficiency in two languages, one of them being English in order to graduate from high school.

What is his/her angle? His angle is suggested in the two-language requirement. Such a requirement would give native English-speakers the benefits of foreign language study while satisfying the demands of those who advocate "English only" or "Official English" legislation.

How strong is this writer's support? How authoritative is his or her overall argument? The argument in this draft is much stronger than in the previous one. Jacob has learned and provided much more hard evidence. What is still missing, however, is some sense of where this information has come from. How do we know Jacob hasn't simply fabricated the facts he presents?

What techniques has this writer used to establish this authority? Jacob presents facts and hard data, but he does not cite enough sources to fully establish his authority.

What specific details, facts, etc., make this argument convincing?

- 44% of Europeans are at least proficient in two or more languages compared to only 9% of Americans who are.
- Finland (16 hours a week) = Reading - 2 Math - 2 (South Korea = 1 in both) Science -1
- U.S.A. (doesn't require foreign language) = Reading – 14 Math – 25 Science 17.
- learning a foreign language is a thinking and problem-solving activity more than simply a language activity
- studying a foreign language helps students develop critical thinking skills, creativity, and mental flexibility
- foreign language learners score higher in the verbal and math sections of standardized tests
- even if the foreign language study takes time away from mathematics, mathematics test scores are higher
- Barack Obama advocated requiring more foreign language learning in American public
- Franklin's fear of Germans
- Teddy Roosevelt's quotation

POSSIBLE STEP 8: Rewrite Opportunity

Jacob decided that the problems remaining in his essay could be fairly easily fixed, and it would be worth his while to take the essay into a third draft. Notice how he has addressed his editor's concerns about citing his sources while not turning this essay into a pseudo research paper.

A major issue in the United States right now centers around whether or not the people who live and work here, who receive public services, and take advantage of whatever benefits our society provides, should be required to speak only English. People are actually offended when they hear some people speaking some other language than English, and in many states there have been attempts at passing legislation to require that public employees speak only English when dealing with the public. People who do not speak English, should not be able to receive services. On the other hand, in other parts of the world, Americans are looked down on because most of us speak only English and cannot speak another language. There are many benefits to being able to speak, read, and write in more than one language. Knowing a second language makes a person smarter than just knowing a second language. Learning a foreign language actually improves the students' performance in all of their academic pursuits. Therefore, in order to receive a high school diploma in our state, every student should be required to be proficient in at least two languages, English and some other.

> This is an important change for Jacob. A fluency requirement in a second language is too severe a requirement; proficiency is more attainable.

One reason American students should be required to learn a second language is that most students in other countries are required to study their own language and some other. A number of articles in The Guardian U.K. and the American Council for Teachers of World Languages magazine show how common foreign language instruction is in Europe. In 1995, the European Commission, the executive body of the European Union, published

> This is a good start. Even if Jacob is unable to cite the specific article, he can at least point his reader in the right direction. His ability to indicate credible sources for his information helps him establish his own authority.

- 191 -

a paper in which they stressed how important it is for children to learn at least two foreign languages before they enter "upper secondary" school. The issue discussed in the 1995 paper isn't only about learning two languages but also beginning the instruction at an early age. Both are important. Almost all students in Europe study at least one foreign language as a mandatory part of their education. According to a January 2011 report on CBS News, in Europe, 44% of citizens are at least proficient in two or more languages compared to only 9% of Americans. The Guardian reports that, in Finland, for example, they devote 16 hours a week to foreign language instruction.

For another example, according to the school's own web site, in order to get accepted into Central European University in Budapest, students have to demonstrate "proficiency in English by submitting standardized English language test scores, e.g., the Test of English as a Foreign Language (TOEFL) or other ... tests." Central European University is in Hungary, where the main language is Hungarian. Most students come from other countries where the main language is not English. It would make more sense for a school in Hungary to require its students to speak Hungarian. To require everyone to speak English is the same as requiring a foreign language for everyone.

Since 2010, every school child in the United Kingdom studies a foreign language beginning at the age of seven.

But Americans have always resisted learning another language. Even Benjamin Franklin expressed fear that, since there were so many Germans living in Pennsylvania, German would replace English as the main language of the state. Later on, President Theodore Roosevelt said, "We have room for but one language here, and that is the English language."

In a world with a global marketplace, in which people on opposite sides of the world can communicate almost instantly, and it takes no effort at all to find a bit of information, the person who knows only one language is at the obvious disadvantage. Some important Americans seem to think so. In July of 2008, during the presidential campaign, ABC News reported that Barack Obama said he believed American students should all be required to learn a second language. A lot of people criticized him, saying he wanted to change American culture, and weaken American unity. Many thought he was making a case for immigrants _not_ learning English. To which he replied, "... absolutely immigrants need to learn English, but we also need to learn foreign languages ... we should want children with more knowledge. We should want our children to have more skills. There's nothing wrong with that! It's a good thing."

This is a very nice, unintrusive way for Jacob to cite his source.

As Mr. Obama points out, having knowledge and skills is a good thing. Learning and knowing a second language have many benefits beyond knowing that second language. When you learn a foreign language, things happen in your brain. Learning language affects how the student's brain works. A study done at the University College of London in 2004 showed that the brains of people who studied their second language at a young age had denser "grey matter" than those who learned one later. Grey matter is the part of the brain that processes information. Other studies show that learning a second language at an early age helps the child develop divergent thinking enabling him to see things from different points of view and to find more than one way to solve a problem.

This is a better transition, but "learning and knowing" are not necessarily the same thing. Jacob needs to clarify which one he is writing about.

As student proficiency in the language grows, the second language gives children another way of expressing themselves. This helps them learn that there is more than one way to look at a problem, and

This sentence reflects a very nice revision. Jacob has managed to bring in a benefit of knowing in addition to the benefits of learning.

there is probably more than one way to solve it. While many of these studies focus on beginning the language instruction at an early age, even if the student begins to study the language as late as middle or high school, he will experience these same benefits.

According to American Council on the Teaching of Foreign Languages, experts believe that learning a foreign language is a thinking and problem-solving activity more than simply a language activity, which is probably why students who study a foreign language do better academically in school than students who don't. Foreign language learners generally score higher in the verbal and math sections of standardized tests than students who have not studied a foreign language. Even if the foreign language study takes time away from mathematics, mathematics test scores of foreign language learners are higher than the scores of students who do not study a foreign language. Increasing the amount of time spent on mathematics has not been shown to improve test scores as much as using that additional time on foreign language learning. Consider Finland where they devote 16 hours a week to foreign language. Despite this amount of time "lost" to other academic subjects, Finland students scored second in reading and math <u>in the world</u> and <u>first</u> in science. By comparison, the United States scored fourteenth in reading, twenty-fifth in math, and seventeenth in science.

Just as Barack Obama explained in 2008, he was not wanting to eliminate any requirements to learn English. He even said that he agreed it was important for immigrants to learn English. But he believed it was important for Americans to learn other languages as well. That is why my plan is so perfect. If every student were required to be proficient in at least two languages—and one of them had to be English—the immigration-language problem would be solved, and all students would get the benefits of studying a foreign language.

Overall, this is a much better draft. The conclusion, however, could still be stronger.

Analyze Jacob's final draft. Has he successfully identified his argument and provided enough information to convince his reader?

What is this writer's purpose?

What is his/her thesis?

Has the writer's new draft strengthened his/her point?

Has the rewrite strengthened the case for his/her thesis?

What new details, facts, etc., have been included to make the argument more convincing?

Does the writer effectively establish his/her argument to any greater degree than in the previous draft? Why or why not?

ASSIGNMENT 2:

The Refutation

In informal logic, a popular view of argumentation that has evolved from Stephen Toulmin's system, a **refutation** is any objection to a general claim. The refutation may assert that the claim itself is false, that it fails because the logic of the warrants is flawed, or that the evidence backing the supporting claims is either incorrect or incorrectly interpreted.

Just as the original claim cannot be mere opinion, however, the refutation cannot be merely an opposing opinion. There must be a logical and factual basis to any legitimate refutation.

A successful refutation identifies the most significant flaw or flaws in the initial argument and attempts to "correct" them in the mind of the reader.

1. **Refute the Logic:** The initial argument is fundamentally flawed if the general claim, any of the supporting claims, or any of the evidence is irrelevant, overly presumptive, or ambiguous.

   • The **irrelevance** of any of the claims weakens the entire argument. One or more irrelevant supporting claims might suggest that the initial writer is not really familiar with the issue he is arguing. Even more important, irrelevant support or evidence might suggest that the writer is trying to distract his reader from an argument he knows is flawed.

      For example, it would have been irrelevant for Jacob to argue that Romance languages like Italian, Spanish, and French are easier to learn than Slavic languages like Polish and Bulgarian.

   • Remember that the warrants are generally agreed upon by both the reader and writer. The initial writer cannot hope to persuade the reader of her general premise if she incorrectly **presumes** that her reader accepts all of her claims and warrants.

      For example, part of Jacob's argument relies on the supporting claim that most other developed countries require their students to learn that nation's language and at least one other. His presumption is that his readers agree it's important for the United States to emulate other nations in this way.

- Any **ambiguity** in terms or in the intent of the claims is grounds for refutation. Like irrelevancies, unclear claims, evidence, or language suggest that the initial writer might be unprepared to put forward his argument or that he is intentionally hiding a flawed argument.

  For example, if Jacob had not specified "English and some other," his general claim would have read, *In order to receive a high school diploma in our state, every student should be required to be proficient in at least two languages,* and it would have been possible for a reader to claim that Jacob did not support English language instruction in United States public schools.

2. **Refute the Definitions of Terms:** This is where a strong knowledge of language conventions will serve you. Words do mean what they mean. Denotations are not arguable, and connotations are generally agreed upon among educated users of the language. Therefore, any time the initial writer bases an argument on specific meanings or uses of key words, you have the opportunity to verify that the terms are indeed being used appropriately. If they are not, any claim based on those terms is flawed.

   For example, one of Jacob's supporting claims is that learning a second language makes the language learner "smarter." Later, he explains what he means by "smarter":

   > ... students who study a foreign language do better academically in school than students who don't. Foreign language learners generally score higher in the verbal and math sections of standardized tests than students who have not studied a foreign language.

   Someone who wanted to refute Jacob's argument might find fault with his definition of "smart" and assert that this weakness calls the validity of Jacob's entire point into question.

3. **Refute the Evidence:** There are several bases on which the evidence supporting the initial argument can be questioned.

   - The facts or data offered in support of one or more of the supporting claims might simply be **incorrect**. This does not necessarily mean that the writer of the initial argument is lying, but she may have chosen weak sources.

     For example, Jacob cites some statistics (44% of Europeans know at least two languages contrasted with only 9% of Americans). If you were to find from reliable sources that the European figure is much lower, or the American figure much higher, you would have strong basis for refutation.

- The data or information offered in support of the initial argument might be **incomplete**. This is especially important if the initial writer has blatantly omitted information that would weaken his own argument.

  For example, if Jacob had told his reader only that 44% of Europeans know at least two languages, you could argue that he was not telling the whole story. By the same token, if he had failed to inform his reader that, although language learners score better on standardized tests, they have a higher failure and dropout rate when they get to college, you could easily refute his evidence as being incomplete.

- As we established above, the initial writer's use of **irrelevant** facts or data to support one or more of her supporting claims might suggest that she is not as informed on her issue as she should be. It might also suggest that she is intentionally trying to distract her reader from the fact that she has a weak argument to begin with.

- Even accurate data interpreted accurately can be taken **out of context**. Suppose Jacob had discovered his 44% of Europeans statistic in a web article that went on to say that the remaining 56% learn only their native language and tend to achieve greater power and wealth in their home countries. You could argue that his use of the figure misrepresents the data.

- Jacob's essay was written in late 2012. If his information about the success of language learners on standardized tests had come from data compiled in the 1980s, you could easily refute his data as being **out of date**.

- Even if the data itself is flawless, the initial writer might have **interpreted** the data **incorrectly**. If you can offer a more thorough or accurate conclusion or view of what the data suggests, you have strong means for refuting the initial argument.

  For example, Jacob concludes that, since students who study a second language perform better than others in mathematics, all students would receive the same benefit if they were required to study a second language. To refute Jacob's interpretation, you might conclude that students who currently choose to study a second language are probably more academic than those who don't, and this academic tendency probably accounts for their improved success in other subjects as well.

In connection with the social studies department's "Contemporary Issues" project, the grade 10 English teachers have their students choose a classmate's essay and write a refutation.

STEP 1: Select a Topic

Maya was troubled by a classmate's essay that examined several recent incidents of cheating in schools and defended the participants' decision to cheat. This was the argument she chose to refute.

STEP 2: Develop an argument

Even though Maya's argument is based on another, she must still organize and present it as a general claim, supporting claims, and evidence. These are the essential steps she followed in developing her refutation:

First, she **read the essay**. She actually read it several times, each time noting any of the flaws described above:

Is the general claim, or are any of the supporting claims, irrelevant?

Given the general claim—

> Since cheating has become so widespread in United States culture, the non-cheater places himself at a disadvantage when competing for school and job placement. Therefore, the decision to cheat is the only logical decision a person who wants to succeed in the United States can make—

the second supporting claim—

> Women cheat in school and the workplace as much as men but in different ways—

is irrelevant.

Does the original author presume logical connections that readers may not accept? The second supporting claim sort of presumes that the reader would expect men to cheat more.

Part of the success of the first supporting claim (Cheating has become ingrained in the United States.) relies on the presumption that relatively few cheaters and cases of cheating are discovered and made public.

Is the general claim, or are any of the supporting claims, ambiguous? I didn't find any ambiguous claims.

Are any key terms used inappropriately or incorrectly? Does the original author rely on specific uses or definitions that are too specific or limited? When "Matthew" says that exposed cheaters become "celebrities," he is probably using the term celebrity too broadly. Their names become publicly known just by having their cheating revealed. Many of them are no longer well known or written about in People magazine or anything.

Does the original writer offer any facts or data that are simply incorrect? It is incorrect for Matthew to claim that Lance Armstrong gained celebrity status and did not become an "outcast."

It is incorrect for him to claim that Stephen Glass, Jayson Blair, and Jonah Lehrer are "celebrities."

Does the original writer offer any facts or data that are incomplete?

When discussing the Harvard incident, Matthew makes no mention of the students' claims that collaboration among students was always allowed in that class—even encouraged. This might show that the students were not really choosing to cheat as much as doing what they thought was allowed.

He also fails to mention any of the punishments that the cheaters she mentions suffered:

- Lance Armstrong was stripped of all of his medals

- Stephen Glass and Jayson Blair were both fired.

Does the original writer offer any facts or data that are irrelevant to the claim they are supposed to support? The fact that Whoopi Goldberg admitted to cheating on her husband is irrelevant. She said it after she was already a celebrity, and cheating on her husband is not the type of cheating Matthew is talking about.

Does the original writer offer any facts or data that would point to alternative conclusions if left in their original context? Instead of proving that the Harvard students felt justified in cheating, their threat to sue Harvard can be interpreted to show that they do not accept accountability or that they really misunderstood the situation and did not intentionally cheat.

The quote from the Van Noort High School student probably shows panic at not doing well more than actual acceptance of a "culture of cheating."

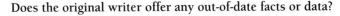

Does the original writer offer any out-of-date facts or data?

The Stephen Glass example is from 1998.

The Jayson Blair thing happened in 2003.

If Matthew can't find more recent examples of cheating, perhaps it's not as common as he claims.

Does the original writer offer any questionable interpretations? Maybe the Harvard and Van Noort examples do show that the students don't care, but the one quote could also show that the students are made to care too much—they are afraid of failure, afraid even of being "average."

Examine the central and supporting claims—Given the flaws you identified in the previous step, what claims will form the structure of your refutation?

> **Central Claim: Since cheating has become so widespread in United States culture, the non-cheater places himself at a disadvantage when competing for school and job placement. Therefore, the decision to cheat is the only logical decision a person who wants to succeed in the United States can make.**
>
> *While on the surface Matthew makes a powerful argument about the pervasiveness and the inevitability of cheating in the United States, a closer examination of the facts show that cheaters are still in the minority and, as the old adage says, "Cheaters never prosper."*

1. **Cheating has become ingrained in the United States.**

   The simple fact that incidents of cheating become such big news stories shows that cheating is the rare exception rather than normal behavior.

2. **Women cheat in school and the workplace as much as men but in different ways.**

   To try to introduce gender into the argument is irrelevant and distracting.

3. **Cheaters who are caught are not outcasts but become celebrities.**

   Exposed cheaters not only suffer negative consequences when they are found out, but they spend the entire rest of their lives known as cheaters.

STEP 3: Independently research the topic

Look especially for information or data to counter what you are refuting as incorrect, incomplete, or out of context. If you are basing any part of your refutation on the fact that some of the original information is out of date, you must be able to provide more recent information that supports your refutation.

STEP 4: Outline

Central Claim: While on the surface Matthew makes a powerful argument about the pervasiveness and the inevitability of cheating in the United States, a closer examination of the facts show that cheaters are still in the minority and, as the old adage says, "Cheaters never prosper."

I. The simple fact that incidents of cheating become such big news stories shows that cheating is the rare exception rather than normal behavior.

   A. 71 students out of a student body of over 3,000

   B. Only 125 students at Harvard—one course, one professor

> These numbers might support a claim that cheaters constitute a minority, but not Maya's claim about the "big news stories."

II. Exposed cheaters not only suffer negative consequences when they are found out, but they spend the entire rest of their lives known as cheaters.

   A. Stephen Glass

      1. fired from The New Republic

      2. Scandal did not help sales or critics' comments about his novel.

      3. A movie about him is based only on his cheating, not on his life before or afterwards

      4. If anyone ever thinks of him, they think about his famous cheating, nothing else.

   B. Jayson Blair

      1. fired from the New York Times.

> This is incorrect. The fact is, Blair resigned. Maya will have to correct this, or it will seriously weaken her refutation.

2. basically unknown today

3. Current life is not a benefit of his cheating "fame."

C. Lance Armstrong

  1. stripped of all titles

  2. resigned from Livestrong charity

  3. Many people feel bitter and let down by him.

III. To try to introduce gender into the argument is irrelevant and distracting.

> Maya is not obligated to base the organization of her refutation on the argument she is refuting.

  1. Whoopi Goldberg's adultery is irrelevant.

    a. She is not famous because of her cheating.

    b. Adultery is not even the kind of cheating we're talking about.

IV. Many of the conclusions leading to Matthew's claim are weak

  A. "For every case found out, how many cases are not disclosed?" is speculation.

    1. Could just as accurately suppose that most cases of cheating are discovered and punished.

    2. Who's to say that every found and punished case of cheating makes national news?

> Maya's outlining is, perhaps, a little unorthodox, but her ideas are, for the most part, valid; and her plan is mostly sound.

  B. Quote from Van Noort student shows panic, not indifference.

    1. Need to "do well"—fear of failure—is too strong for many.

    2. He knows he is doing wrong, but does not feel he has a choice.

  C. Cheating is not common or generally accepted or famous cases of cheating and cheaters wouldn't attract so much attention.

> This final point merely repeats Maya's first supporting claim. She'll have the opportunity to realize this and fix it when she drafts and revises her essay.

STEP 5: First Draft

This is a fairly bland opening sentence. The phrase "in life today" is essentially meaningless and might invite the reader to prejudge Maya as an immature writer and thinker.

Maya has chosen an interesting approach to introducing her refutation. It could work well for her except that she should not cast aspersions about those whose claim she is going to refute—especially since she is going to name one of those persons.

Maya makes a common grammatical error here. The true subject of the sentence is "examination," so the verb must be "shows."

This is a fairly typical introductory paragraph. Since Maya is refuting Matthew's argument, it is perfectly acceptable for her to mention the specific claims of Matthew's that she is going to refute.

Maya is following her outline, but she has not rethought the relationship between her supporting claim and her interpretation of these statistics.

Cheating is a big issue in school and in life today. Everyone cheats. Even our biggest heroes are eventually found out to be cheaters. In fact, cheating is so common today that the person who does not cheat is at a disadvantage. Successful people cheat. At least, that's what some people might have us believe—probably cheaters themselves. In a recent Contemporary Issues essay, Matthew argues just that case: cheating is pervasive, and the decision not to cheat is foolish. While on the surface, Matthew seems to make a powerful argument about the pervasiveness and the inevitability of cheating in the United States, a closer examination of the facts show that cheaters are still in the minority and, as the old adage says, "Cheaters never prosper." If cheating really were as widespread as Matthew claims, then the famous cases he gives as evidence would not have been so famous. His claim that cheaters are rewarded with fame and success is also not true. When his weak evidence fails to prove his point, Matthew resorts to distraction to try to win his case. Basically, the justification for cheating based on the claim that "everybody's doing it" is just that—a justification.

The simple fact that incidents of cheating become such big news stories shows that cheating is the rare exception rather than normal behavior. Matthew makes a big deal out of the students at Van Noort High School in the Bronx and their "massive cheating ring." It was 71 students out of a student body of over 3,000. That's hardly massive. The big Harvard scandal he cites involved only 125 students and one professor. It all happened in one course. Even if the students really were cheating, these small numbers can hardly be considered "pervasive" and "systemic," as Matthew claims.

Also, exposed cheaters not only suffer negative consequences when they are found out, but they spend the entire rest of their lives known as cheaters. Stephen Glass <u>was</u> fired from <u>The New Republic</u>. He did write a novel kind of based on his experience, but the fact that he was a "famous cheater" did not make the book a bestseller, and the critics didn't like it either. The movie Matthew mentions, <u>Shattered Glass</u>, starring Hayden Christiansen as Stephen Glass, is based <u>only</u> on his cheating and getting caught, not on any other part of his life. So, if anyone ever thinks of him, they think about his famous cheating, nothing else.

Jayson Blair is another example. Contrary to what Matthew claims, he was fired from the <u>New York Times</u> because of his plagiarism, and he is basically unknown today. Wikipedia says he is a "life coach," and I sincerely doubt that his history as a famous cheater is helping him with that.

While there is nothing wrong with Maya's basing her refutation directly on Matthew's essay, she is not providing her reader with enough exposition to appreciate the point she is refuting. Her claim that Blair was fired is still a misstatement of fact that she must fix.

Finally, Lance Armstrong's fame and reputation certainly weren't helped by his cheating. He was stripped of all titles. He resigned from his well-known and popular Livestrong charity, and many people feel bitter and let down by him. The same three examples that Matthew gives to prove that cheaters get famous actually prove that, if anything, being found to be a cheater destroys your fame.

This is an ironic word choice error. Armstrong's fame was enhanced by his cheating; Maya means that his celebrity was not helped by the discovery of his cheating.

Throughout this first draft, Maya has been careless with word choice, especially lapses into first and second person and a conversational, colloquial tone that is not appropriate for a formal essay like this.

Another claim Matthew makes is that women cheat as much as men. Maybe it's because all of the examples he gives of famous cheaters are men, but so what? To try to introduce gender into the argument is irrelevant and distracting. Whoopi Goldberg's adultery is irrelevant. She is not famous because of her cheating, and adultery is not even the kind of cheating we're talking about.

To refute the relevance of a claim or of evidence is fine, but Maya's approach reads more like a rant than a rational refutation.

Many of the conclusions leading to Matthew's claim are weak. "For every case found out, how

In this paragraph, all Maya has done is transcribe her outline. She's stating her claims but not making any effort to explain, illustrate, or provide evidence to support them.

Again, Maya is offering a reinterpretation of some information, but her reader can only, at best, infer what that information was and how the writer whose argument she is refuting originally interpreted it.

Some parts of this refutation are much stronger than others. One general weakness is that Maya herself presumes her reader's knowledge of Matthew's essay, so she does not lay sufficient groundwork to establish her claims as valid in their own right. Word choice and tone are also problems. Too often Maya allows herself to lapse into an informal, colloquial tone that might endear her to some readers but will most likely weaken her argument for most readers.

many cases are not disclosed?" is speculation. You might just as well suppose that most cases of cheating are discovered and punished. Who's to say that every found and punished case of cheating makes national news? That one quote from that one Van Noort student probably shows panic, not indifference. For students in such high-stress and competitive schools like Van Noort, the need to "do well," the fear of failure, is too strong. Most students in those schools cannot even afford to be average. They all have to be at the top of their class. The quoted student probably knows he was doing wrong but did not feel he had a choice.

In short, cheating is not common or generally accepted or famous cases of cheating and cheaters wouldn't attract so much attention.

STEP 6: Peer Edit

What is this writer's point? Maya's point is that cheating in school and professional advancement is not as prevalent and inevitable as some suggest, specifically the author of a previous essay justifying the decision to cheat.

What is his/her angle? Her angle is that the examples chosen by the original writer do not really illustrate his points and that he often misstates and misinterprets data in order to prove his point. She also accuses him of using distraction techniques to mask his lack of solid support.

How strong is this writer's support? How authoritative is his or her overall argument? Maya really offers no support of her own. Her entire refutation is based on simple contradiction.

What techniques has this writer used to establish this authority? At this point, Maya has not established a sense of authority.

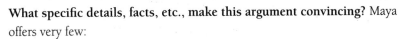

What specific details, facts, etc., make this argument convincing? Maya offers very few:

- Stephen Glass and Jayson Blair were fired from their respective jobs—but this is a misstatement of fact about Blair.

- Lance Armstrong was stripped of his titles and resigned from Livestrong.

NOW plan your own refutation.

STEP 1: Select a Topic

STEP 2: Develop an argument

STEP 3: Independently research the topic

STEP 4: Outline

STEP 5: Write your first draft

STEP 6: Peer Edit

What is this writer's point?

What is his/her angle?

How strong is this writer's support? How authoritative is his or her overall argument?

What techniques has this writer used to establish this authority?

What specific details, facts, etc., make this argument convincing?

STEP 7: Revised/Final Draft

Here are Maya's peer editor's comments and analysis as well as Maya's responses.

- This is a fairly bland opening sentence. The phrase "in life today" is essentially meaningless and might invite the reader to prejudge Maya as an immature writer and thinker.

- Maya has chosen an interesting approach to introducing her refutation. It could work well for her except that she should not cast aspersions about those whose claim she is going to refute—especially since she is going to name one of those persons.

- Maya makes a common grammatical error here. The true subject of the sentence is "examination," so the verb must be "shows."

- This is a fairly typical introductory paragraph. Since Maya is refuting Matthew's argument, it is perfectly acceptable for her to mention the specific claims of Matthew's that she is going to refute.

- Maya is following her outline, but she has not rethought the relationship between her supporting claim and her interpretation of these statistics.

- While there is nothing wrong with Maya's basing her refutation directly on Matthew's essay, she is not providing her reader with enough exposition to appreciate the point she is refuting. Her claim that Blair was fired is still a misstatement of fact that she must fix.

- This is an ironic word choice error. Armstrong's fame was enhanced by his cheating; Maya means that his celebrity was not helped by the *discovery* of his cheating.

- Throughout this first draft, Maya has been careless with word choice, especially lapses into first and second person and a conversational, colloquial tone that is not appropriate for a formal essay like this.

- To refute the relevance of a claim or of evidence is fine, but Maya's approach reads more like a rant than a rational refutation.

- In this paragraph, all Maya has done is transcribe her outline. She's stating her claims but not making any effort to explain, illustrate, or provide evidence to support them.

- Again, Maya is offering a reinterpretation of some information, but her reader can only, at best, infer what that information was and how the writer whose argument she is refuting originally interpreted it.

- Some parts of this refutation are much stronger than others. One general weakness is that Maya herself presumes her reader's knowledge of Matthew's essay, so she does not lay sufficient groundwork to establish her claims as valid in their own right. Word choice and tone are also problems. Too often Maya allows herself to lapse into an informal, colloquial tone that might endear her to some readers but will most likely weaken her argument for most readers.

And here is Maya's reaction:

> I can improve my language. That's something I would have worked on in the revision anyway.
>
> I'll have to look at my outline and see why some of my evidence doesn't logically support the claim. I guess I also need to find more evidence—but would this be new evidence or information about the cases Matthew already mentions? I still think, since this is a refutation, I should stick to what Matthew says and argue against it.

Maya is making the correct assumption here. She needs to research the same cases Matthew did, but she needs concrete information to support her claims.

> I didn't think I was supposed to repeat or summarize Matthew's essay, but I can see that, if my reader hasn't read it, how would they know that I'm right, and he's wrong?
>
> All right. I think I understand a little better. This is an essay that's based off another essay, but it's also its own essay as well.

Maya seems to have really paid attention to her editor's comments and to take them to heart.

Analysis of First Draft

What is this writer's point? Maya's point is that cheating in school and professional advancement is not as prevalent and inevitable as some suggest, specifically the author of a previous essay justifying the decision to cheat.

> *Yes. At least my point is clear.*

What is his/her angle? Her angle is that the examples chosen by the original writer do not really illustrate his points and that he often misstates and misinterprets data in order to prove his point. She also accuses him of using distraction techniques to mask his lack of solid support.

> *At least I got that across, too. Maybe my logic attack could be stronger, or I should just leave them out.*

How strong is this writer's support? How authoritative is his or her overall argument? Maya really offers no support of her own. Her entire refutation is based on simple contradiction.

> *I understand that now. I need to show that I am familiar with the examples Matthew gives. I think I do do that a little when I point out more information about the famous cheaters Matthew talks about. I guess I need to do it more and more consistently in the entire essay.*

What techniques has this writer used to establish this authority? At this point, Maya has not established a sense of authority.

> *They also seem to say that my tone might weaken my authority.*

What specific details, facts, etc., make this argument convincing? Maya offers very few:

- Stephen Glass and Jayson Blair were fired from their respective jobs—but this is a misstatement of fact about Blair.

- Lance Armstrong was stripped of his titles and resigned from Livestrong.

So when I talk about the Van Noort and the Harvard incidents, maybe I should find quotations from the students (or at least repeat Matthew's). I don't mention in the essay that some of the Harvard kids are suing Harvard, so that might be important. Anyway, I think I know what I need to do to make a stronger refutation. It's almost as if I'm writing my own argumentative essay, but my argument is a refutation of someone else's.

Maya has arrived at an important realization here.

Here is Maya's revised draft.

Cheating is a big issue in American society. Everyone cheats. Even America's biggest heroes are eventually found out to be cheaters. In fact, cheating is so common that the person who does not cheat is at a disadvantage. Successful people cheat. At least, that's what <u>some</u> people insist, and they offer this argument as a defense for the decision to cheat. In a recent Contemporary Issues essay, Matthew makes just that claim: cheating is pervasive, and the decision not to cheat is foolish. While on the surface, Matthew seems to make a powerful argument about the pervasiveness and the inevitability of cheating in the United States, a closer examination of his own evidence shows that cheaters are still in the minority and, as the old adage says, "Cheaters never prosper." If cheating really were as widespread as Matthew claims, then the famous cases he gives as evidence would not have been so famous. His claim that cheaters are rewarded with fame and success is also not true. When his weak evidence fails to prove his point, Matthew resorts to distraction to try to win his case. Basically, the justification for cheating based on the claim that "everybody's doing it" is just that—a justification.

This is a more accurate restatement of Matthew's original claim, and it removes the allegation that Matthew himself is probably a cheater.

Since Maya has chosen to keep this as a supporting claim, she will have to defend it better than she did in her first draft.

Again, Maya has chosen to keep a supporting claim that she did not successfully argue in her first draft. Hopefully, she is prepared to handle it better in this revision.

Since Maya has not made substantial changes to her introduction, we hope to see strong improvement in the body of her essay.

So far Maya avoids her factual error about Jayson Blair by simply stating that he was "found guilty."

Slang. Generally, however, Maya has achieved a more even tone.

Maya's voice is a little improved. Her discussion is considerably better.

Rather than simply repeating Matthew's statistics, Maya has reinterpreted the significance of those statistics. This is a strong improvement.

The simple fact that incidents of cheating become such big news stories shows that cheating is the rare exception rather than normal behavior. Matthew presents an impressive list of examples of cheaters: Stephen Glass, who was fired from The New Republic in 1998 for fabricating his critically acclaimed and award-winning news articles and Jayson Blair, who was similarly found guilty of plagiarism and fabricating stories for the New York Times in 2003. The international, twenty-four/seven coverage that the discovery that Lance Armstrong had cheated through just about his entire career got does not prove that everyone cheats, and cheating is to be expected.

Matthew also discusses an infamous cheating incident in the famous and exclusive Van Noort High School in the Bronx and an equally famous case at Harvard University. Matthew claims that these cases illustrate how pervasive cheating is. Journalists cheat. Students in even the country's "best schools" cheat. The fact is, however, that if cheating were commonplace, these particular incidents would not have become well known. Journalists do not make names for themselves by covering the ordinary and commonplace. These incidents do not prove that cheating is common. Au contraire, they prove that cheating is rare, and incidents of cheating are worth reporting.

The Van Noort and Harvard incidents especially do not help Matthew's case. He himself quotes the statistics: 71 students were involved in Van Noort's cheating ring. Van Noort High School, however, has a student body of over 3,000 students. The small percentage of students (just a little more than 2%, which cannot be reasonably called "massive" or "prevalent." Similarly, the Harvard scandal he cites involved only 125 students and one professor. It all happened in one course. Again, given the entire student body of a school like Harvard and the number of professors who teach there and the number of courses offered, this is hardly a "systemic" problem as Matthew asserts.

Matthew also argues that cheating has become so common in the United States that it is virtually accepted, maybe even encouraged. In every case of cheating Matthew discusses, the cheaters are exposed and punished. Even in the cases where the cheaters do not think they cheated, punishments have been handed down. All 71 of the Van Noort students were suspended "pending further investigation." The incident has been noted on their permanent records, and even if a few are found to be innocent, the disgrace of the accusation will hang over them for the rest of their lives. The Harvard students were also suspended for the remainder of the semester, and their permanent records were marked. Most of these students claim that they did not know what they did was actually cheating, and some have actually threatened to sue Harvard, but at this point, they stand punished for doing wrong. It is simply not true for Matthew to say they suffer no bad consequences for their cheating.

> Maya does need to be careful here. She is accurate to say that Matthew claims cheating is accepted. It might not be as accurate for her to claim that he says it is "encouraged."

Exposed cheaters not only suffer negative consequences when they are found out, but they spend the entire rest of their lives known as cheaters. Stephen Glass <u>was</u> fired from <u>The New Republic</u>. He did write a novel kind of based on his experience, but it sold poorly. The fact that he was a "famous cheater" did make people buy his book. The movie Matthew mentions, <u>Shattered Glass</u>, starring Hayden Christiansen as Stephen Glass, is based <u>only</u> on his cheating and getting caught, not on any other part of his life. So, if anyone ever thinks of him, they think about his famous cheating, nothing else. Even his Wikipedia article begins with a summary of his cheating.

> This is just the type of additional information Maya needed to bolster her refutation.

Jayson Blair is another example. He did leave the <u>New York Times</u> because of his plagiarism, and he is basically unknown today. Wikipedia says he is a "life coach." It is doubtful that his history as a famous cheater is enhancing his career.

This "it is doubtful" is Maya's weakest support so far.

Finally, Lance Armstrong's fame and reputation certainly weren't helped by the discovery of his cheating. He was stripped of all titles. He resigned from his well-known and popular Livestrong charity, and many people feel bitter and let down by him. The same three examples that Matthew gives to prove that cheaters get famous actually prove that, if anything, being found to be a cheater destroys the cheater's fame.

Matthew probably realizes that his evidence really does not support his claim because, after he offers everything he's got, he tries to distract his reader with irrelevancies. His claim that women cheat as much as men is irrelevant and distracting. First of all, gender has nothing to do with the argument. Second, the only example Matthew offers is Whoopi Goldberg admitting that she committed adultery. This example does not support any of Matthew's claims because neither her cheating nor her adultery helped her become famous, and adultery is not the kind of "cheating" Matthew is talking about in his essay.

Many of the conclusions leading to Matthew's claim are weak. He writes, "For every case found out, how many cases are not disclosed?" This is speculation. It is just as logical to speculate that there are <u>no</u> cases of cheating that are not disclosed. When cheaters cheat, they <u>are</u> caught, and their cheating is made public.

Providing the actual quotation was an excellent choice.

Matthew quotes a Van Noort student who said, "You could study for two hours and barely pass, or you could take a risk and ace the exam." This, Matthew claims, proves a sense of justification.

- 214 -

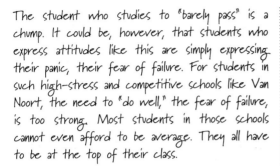

The student who studies to "barely pass" is a chump. It could be, however, that students who express attitudes like this are simply expressing their panic, their fear of failure. For students in such high-stress and competitive schools like Van Noort, the need to "do well," the fear of failure, is too strong. Most students in those schools cannot even afford to be average. They all have to be at the top of their class.

In short, cheating is not common or generally accepted. The decision to cheat is still so rare that it is newsworthy, and cheaters suffer consequences that include losing whatever it was they cheated for and living the entire rest of their lives with the shame of being known as a cheater. So far, in the United States, cheaters still never prosper.

For Maya to return to this quotation provides some nice structure and a good sense of closure to her essay.

Analysis of Revised Draft

What is this writer's point? Maya's point is a clear refutation of a previous essay justifying the decision to cheat on the grounds that cheating is ubiquitous and inevitable. Maya counters that cheating is actually not as prevalent as some would like to believe.

What is his/her angle? Her angle is that the examples chosen by the original writer do not really illustrate his points and that he often misstates and misinterprets data in order to prove his point. She also accuses him of using distraction techniques to mask his lack of solid support.

How strong is this writer's support? How authoritative is his or her overall argument? In this draft, Maya's treatment of the original writer's support and her own new support are much stronger.

What techniques has this writer used to establish this authority? Maya cites statistics from the original essay as well as additional figures and statistics from her own examination of the cases presented. She truthfully and authoritatively presents facts about the cases discussed that the original writer does not disclose.

What specific details, facts, etc., make this argument convincing? This is possibly Maya's strongest improvement. Her specific evidence includes:

- Stephen Glass was fired from *The New Republic* in 1998 for fabricating news articles.

- Jayson Blair was similarly found guilty of plagiarism and fabricating stories for the *New York Times* in 2003. He, as a result, resigned.

- Journalists do not make names for themselves by covering the ordinary and commonplace; therefore, incidents of cheating are rare and worth reporting.

- 71 of a student body of over 3,000 students, or two percent of the student body cannot be reasonably called "massive" or "prevalent."

- All 71 of the Van Noort students were suspended "pending further investigation."

- The incident has been noted on their permanent records.

- The 125 Harvard students were also suspended for the remainder of the semester, and their permanent records were marked.

- At least one quotation from the original essay in order to refute the original writer's interpretation.

POSSIBLE STEP 8: Rewrite Opportunity

MINI LESSON 1:

The Test or Exam Essay (Support, refute, or qualify the thesis that...)

Of all of the forms and purposes of writing covered in these books, the exam essay is probably the least "real" or "authentic." Even its name, "The Exam Essay," suggests that the only time you will ever write one will be when you are taking an exam. Still, when you consider that, through the course of your education, these "exams" will include mid-term and final exams, writing samples for whatever state or national exams you may be required to take, SATs, ACTs, an IB or AP exam, you might decide that these exam essays might possibly be the most important writing you're going to be doing—at least while you are in school (including college, graduate school—however far you take your formal education).

When you are sitting for an exam, and you are instructed to write an essay— often the instructions will include qualifiers like "thoughtful," "well-organized," "well-supported," etc.—know that you *must write an essay*.

It is true that the scorer of your exam essay might care more about the quality of the information than the quality of your presentation, but there are several reasons the exam question asks for an essay rather than, say, a list:

- Your scorer must be able to understand your answer. The organizational pattern of an essay, the relationship between thesis, supporting points, and information, and the simple fact of sentence structure help your scorer know, not only that you can spit out facts, but that you are able to explain relationships, share insights, explore ideas.

- The process of planning an essay will help you eliminate needless repetition and tangents into irrelevant trivia. It is possible to give too much information (even if all of the information is correct), and it is possible to see your grade lowered because you ultimately failed to answer the question simply by dumping in too much.

- The process of planning an essay might stop you from leaving out important information. You don't get "credit" for knowing what you don't tell. You won't receive a top score for an exemplary essay if you leave out crucial ideas or facts.

- Giving some thought to presentation might help you maintain your focus, stick to your topic, and discuss only your thesis.

- A well-written essay will almost always receive a higher score than an equally informative but badly written answer.

Still, since you've got only *hours* to write an exam essay (maybe even only *minutes*), instead of the several days to several weeks you might usually have to write something, you've got to be skilled at generating your information, drafting a thesis, organizing your thoughts, and writing your essay in whatever time is allowed you.

In Maya and Kyle's school, most of the tenth graders read William Shakespeare's *Romeo and Juliet* at some point during the year. This is an essay prompt that occasionally appears on the tenth-grade English final exam:

> In Act II, scene iii of Romeo and Juliet, Friar Lawrence says, "Young men's love then lies not truly in their hearts, but in their eyes." Consider the character of Romeo and his behavior throughout the entire play. Then write a well-organized and well-supported essay in which you defend, refute, or qualify Friar Lawrence's assessment of Romeo's love for Juliet. Be certain to provide evidence from the play to support all of your claims.

Students are given a total of 3 hours (180 minutes) for their exam, 30 minutes for approximately 50 multiple-choice questions, and then one hour (60 minutes) each for two essays. Some standardized assessments allow as little as 20 minutes for their essay portion. You need always to be aware of how much time you have and how much time you are devoting to each step so you can write at least a full first draft.

STEP 1: Draft a Thesis (no more than 5 min. out of 60)

For the above prompt, this is a relatively easy step since *your* thesis is simply a reaction to someone else's. Basically, which view of Lawrence's statement can you best argue?

Here is Maya's first attempt at a thesis:

— In Romeo and Juliet, Friar Lawrence essentially dismisses the possibility that Romeo really loves Juliet when he says that men only love with their eyes and not with their heart.

> This thesis merely summarizes Lawrence's claim without making any claims of its own. The prompt does not ask students to explain the Friar's point but essentially to agree or disagree with it.

— Friar Lawrence is right when he criticizes men in love as shallow and obsessed with physical appearance.

> As the prompt requires, this thesis does defend Lawrence's thesis, but Maya does not establish Romeo as the basis of her defense. Such a general statement of agreement can entice Maya into any number of tangents.

Here are Kyle's attempts:

— Since Friar Lawrence seems to have been Romeo's confidant and advisor while he was in love with Rosaline, he knows what he's talking about when he says that Romeo loves with his eyes and not his heart.

> There is a good deal wrong with this sentence, especially with helping the reader keep the antecedent for "he" straight, but Kyle does have a sense of responding to Friar Lawrence's assessment.

— Romeo's actions in Act II, scene iii of <u>Romeo and Juliet</u> do seem to show that he is what Friar Lawrence says, a man who loves with his eyes and not his heart, but his actions throughout the rest of the play show that Friar Lawrence is being unfair in this assessment of him.

> This is the best, most complex statement of qualification or disagreement that we have seen, but Kyle still has a number of problems with pronoun/ antecedent clarity.

> **TIME SPENT: 5 MIN.—TIME REMAINING: 55 MIN.**

STEP 2: Brainstorm, jot notes (no more than 10 min. out of 60)

Once you have a workable thesis, you might be tempted to jump right in and begin writing your essay. *Such a strategy can only lower your score* as the thesis alone cannot guarantee that you will present complete information in an easily followed form and organizational pattern.

You want this essay to reflect how well you understand the play, so you want to make sure you take the time to think about and jot down all the ideas you want to explore and all the information from the play to support those ideas.

Here are Maya's notes:

- Romeo first loves Rosaline, then loves Juliet
- Paris has not even met Juliet and says he loves her
- Capulet tells Paris to wait a year or two but then sets up the marriage for less than a week later
- Even the Friar allows Romeo to be fickle when he agrees to marry them
- They're only, what? Fourteen years old?
- Capulet tells us how old Juliet is—twelve summers, or something like that.

> Maya's plan so far still does not address the prompt, which instructs the students to "Consider the character of Romeo and his behavior throughout the entire play."

Here are Kyle's notes:

- Romeo first pines for Rosaline—our introduction to him is his exaggerated despair for loving her.
- Romeo's love is pointless—Rosaline has sworn a vow of chastity—like a nun or something.
- Benvolio encourages Romeo to forget her and move on.
- ben + volio = "good" + "will" or "intentions" so Benvolio is a giver of good advice.
- Benvolio is the attempted peacemaker in the play
- End of Act I, scene i, Benvolio tempts Romeo with other beautiful women, but Romeo says his heart and mind cannot be turned from Rosaline.

> Already we can see that Kyle is building a case to disagree with Friar Lawrence. He is clearly drawing on material taught in class (the meaning of Benvolio's name and his role in the play), and he is careful to make specific references to the play, even if he is not able to quote directly.

- Rosaline is Capulet's niece and invited to the party
- BUT ... Benvolio tempts Romeo to go to the party to compare Rosaline's beauty with other girls, the idea being that Romeo will see how plain she is compared to other girls, so this would make Friar Lawrence seem right.
- Entire notion of love is different. Juliet not met Paris but mom asks if she can love him

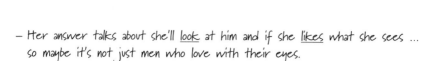

- Her answer talks about she'll <u>look</u> at him and if she <u>likes</u> what she sees ... so maybe it's not just men who love with their eyes.
- Once he meets Juliet, Romeo remains completely faithful to her
  - Stays in orchard to see her
  - Doesn't back away when she insists on marriage
  - Tries not to fight with Tybalt
  - Rushes to her side when he thinks she's dead
  - Dies for her

TIME SPENT: 15 MIN.—TIME REMAINING: 45 MIN.

STEP 3: Outline (no more than 5 min. out of 60)

Yes, even though you have only an hour to plan and write this essay, it will be in your best interest to draft some kind of outline. Given your thesis and the information you've brainstormed, you might find it helpful to rely on a pre-fabricated organizational plan like the five-paragraph essay.

Here is Maya's attempt at an outline:

Thesis: Friar Lawrence is right when he criticizes men in love as shallow and obsessed with physical appearance.

I. Men are shallow and fickle.

   A. Romeo w/Rosaline and then Juliet

   B. Paris and Juliet

II. Immature

   A. Capulet tells Paris to wait a year or two but then sets up the marriage for less than a week later

      1. Capulet says she's too young to marry

      2. Paris insists many her age are already mothers

III. But even the Friar is fickle when he agrees to marry them

   A. His marriage is for political reasons, not for love

IV. It's almost like no one in the play really knows what love is.

> There is nothing blatantly wrong with any of Maya's intention. She is clearly familiar with the play and has some ideas that she is able to discuss and support, but nothing in her preparation so far will yield an answer to the specific question she has been assigned to address.

Here is Kyle's:

Thesis: Romeo's actions in Act II, scene iii of Romeo and Juliet do seem to show that he is what Friar Lawrence says, a man who loves with his eyes and not his heart, but his actions throughout the rest of the play show that Friar Lawrence is being unfair in this assessment of him.

I. R's actions leading up to F.L.'s criticism make F.L. look right

   A. Pines for Rosaline

   B. Goes to party on a dare to prove that Ros is beautiful/or not

> Remember that this is a timed essay on an exam. The scorer has probably been instructed not to look at any notes or preliminaries but to score only the essay. Since this outline is for Kyle's benefit only, his shorthand is perfectly acceptable. It would be foolish for him to waste time drafting and polishing a perfect, formal outline.

II. But there are "extenuating circumstances"

   A. Rom knows his love for Ros is hopeless; she has sworn vow of chastity

   B. Benvolio equates love w/ beauty when he dares Rom to crash the party

      1. ben + volio = "good" + "will" or "intentions" so Benvolio is a giver of good advice.

      2. Benvolio is the attempted peacemaker in the play

   C. Before he meets J, Rom says his heart and mind cannot be changed

> The etymology and meaning of Benvolio's name might not be relevant to Kyle's thesis.

III. Once he meets J, Rom is faithful to her

   A. Stays in orchard to see her

   B. Doesn't back away when she insists on marriage

   C. Tries not to fight with Tybalt

   D. Rushes to her side when he thinks she's dead

   E. Dies for her

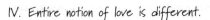

IV. *Entire notion of love is different.*

> This last point is a nice example that the order of ideas in the outline (and thus in the essay) does not need to follow simply the order in which you think of them. That is why the brainstorming and the outlining are two separate steps.

    A. *Juliet not met Paris but mom asks if she can love him*

        1. *Her answer talks about she'll <u>look</u> at him and if she <u>likes</u> what she sees ... so maybe it's not just men who love with their eyes.*

    B. *P claims to love J even though they have never met*

> While it is not identical, Kyle's plan for his essay is not too very different from a five-paragraph essay format.

> **TIME SPENT: 20 MIN.—TIME REMAINING: 40 MIN.**

STEP 4: Write your essay (35 min. out of 60)

With a reasonably strong thesis, some clear and specific notes, and a sense of where you want to take your reader, writing the essay should almost be the easiest step.

Here is Maya's essay:

In Act II, scene iii of Romeo and Juliet, Friar Lawrence says, "Young men's love then lies not truly in their hearts, but in their eyes." He is right when he criticizes men in love as shallow and obsessed with physical appearance. As you can tell from examining characters' attitudes toward love in the play, men are shallow and fickle. People who claim to be in love are immature. Even Friar Lawrence is fickle when he agrees to marry Romeo and Juliet after criticizing Romeo for being fickle himself.

On the plus side, Maya is following her thesis and outline, and her thesis is a reaction to Friar Lawrence's Act II, scene iii statement. On the negative side, however, the writing prompt asks her to write about Romeo, not characters or men in general.

Based on the play, men are shallow and fickle. At first, Romeo is madly in love with Rosaline. His entire first scene is the play is a conversation with Benvolio where he moans and groans about

If this last sentence is an attempt at humor, it doesn't really work. It gives the impression that Maya does not understand that Romeo and Juliet, being the title characters, will indeed be the focus of the play.

This is a rambling and largely tangential paragraph. Even disregarding the fact that a discussion of Paris does not meet the requirements of the prompt, in this one paragraph, Maya offers Paris as an example of a fickle lover, claims he is not fickle, and shifts the focus from "men as fickle" to "men whose love is questionable." The discussion of Juliet's age, and Maya's speculation about Paris's motivation for wanting to marry Juliet are irrelevant at best.

Who are "they"?

Scorers will be more forgiving in a timed, on-demand setting, but a good writer should establish good habits like avoiding second person and rhetorical questions. Maya apparently assumes her reader interprets these characters' actions the way she does, but one purpose of an exam essay like this would be for Maya to make clear to her reader how she interprets the play and why.

Maya might feel she is running out of time. Her voice sounds rushed, and her flow of ideas is nearly impossible to follow. We almost lose complete track of Maya's pronouns and antecedents.

how in love he is with Rosaline and that she does not love him back. He only goes to the party where he meets Juliet because Rosaline is going to be there. At the party, he meets Juliet, and for the entire rest of the play, we never hear about Rosaline again. It's all Romeo and Juliet.

Paris's love is also questionable. He claims to love Juliet and to want to marry her before he even meets her. I think what he loves is Capulet's fortune, because the servant even refers to Capulet as "great rich Capulet." He seems to be in a hurry to marry Juliet, even though Capulet has not said no, only to wait. And it makes sense for Capulet to want Paris to wait. After all, Juliet is only something like fourteen years old. Still, Paris is not as fickle as Romeo because, once he says he loves Juliet, he does not change his mind. He even visits her at the Capulet family tomb and brings her flowers.

They are immature. Capulet tells Paris to wait a year or two but then he sets up the marriage for less than a week later. Capulet says she's too young to marry, even though Paris insists that many women her age are already mothers. Why is Paris in such a hurry? Why does Capulet change his mind like that?

But even the Friar is fickle when he agrees to marry Romeo and Juliet. One minute, he's teasing Romeo about dropping Rosaline so suddenly—this is what's happening in the Act III, scene iii lines—and the next minute he's all about going to marry them because if they get married then the feud will end. His reason for the marriage is for political reasons, not for love.

It seems as if no one in the play really understands what love is, so when Friar Lawrence says in Act II, scene iii, "Young men's love then lies not truly in their hearts, but in their eyes," he is right. This not understanding what love is might be the real source of the tragedy in the play. If Romeo and Juliet had known what true love was, then maybe they wouldn't have killed themselves and each other.

> This unfortunate essay ends on a completely unrelated issue—the source of tragedy in the play. From the beginning, Maya has either misread or disregarded the writing prompt. Even putting that aside, however, this essay treats its topic too broadly and summarily with insufficient clarification of, and support for, each point.

Analysis of Exam Essay

What is this writer's point? In this essay, Maya seems to want to discuss various characters' views of love, arguing that these views do not reflect an understanding of what love really is.

In what way(s) does this thesis fulfill the requirements of the prompt? It doesn't. Students were instructed to defend, refute, or qualify Friar Lawrence's statement in terms of Romeo's actions throughout the play. Maya discusses Romeo very briefly in her first body paragraph and then spends the bulk of her essay discussing other characters and their views and actions.

What information does the writer provide to demonstrate her understanding of the tested subject matter? Maya does demonstrate a decent understanding of some of the play's overarching issues:

- Romeo's excitable and fickle nature,
- Juliet's youth and her father's caution,
- Paris's apparent, inexplicable haste,
- Friar Lawrence's lack of common sense and skewed values.

What techniques has this writer used to present this information in a coherent, cohesive essay? Maya's essay is modeled after a basic five-paragraph essay.

What type of score is this essay likely to receive? Why? Unfortunately, this essay is likely to earn a failing grade. If the scorer is allowed to reward her for *any* demonstration for understanding the play, the might receive the lowest possible passing score.

- It does not address the requirements of the prompt: Defend, refute, or qualify the Friar's statement *in terms of Romeo's behavior*.
- It provides only minimal direct reference to events in the play.

- It speculates on character action and motivation, providing no support for the speculation.

- It is badly written, full of pronoun-antecedent errors and overused, unnecessary rhetorical questions.

Here is Kyle's essay:

Both Maya and Kyle began their essay by quoting verbatim from the prompt. As long as it helps the writer focus on the assigned topic, there is nothing wrong with this technique.

At this point, the five-paragraph structure might seem too obvious, but remember that this is a timed, on-demand, exam essay. The scorer has most likely been instructed to focus on the answer and not penalize for lack of originality in the composition—as long as the essay is appropriately written and structured.

Rather than merely transcribing what he has already written in his notes and outline, Kyle is allowing the outline to spur his memory. His discussion of these points is much more thorough than indicated in the outline.

In Act II, scene iii of Romeo and Juliet, Friar Lawrence says, "Young men's love then lies not truly in their hearts, but in their eyes." Even though Romeo's actions up to and in Act II, scene iii do seem to show that he is what Friar Lawrence says, his actions throughout the rest of the play show that Friar Lawrence is being unfair in this assessment of him.

Romeo's actions leading up to Friar Lawrence's criticism do make Friar Lawrence look right. The audience's first introduction to Romeo sees him pining for Rosaline, whom he describes as beautiful. His only reason for attending the Capulets' feast, where he will meet Juliet, is because Benvolio dares him to judge Rosaline's beauty against other beautiful women's. But even in the dare, the focus is on the physical beauty of the woman.

But there are "extenuating circumstances." Romeo's search for a beautiful woman is not the whole story. In Act I, when we first meet Romeo, he admits that his love for Rosaline is hopeless. She has sworn a vow of chastity, and he knows he will never win her heart. It makes sense that, since he knows to continue pursuing Rosaline is pointless, he would be open to meeting and falling in love with someone else. It's also possible that Rosaline is not all that beautiful. It is Benvolio who dares Romeo to crash the Capulets' party and compare Rosaline to the other beauties who will be there. Benvolio, whose name means "good will" or "good intentions" must know that, compared to others, Rosaline isn't all that. This would mean that

Romeo finds her beautiful because he loves her, not that he loves her because she is beautiful, which is what Friar Lawrence is accusing him of. In his defense, before he meets Juliet, Romeo says his heart and mind cannot be changed.

Romeo's sudden love for Juliet might be surprising and show him to be fickle—though we have already shown that he knows it will be foolish to keep pursuing Rosaline—but once he meets Juliet, he is completely faithful to her. After he has been unmasked as a party crasher, he still stays in the Capulets' orchard to see Juliet. He doesn't back away when she insists on marriage. In fact, it is when he goes to Friar Lawrence to arrange that marriage that Lawrence chastises him for being fickle. After the marriage, Romeo tries not to fight with Tybalt, and, in spite of the danger of breaking the law, he returns to Verona and rushes to her side when he thinks she's dead. All of these actions show love, not just infatuation, and not just something based on the fact that Juliet is beautiful. Romeo has to be "loving with his heart and not his eyes," or he would not have suffered everything that he did.

He even dies for her, and it is not likely that he would kill himself if all he was attracted to was her beauty.

What Friar Lawrence says to Romeo in Act II, scene iii really isn't fair. Not only do Romeo's actions throughout the entire play show him to be truly in love with Juliet, heart <u>and</u> eyes, the entire notion of love in this play is different. Juliet has not yet met Paris when her mother asks if she can love him. Juliet's answer has something to do with her willingness to <u>look</u> at him and decide whether she <u>likes</u> what she sees. Apparently it's not just men who "love with their eyes."

Unlike Maya, Kyle supports his speculation with the reasoning and the text behind it. The reader need not agree, but at least we know its basis.

This is not a direct quotation, but it is effective for Kyle to return to the language of the quotation in the prompt to remind his reader of the point he is trying to establish.

Kyle knows it's an effective technique to return to some version of his thesis at the beginning of his conclusion.

It's also effective for him to repeat some language from the question he is answering. This keeps him on track and points out to the scorer that he is on track.

This last sentence doesn't add anything to Kyle's discussion, but it shouldn't hurt his grade any, either.

Analysis of Exam Essay

What is this writer's point? Kyle's point is a refutation of Friar Lawrence's comment, based on the ground that Lawrence is being unfair in his assessment of Romeo.

What information does the writer provide to demonstrate his understanding of the tested subject matter? Kyle presents information that clearly shows his understanding of Romeo's character and the situation in which he finds himself. Kyle also shows some understanding of the nature of romantic love in the Elizabethan mind.

- the reason behind Romeo's impossible love for Rosaline and his willingness to surrender it,
- Benvolio's suggestion that Rosaline is, perhaps, not as beautiful as Romeo believes,
- Romeo's constancy, even up to death, once he meets Juliet and professes love for her.

What techniques has this writer used to present this information in a coherent, cohesive essay? Kyle basis his organizational plan on the five-paragraph essay. He refers directly to, and quotes from, the prompt and the quotation on which the question is based. He repeats some of the actual words and phrases from his introduction in his conclusion, thus indicating to his reader that he is about to wrap up his discussion.

What type of score is this essay likely to receive? Why? Kyle's essay should receive a very high score. He fully addresses the prompt, both offering a refutation of the Friar's criticism and using the portrayal of Romeo throughout the entire play as his illustration. He demonstrates a full and accurate understanding of the play, including character relationships and the roles of various characters in the narrative structure. He is able to summarize and at times almost paraphrases or quotes from the play. The writing itself is clear, organized, and relatively free of conventional errors.

TIME SPENT: 55 MIN.—TIME REMAINING: 5 MIN.

STEP 5: Review, proof, and edit (5 min. out of 60)

Even though you probably do not have time to complete a full second draft, before you turn your essay in, you should give it one last quick read and correct any surface errors you find that might erode your score. Misspellings of key words or prominent people's names are especially damaging.

Maya's essay did contain a number of conventional errors, but here is what a portion of her essay might have looked like had she taken even only a few minutes to proofread:

All of the characters, even the supposed adults, ~~They~~ are immature.

Capulet tells Paris to wait a year or two ^ but then he ~~sets up the~~ *arranges*

claims that Juliet's

marriage for less than a week later. Capulet ~~says~~ she's too young to

marry, even though Paris insists that many women her age are

already mothers. Why is Paris in such a hurry? Why does Capulet

change his mind like that?

E   Romeo and Juliet.

   But even the Friar is fickle when he agrees to marry them. One

minute, he's teasing Romeo about dropping Rosaline so suddenly—this is

what's happening in the Act III, scene iii lines—and the next

encourages the marriage.

minute ~~he's all about going to marry them because~~ if they get married ^

might

then the feud will end. His reason for agreeing to perform the

marriage is for political reasons, ~~not for love.~~

TIME SPENT: 60 MIN.—TIME REMAINING: 0 MIN.
Time to turn in your exam.

ASSIGNMENT 3:

The Academic Thesis-Proof Essay

An academic essay is something you'd write for school, or for your field of study if you were a research scientist or something like that. While you are in school, the main purpose of this type of essay is to prove to your teacher or the scorers of an exam that you have learned whatever it is you were supposed to have learned in the class.

In college, graduate school, and professional research, the purpose of your essay might be to share your new discovery with other professionals in your field and demonstrate the validity of your findings.

In that sense, this essay is not terribly different from your research paper.

It is important enough to warrant being studied and practiced independently because just about every essay you will write for every course you take, every answer you compose for a mid-term or final exam, or a state assessment, or the SAT, ACT, or AP exams will be academic essays.

And if you accept the notion that every academic essay should be a thesis-proof essay, you will find yourself scoring higher on those exams and assessments than your classmates who simply write a mind-dump of facts.

After completing a long unit on "tragedy in literature," during which they studied Shakespeare's *Romeo and Juliet*, F. Scott Fitzgerald's *The Great Gatsby*, and Arthur Miller's *Death of a Salesman*, **Kyle's** teacher wanted to begin preparing her class for their essay-rich final exam. The class's end-of-unit assessment took the form of the following writing assignment:

> In 1949, playwright Arthur Miller wrote a groundbreaking essay titled "Tragedy and the Common Man," in which he argued this thesis:
>
> > As a general rule…the tragic feeling is evoked in us when we are in the presence of a character who is ready to lay down his life, if need be, to secure one thing—his sense of personal dignity. From Orestes to Hamlet, Medea to Macbeth, the underlying struggle is that of the individual attempting to gain his 'rightful' position in his society.

> *From a novel or play you have studied, choose a character who might legitimately be considered a tragic hero and use him or her as the basis to support, refute, or qualify Miller's thesis. Be certain to support all of your assertions with direct evidence from the novel or play and with references to other reliable literary criticism.*
>
> *Because the purpose of this assignment is to assess your ability to discuss the literature studied in class, you may choose one of the following characters:*
>
> *Romeo or Juliet (NOT BOTH)*
> *Jay Gatsby*
> *Willy Loman*

To complete this assignment, Kyle followed a predictable, but reliable, planning and writing process:

STEP 1: Select a Topic

...individual attempting to gain his 'rightful' position in his society...

Willy Loman: this would be the easiest because Miller was clearly talking about Willy. But everyone will do Willy. Does Ms. Stern expect us to do Willy? But Death of a Salesman was the last play we studied, and this assignment is supposed to test the whole unit, so it might be a good idea to go back to look at some of the early ones.

Kyle is actually being pretty smart right now. He is considering the entire unit, not just the last play studied.

Early in the unit, the class read this essay in its entirety, and it was often mentioned during their study of all three titles.

Romeo: what would be his "rightful position"? What is he trying to gain? What makes him a tragic hero, just the fact that he dies in the end? But he doesn't have any of the other traits tragic heroes are supposed to have ... I don't think he's a tragic hero.

Juliet: rightful position ... she was a woman with no choices, but she wanted to have the choice. Self determination!!! She tells her mother something like, I won't get married next week, and when I do get married, I will marry Romeo! And because she asserts <u>her</u> independence, she must die.

> You can tell by the exclamation points that Kyle is a little excited about the possibility of using Juliet as his tragic hero.

Jay Gatsby: I know I'm going to do Juliet, but I guess I have to at least consider that Gatsby sees himself as Daisy's rightful lover, and that's the whole thing with him trying to get her to say she never loved Tom. He dies "protecting" her, and in his warped mind, this is maybe supposed to earn him top place in her memory? Yeah ... but it doesn't work ... but he does support Miller's thesis.

> As you might already have learned, you know you've got a strong possible topic when the essay begins to lay itself out for you like this.

STEP 2: Brainstorm, discuss, research

Even without the prompt's specifying it, Kyle knows that whatever he says about Juliet's independence or strong will is going to have to be supported from the play itself. There has to be some basis for his inference, and he must be able to explain that basis with someone else.

Juliet is strong willed and independent.

Act III, scene v: I will not marry yet; and, when I do, I swear, / It shall be Romeo ...

and after Nurse tells her to go ahead and marry Paris ... which would be a crime and a sin since she is already married ...

I'll to the friar, to know his remedy: / If all else fail, myself have power to die.

So ... she's not passive. She takes action here.

Maybe this is also where she tells us what her "rightful place in society is" that she needs to secure.

O, how my heart abhors / To hear him named, <u>and cannot come to him.</u> / <u>To wreak the love I bore my cousin</u> / <u>Upon his body</u> [she's talking about Romeo's body] that slaughter'd him!

- 232 -

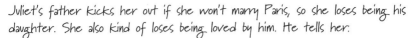

Juliet's father kicks her out if she won't marry Paris, so she loses being his daughter. She also kind of loses being loved by him. He tells her:

> doth she not count her blest, / <u>Unworthy as she is</u>, that we have wrought / So worthy a gentleman to be her bridegroom?

So now she's "unworthy" of Paris. In Act I, scene ii, he said that even though he liked Paris and was willing to let Paris marry her, he would not force Juliet to marry someone she didn't want to:

> … woo her, gentle Paris, get her heart, / My will to her consent is but a part; / An she agree, within her scope of choice / Lies my consent and fair according voice.

Kyle continued by finding a few Internet sources to support his claim that Juliet could be considered a tragic hero and also argued that she is a strong character, not demonstrating the stereotypically female traits of passivity and weakness. He also reviews Miller's essay and pulls some key quotations to show how Miller's model can be applied to Juliet.

STEP 3: Draft a Thesis

Kyle knows that his thesis is dependent on the thesis of Miller's article. He has been assigned to "support, refute, or qualify" it. He is, of course, going to use Juliet as the means to support Miller's contention. To make sure that he stays close to his assigned topic, he begins with a direct restatement of Miller's thesis:

> As a general rule…the tragic feeling is evoked in us when we are in the presence of a character who is ready to lay down his life, if need be, to secure one thing—his sense of personal dignity. From Orestes to Hamlet, Medea to Macbeth, the underlying struggle is that of the individual attempting to gain his 'rightful' position in his society.

Then he more or less "customizes" it into a statement about Juliet:

> Juliet evokes in us the tragic feeling because she is ready to lay down her life to secure one thing—her sense of personal dignity. Juliet is truly an individual attempting to gain her rightful position in her society.

In terms of content and intent, this is a fine thesis that directly addresses the assignment. Kyle will have to revise it, however, both to reduce the amount of material he is taking directly from Miller's sentence and to credit Miller for his contributions to Kyle's thesis.

STEP 4: Outline

Thesis: Juliet evokes in us the tragic feeling because she is ready to lay down her life to secure one thing—her sense of personal dignity. Juliet is truly an individual attempting to gain her rightful position in her society.

Revised Thesis: Juliet, the most famous of all of Shakespeare's heroines, evokes the tragic feeling in audience members because she is ready to lay down her life to secure one thing—her sense of personal dignity. Juliet is truly an individual attempting to gain her rightful position in her society.

> Kyle has changed some of the sentence structure, but he really has not revised the thesis in terms of clarity and specificity.

I. Before Romeo, Juliet enjoys two statuses in her family.
   A. She is loved by her father.
   B. She has freedom of choice.
   C. She is strong and independent.

II. Social rules and expectations ruin it
   A. Can't choose Romeo
   B. Feud gets in way
      1. Loses Romeo
      2. Isolates Juliet
   C. Can't admit to marrying Romeo
      1. Loses father's love
      2. Loses freedom of choice

III. Visit to Friar Laurence is her attempt to get it back.
   A. She chooses her destiny
   B. She identifies as Romeo's wife
   C. Dies in her attempt to achieve her proper role

> There may be a few inconsistencies in this outline, but Kyle does seem to have a good grasp on this essay. Remember that he is writing his first draft, so any problems that are the result of flaws in the outline can be identified and corrected in the revision stage.

STEP 5: Write your first draft

When people talk about tragedy and tragic heroes, they don't usually take into account Arthur Miller's groundbreaking 1949 essay, "Tragedy and the Common Man." In this essay, the writer who is most famous for his play <u>Death of a Salesman</u> and because he was married to Marilyn Monroe before she died, redefines what is "tragic" so that common people, too, can be tragic heroes. What he says essentially boils down to the idea that, even the most famous tragic heroes like Macbeth, Hamlet, and Julius Caesar, are tragic because their sense of self has been challenged, and they are willing to do anything necessary, even die, in order to regain their sense of who they are. It will not be the purpose of this paper to prove that Miller's thesis is right. I am simply going to say that, if you accept Miller's definition, then Juliet fills the bill as a tragic hero according to Arthur Miller's definition.

The main point of "Tragedy and the Common Man" can be summed up by Miller's statement, "As a general rule...the tragic feeling is evoked in us when we are in the presence of a character who is ready to lay down his life, if need be, to secure one thing—his sense of personal dignity. From Orestes to Hamlet, Medea to Macbeth, the underlying struggle is that of the individual attempting to gain his 'rightful' position in his society." This statement can define William Shakespeare's Juliet, the most famous of all of Shakespeare's heroines. Juliet is a character who is a strong and independent woman who is beloved by those around her. When her status in her family is threatened, she does everything she can to regain her beloved status. The tragic fact is, though, that she dies.

Granted, this is an academic essay, and the occasion for writing is contrived, but to imply there might actually be times when people sit around, drink tea (or soda), and "talk about tragedy and tragic heroes" is really silly.

Without meaning to, Kyle has introduced a new argument: whether or not those who debate tragedy consider Miller.

Death of a Salesman might be important to mention, but the fact that Miller was married to Marilyn Monroe is irrelevant, and it is almost comic for Kyle to observe that Miller was married to her "before she died."

Kyle says he is naming tragic heroes, not tragic plays. Brutus is generally considered to be the tragic hero of Julius Caesar.

In some academic circles, this technique of referring to one's own paper is allowed, but it is never considered the best option.

Kyle is not ever really wrong in anything he says in this introductory paragraph, but his word choice, tone, and stance are immature and mildly humorous. These are not qualities he wants in his academic essay.

These final sentences about Juliet are Kyle's best iteration of his thesis so far.

Kyle needs to avoid silly clichés like this.

Because he has already identified the play, act, and scene, Kyle does not need any form of documentation.

Confusing use of pronouns. Who tells whom?

There are a number of problems with this short paragraph. The language is too informal, almost conversational. The character should not be referred to as "Mrs." and who is consenting to what and to whom at the end of the final sentence?

As was the case in the other paragraphs, Kyle has some decent ideas here, but he is not elaborating sufficiently on them, and his language choices weaken the overall academic quality of this essay.

From the beginning of the play, Shakespeare makes it clear that Juliet is the apple of her family's eye. In Act I, scene ii, Juliet's father tells Paris, who has come to marry her:

> The earth hath swallow'd all my hopes but she,
>
> She is the hopeful lady of my earth

Later, he tells him:

> My will to her consent is but a part;
>
> An she agree, within her scope of choice
>
> Lies my consent and fair according voice.

So Juliet's father is a nice guy, and he does not seem to want to treat his daughter like property to be given away or sold. Mrs. Capulet also seems to love Juliet enough that it is important for her to also like Paris and consent to marry him before she will also give her consent.

When Juliet first meets Romeo, we catch a glimpse of Juliet's view of herself in her society. She is immediately interested in Romeo and asks her nurse who he is. Why would she worry that he might be a Montague if she didn't think there was the possibility that she might marry him? Even though she's already been told that her father has been considering Paris for a husband for her, it seems that she knows it will be her choice whom to marry. So there is a real chance she will be able to marry Romeo—unless he is a member of the one family she cannot marry into.

And that's when she first says she'll die if she can't marry him.

The tragedy of Juliet's losing what Miller calls her "'rightful' position in [her] society" does not begin with her meeting Romeo. It doesn't even begin when Juliet sneaks off to Friar Laurence's cell to marry Romeo. It begins when the "unjust society" that Miller mentions in his essay intrudes. Romeo kills Juliet's cousin Tybalt. The feud between the Montagues and Capulets is completely beyond Juliet's control. She did not cause it, and nothing in the play says she even participated in it. That she knew about it explains her fear that Romeo might be a Montague and why she had to hide her intent to marry, but it is a factor in her life over which she has no control.

But now that Tybalt is dead at Romeo's hand, even the nurse has taken away her unconditional love. When she refuses to marry Paris—not because she doesn't like him or is disobedient but because <u>she is already married</u>—she loses her standing with her father and mother and is no longer the favored or beloved daughter that she was at the beginning of the play:

In Act III, scene v, after she has refused to marry Paris, making it seem as if she would never marry anyone, her father asks his wife,

> doth she not count her blest,
>
> <u>Unworthy as she is</u>, that we have wrought
>
> So worthy a gentleman to be her bridegroom?

In Act I, Juliet was "the hopeful lady of [her father's] earth. Now she is "unworthy" to marry such a man as Paris. Earlier, the father insisted he could consent to Juliet's match to Paris, only if she also consented. Now he berates her for being disobedient. At this point, what Miller calls "[her] sense of personal dignity" and her "'rightful' position in [her] society" is threatened. She could maybe restore it if she told her parents that she was already married, but the added complication of Romeo having killed Tybalt makes that impossible. At least, she believes it is impossible. So, as a person whose "unjust society" has threatened her ability to be who and what she believes herself to be, Juliet must be shown to be "a character who

If losing the nurse's love is part of Juliet's loss of status, then having that love it must be established earlier. It is also not clear whether Kyle is being ironic when he writes of Juliet's losing "unconditional" love.

This is not a bad paraphrase of another part of Miller's discussion.

When he reviews this draft, Kyle will probably feel that he is being repetitive. The passive is also a bad word choice here.

As he does in the second paragraph, Kyle refers to his own paper, wasting time and space telling the reader what he's not going to write.

At this point, Kyle seems to have completely given up on trying to create a formal, academic tone for his essay.

Kyle is apparently forgetting the fact that Romeo killed Paris earlier in this scene.

The one-sentence paragraph only contributes to the overall informal, conversational tone of this essay.

is ready to lay down [her] life, if need be, to secure one thing," which is that sense of personal dignity and that rightful position in society.

This happens when she goes to Friar Laurence. I don't think I need to summarize the play and what happens, but the only reason for Juliet's going to the Friar is to find a solution to her problem. The Nurse knows she is already married, but the Nurse's solution was for Juliet to just go ahead and marry Paris. This would be illegal, immoral, and would not really restore Juliet to her view of who she is. She would be demeaning herself—lying and violating an oath—only to sacrifice her independence and the freedom of choice she had at the beginning of the play.

The only way to restore all of things in Juliet's mind is to be reunited with Romeo.

Now, you shouldn't be fooled to think that the death-like sleeping potion that Laurence gives to her is her willingness to "lay down [her] life." You might want to see symbolism in her funeral and being placed into her family's tomb, but she knows full well that she is not really dying for her cause. She will awaken, and when she does, Romeo will be there, and she will be restored to her status as beloved, independent woman.

The "lay down [her] life" part comes when she wakes up and sees Romeo dead. With Romeo dead, it is now impossible for her to be restored to her earlier status. If her parents come and see her alive, and she is now a widow, so she can legally marry Paris, then she will never regain the independent and able-to-choose status that she enjoyed before Romeo killed Tybalt.

So, she kills herself.

The story is a tragedy, according to Arthur Miller's "Tragedy and the Common Man," because

Juliet is a person whose personal dignity, her sense of who and what she is, is challenged by a dysfunctional, unjust society, and she fights to regain it. She's even willing to die rather than live life as someone or something she isn't. Juliet Capulet is a perfect example of Arthur Miller's tragic hero.

Kyle's understanding of the topic is sound, and his thesis is valid. He does not, however, discuss that thesis as fully and as academically as he should.

Analysis of First Draft

What is this writer's point? Kyle's point is that the Shakespearean heroine Juliet both illustrates and supports the central thesis of Arthur Miller's 1949 essay, "Tragedy and the Common Man."

What is his/her angle? Because this is an academic essay, there is no strong angle. Kyle is making a case for Miller's thesis but not necessarily trying to "convince" the reader to agree with him.

How strong is this writer's support? How authoritative is his or her overall argument? Kyle's support is quite strong. He presents summary and paraphrase, and direct quotations, from both the play and Miller's article. There are a couple of points, most notably the loss of the Nurse's love, that would benefit from more complete discussion.

What techniques has this writer used to establish this authority? As noted, Kyle presents a good amount of support, and his thesis is well founded. What he needs to work on is his word choice and the resultant tone, which tends to be too conversational.

What specific details, facts, etc., make this argument convincing? Kyle cites Juliet's status as only surviving daughter, loved enough by her father that he says she must consent to his choice of a husband for her, as his chief example of the rightful status that Miller contends is at the core of tragedy.

Tybalt's death at the hand of Romeo is the event that threatens Juliet's sense of her rightful place.

Her suicide is her willingness to lay down her life in her attempt to secure that status.

NOW plan an essay to one of the following prompts or one assigned by your teacher. Notice that, while most of our examples address English language and literature topics, some address topics in other fields. You will most likely find yourself writing this kind of academic essay in just about every subject you study in school, college, and graduate school.

The main conflict of many novels or plays is based on the difference between how a character sees him or herself and how other characters see him or her. Choose a character from a novel or play that you have studied in class and write a well-organized essay in which you explore the nature of this difference and what it contributes to the plot and meaning of the work. Be certain to provide support from the text for all of your claims.

Characters who might lend themselves to this type of discussion include:
Arthur Dimmesdale in The Scarlet Letter
Holden Caulfield in The Catcher in the Rye
Atticus Finch in To Kill a Mockingbird
Blanche in A Streetcar Named Desire
Don Quixote
Jay Gatsby
Willy Loman in Death of a Salesman

An important idea in a Marxist reading of literature is Marxism's strong focus on the material rather than the spiritual (the belief that things are more important to a person's satisfaction in life than ideals). According to Marx, persons are not destroyed by a failure to attain their ideals but by a failure to secure their material needs. Choose a novel or play that lends itself to a Marxist reading and analyze the central conflict and final outcome of the plot in terms of the characters' material failures.

Novels and plays that lend themselves to this type of reading include:
The Great Gatsby
The Glass Menagerie
Of Mice and Men
The Grapes of Wrath
The Pearl
The Old Man and the Sea

While the terms *theory* and *hypothesis* are often used interchangeably, in the advancement of scientific knowledge, they describe two very different ideas. Write a well-organized and well-supported essay in which you explain the difference between a theory and a hypothesis and argue which is the more scientifically significant.

The working of the court system—especially the federal courts, which culminate in the Supreme Court—may seem distant and irrelevant to the everyday life of a high school student, but many of the cases argued before federal justices and the decisions these justices deliver do have a direct impact on what students learn and what they can and cannot do while in school. Research one of the following landmark cases and write an essay in which you describe the significance of this case to a high school student's life and explore how the high school experience might be different if the case had been settled differently.

Brown v. Board of Education (1955)
Schenck v. United States (1919)
Tinker v. Des Moines Independent Community School District (1969)
Hazelwood v. Kuhlmeier (1988)
Cantwell v. Connecticut (1940)
New Jersey v. T.L.O. (1985)
Vernonia School District 47J v. Acton (1995)
Brown v. Entertainment Merchants Association (2011)
Kitzmiller v. Dover Area School District (United States District Court for the Middle District of Pennsylvania, 2005)

STEP 1: Select a Topic

STEP 2: Develop a(n) slant/angle/hook

STEP 3: Brainstorm, discuss, research

STEP 4: Outline

STEP 5: Write your first draft

STEP 6: Peer Edit

What is this writer's point?

What is his/her angle?

How strong is this writer's support? How authoritative is his or her overall argument?

What techniques has this writer used to establish this authority?

What specific details, facts, etc., make this argument convincing?

STEP 7: Revised/Final Draft

Here are Kyle's editor's comments and analysis as well as his responses.

- Granted, this is an academic essay, and the occasion for writing is contrived, but to imply there might actually be times when people sit around, drink tea (or soda), and "talk about tragedy and tragic heroes" is really silly.

- Without meaning to, Kyle has introduced a new argument: whether or not those who debate tragedy consider Miller.

- *Death of a Salesman* might be important to mention, but the fact that Miller was married to Marilyn Monroe is irrelevant, and it is almost comic for Kyle to observe that Miller was married to her "before she died."

- Kyle says he is naming tragic heroes, not tragic plays. Brutus is generally considered to be the tragic hero of *Julius Caesar*.

- In some academic circles, this technique of referring to one's own paper is allowed, but it is never considered the best option.

- Kyle is not ever really wrong in anything he says in this introductory paragraph, but his word choice, tone, and stance are immature and mildly humorous. These are not qualities he wants in his academic essay.

- These final sentences about Juliet are Kyle's best iteration of his thesis so far.

- Kyle needs to avoid silly clichés like this.

- Because he has already identified the play, act, and scene, Kyle does not need any form of documentation.

- Confusing use of pronouns. Who tells whom?

- There are a number of problems with this short paragraph. The language is too informal, almost conversational. The character should not be referred to as "Mrs.," and who is consenting to what and to whom at the end of the final sentence?

- As was the case in the other paragraphs, Kyle has some decent ideas here, but he is not elaborating sufficiently on them, and his language choices weaken the overall academic quality of this essay.

- If losing the nurse's love is part of Juliet's loss of status, then having that love must be established earlier. It is also not clear whether Kyle is being ironic when he writes of Juliet's losing "unconditional" love.

- This is not a bad paraphrase of another part of Miller's discussion.

- When he reviews this draft, Kyle will probably feel that he is being repetitive. The passive is also a bad word choice here.

- As he does in the second paragraph, Kyle refers to his own paper, wasting time and space telling the reader what he's not going to write.

- At this point, Kyle seems to have completely given up on trying to create a formal, academic tone for his essay.

- Kyle is apparently forgetting the fact that Romeo killed Paris earlier in this scene.

- The one-sentence paragraph only contributes to the overall informal, conversational tone of this essay.

- Kyle's understanding of the topic is sound, and his thesis is valid. He does not, however, discuss that thesis as fully and as academically as he should.

And here are Kyle's reactions:

> My biggest problem seems to be language and tone. So I guess that means no first or second person, no one-sentence paragraphs, and not flippant or sarcastic off-the-cuff comments. I guess that's a fair criticism since this academic essay is supposed to be about the topic—the thesis and support—not the writer. If I make myself too obvious, maybe I'm distracting my reader from my point.
>
> Wow, that's a pretty good realization.
>
> I also need to give more discussion of the nurse.

Analysis of First Draft

What is this writer's point? Kyle's point is that the Shakespearean heroine Juliet both illustrates and supports the central thesis of Arthur Miller's 1949 essay, "Tragedy and the Common Man."

> Right

What is his/her angle? Because this is an academic essay, there is no strong angle. Kyle is making a case for Miller's thesis but not necessarily trying to "convince" the reader to agree with him.

> So I guess it's good that I don't have an angle.

How strong is this writer's support? How authoritative is his or her overall argument? Kyle's support is quite strong. He presents summary and paraphrase, and direct quotations, from both the play and Miller's article. There are a couple of points, most notably the loss of the Nurse's love, that would benefit from more complete discussion.

> Okay ... I need to look at my discussion of the nurse.

What techniques has this writer used to establish this authority? As noted, Kyle presents a good amount of support, and his thesis is well founded. What he needs to work on is his word choice and the resultant tone, which tends to be too conversational.

What specific details, facts, etc., make this argument convincing? Kyle cites Juliet's status as only surviving daughter, loved enough by her father that he says she must consent to his choice of a husband for her, as his chief example of the rightful status that Miller contends is at the core of tragedy.

Tybalt's death at the hand of Romeo is the event that threatens Juliet's sense of her rightful place.

Her suicide is her willingness to lay down her life in her attempt to secure that status.

He does need to elaborate on some of the more summary statements he makes in the final paragraphs.

> So this is good. I can also quote the nurse when she turns her back on Juliet.

Here is Kyle's revised draft. Notice that he has revised his thesis and really worked to establish a more academic tone.

> *In 1949, playwright Arthur Miller wrote a groundbreaking essay titled "Tragedy and the Common Man," in which he argued this thesis:*
>
> > *As a general rule…the tragic feeling is evoked in us when we are in the presence of a character who is ready to lay down his life, if need be, to secure one thing—his sense of personal dignity. From Orestes to Hamlet, Medea to Macbeth, the underlying struggle is that of the individual attempting to gain his 'rightful' position in his society.*
>
> *From a novel or play you have studied, choose a character who might legitimately be considered a tragic hero and use him or her as the basis to support, refute, or qualify Miller's thesis. Be certain to support all of your assertions with direct evidence from the novel or play as well as references to other reliable literary criticism.*
>
> *Because the purpose of this assignment is to assess your ability to discuss the literature studied in class, you may choose one of the following characters:*
>
> *Romeo or Juliet (NOT BOTH)*
> *Jay Gatsby*
> *Willy Loman*

Revised thesis: In his groundbreaking 1949 article, "Tragedy and the Common Man," Arthur Miller suggests a new "take" on our understanding of what makes a tragic hero tragic. Given his new view, even famous characters who are not generally thought to be tragic heroes can be seen as tragic. Juliet, from William Shakespeare's tragedy Romeo and Juliet almost perfectly meets Miller's new criteria for a tragic hero. She is "ready to lay down [her] life ... to secure one thing—[her] sense of personal dignity." Juliet is truly what Miller says a tragic hero is: "[an] individual attempting to gain [her] "rightful" position in [her] society."

By specifically mentioning the article and then placing Miller's words in quotation marks, Kyle has improved his thesis and saved himself from a possible charge of plagiarism. There are still, however, some word choice problems that Kyle should address.

Revised draft:

On the positive, Kyle's mention of Aristotle helps him to introduce the topic without setting up a ridiculous writing situation. He is also making an effort to adopt a more academic tone. Still, he tends to be repetitive and to create errors like sentence fragments.

Kyle has apparently done a little additional research. The facts he mentions here were certainly not hard to find.

Most discussion of tragedy and the tragic hero eventually turns to a discussion of Aristotle and his definition of the tragic hero in his famous Poetics. Aristotle established what everyone would quote as the definition of a tragic hero when he wrote that the tragic hero was an important or powerful person, someone with great influence in his or her society, who had a flaw, a trait that would first cause this person to rise in status and then to fall. The fall that was caused by this fault would be total. The tragic hero would lose everything. Even his life. After the opening of Death of a Salesman in 1949, playwright Arthur Miller wrote an essay in which he claimed that Willy Loman, the salesman in his Pulitzer Prize winning play was a tragic hero.

In this groundbreaking 1949 essay, "Tragedy and the Common Man," Miller argues that, even the most famous tragic heroes like Macbeth, Hamlet, and Brutus are tragic because their personal dignity, their sense of who they are and how they fit into their societies, has been challenged. They are heroes because they are willing to do anything necessary, even die, in order to regain their sense of who they are. They are tragic because, in most cases, they do die in their attempt. The main point of "Tragedy and the Common Man" can be summed up by Miller's statement:

> As a general rule...the tragic feeling is evoked in us when we are in the presence of a character who is ready to lay down his life, if need be, to secure one thing—his sense of personal dignity. From Orestes to Hamlet, Medea to Macbeth, the underlying struggle is that of the individual attempting to gain his 'rightful' position in his society.

William Shakespeare's Juliet is an excellent example of the type of tragic hero Miller is talking about, and she helps to support Miller's thesis as valid. She is "ready to lay down [her] life ... to secure one thing—[her] sense of personal dignity." Juliet is truly what Miller says a tragic hero is: "an individual attempting to gain [her] 'rightful' position in [her] society."

From the beginning of the play, Shakespeare makes it clear that Juliet enjoys a high status in her family and in her father's affections. In Act I, scene ii, Juliet's father tells Paris, who has come to marry her:

> The earth hath swallow'd all my hopes but she,
>
> She is the hopeful lady of my earth.

When he says that all of his other hopes have been swallowed by the earth, Capulet probably means that all of his other children have died. Whether or not Juliet is his "favorite" child, she is his <u>only surviving daughter</u>. Later, Capulet tells Paris:

> My will to her consent is but a part;
>
> An she agree, within her scope of choice
>
> Lies my consent and fair according voice.

Capulet will not force his daughter to marry someone she does not like. Although in his time period, place, and social class, it would have been

This is an interesting insight that Kyle did not share in his first draft. Perhaps he realized it while working on his revision.

his right to give his daughter in marriage to anyone he chose, he has decided that she must consent to his choice.

Lady Capulet also seems to love Juliet enough for her to want Juliet to like Paris before agreeing to marry him. When she first tells Juliet of Paris's proposal in Act I, scene iii, Lady Capulet tells Juliet to look at him during their party. If she likes what she sees, then she can agree to marry him.

> What say you? Can you love the gentleman?
>
> This night you shall behold him at our feast;
>
> Read o'er the volume of young Paris' face,
>
> And find delight writ there with beauty's pen;
>
> Examine every married lineament,
>
> And see how one another lends content
>
> And what obscured in this fair volume lies
>
> Find written in the margent of his eyes.

So Juliet seems to enjoy a special status in her family. She is the only surviving daughter, maybe even the only surviving <u>child</u>, and even though her father has the right to choose her husband, he says he will choose only someone she will agree to. It is also important to point out that, unlike many fathers who seem very eager to get their daughters married off and out of the house, Capulet wants to keep her home for another year. In Act I, scene ii, he tells Paris that she is not even fourteen years old. Paris insists that there are girls younger than her who are married and already have children:

"Younger than she [is]" is actually correct and what Kyle should have written as well.

> Younger than she are happy mothers made.

Capulet's answers shows that he is concerned with Juliet's well-being as well as seeing her married off:

> And too soon marr'd are those so early made.

Maybe he's actually talking about his own wife, who says in the next scene that she was only Juliet's age when Juliet was born, and whose children have all died except for one. Still, it is clear that Capulet is not rushing to marry off his only daughter and that he will arrange for her to marry only someone she herself likes. This is the status that Juliet enjoys and loses and fights to regain in her tragic story.

This is interesting speculation but not at all supported and not really relevant to this topic.

However, in order for Juliet to be tragic according to Miller, she has to consider this status her "rightful position," and she must lose it and try to get it back. When Juliet first meets Romeo, there is a hint that Juliet has this same view of herself in her society. She is immediately interested in Romeo and sends her nurse to find out who he is and whether or not he's married. It doesn't make any sense for her to show interest in Romeo or to care whether or not he's married if she doesn't believe she'll be allowed to pursue a relationship with him. She already knows Paris wants to marry her, but she also knows that her parents want her to <u>like</u> Paris and <u>agree to</u> marry him. So, until she finds out that Romeo is a Montague, she seems to think she will be allowed to choose him as her husband.

The sentence itself might be a little unwieldy, but it is good that Kyle has brought this discussion back around to the point of Miller's essay.

This is a nice attempt at a transition, but the two consecutive sentences are redundant, adding only the idea that Juliet must be aware of her status.

Again, there are some excellent ideas here, but Kyle is not paying enough attention to word choice and sentence structure.

The tragedy of Juliet's losing this "'rightful' position in [her]society" does not begin with her meeting Romeo. It doesn't even begin when Juliet sneaks off to Friar Laurence's cell to marry Romeo. It begins when the "unjust society" that Miller mentions in his essay intrudes. Friar Laurence hoped a marriage between Romeo and Juliet would end the feud between the Montagues and Capulets, but in Act III, scene i, that feud erupts only minutes after the wedding. Romeo kills Juliet's cousin Tybalt, and everything in Juliet's life begins to fall apart.

If Tybalt had not been killed, Juliet's marriage to Paris might not have been so rushed. Act III, scene iv, doesn't make much sense unless the hasty wedding is Capulet's way of consoling Juliet in her grief. After all, earlier, he wanted to wait two more years before arranging Juliet's marriage. In addition, if Tybalt had not been killed by <u>Romeo</u>, when the issue of Juliet's marriage to Paris did come up again, Juliet would be able to confess that she was already married.

But this feud, which is completely beyond Juliet's control, is the cause of her tragic story. When she refuses to marry Paris—not because she doesn't like him or is disobedient but because <u>she is already married</u>—she loses her standing with her father and mother and is no longer the favored or beloved daughter that she was at the beginning of the play. In Act III, scene v, after she has refused to marry Paris, making it seem as if she would never marry anyone, her father asks his wife:

> doth she not count her blest,
>
> <u>Unworthy as she is</u>, that we have wrought
>
> So worthy a gentleman to be her bridegroom?

In Act I, Juliet was "the hopeful lady of [her father's] earth." Now she is "unworthy" to marry such a man as Paris. Earlier, the father insisted he could consent to Juliet's match to Paris, only if she also consented. Now he berates her for being disobedient. At this point, what Miller calls "[her] sense of personal dignity" and her "'rightful' position in [her] society" is threatened. She could maybe restore it if she told her parents that she was already married, but the added complication of Romeo having killed Tybalt makes that impossible. At least, she believes it is impossible. Juliet, then, truly is a person whose "unjust society" has threatened her ability to be who and what she

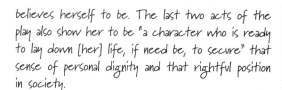

believes herself to be. The last two acts of the play also show her to be "a character who is ready to lay down [her] life, if need be, to secure" that sense of personal dignity and that rightful position in society.

This happens when she goes to Friar Laurence. In her mind, the only way to restore the status she has lost is to be reunited with Romeo, and she will prove that she is willing to "lay down [her] life, if need be," to make that reunion happen. This element of Miller's definition is not fulfilled when she takes the sleeping potion that Laurence gives to her. There is indeed symbolism, irony, and foreshadowing in the discovery of her body and her being laid in the tomb, but she knows full well—just as the audience does—that she is not really dying for her cause. She will awaken, and when she does, Romeo will be there, and she will be restored to her status as a beloved, independent woman.

But she does "lay down [her] life" when she wakes up and sees Romeo dead. With Romeo dead, it is impossible for her to be restored to her earlier status. There is nothing she can do to regain her standing in the family that disowned her, and she cannot be reunited with Romeo. The only alternative to living as someone she does not believe herself to be is to die.

The story is a tragedy, according to Arthur Miller's "Tragedy and the Common Man," because Juliet is a person whose personal dignity—her sense of who and what she is—is challenged by a dysfunctional, unjust society, and she fights to regain it. She is even willing to die rather than live life as someone or something she isn't. Juliet Capulet is a perfect example of Arthur Miller's tragic hero.

While Kyle still needs to pay attention to tone, word choice, and sentence structure, this draft is indeed a significant improvement over the original.

Analysis of Final Draft

What is the writer's thesis?

Has the writer's new draft strengthened his/her point?

Has the rewrite strengthened the case for his/her thesis?

What new details, facts, etc., have been included to make the thesis more valid?

Does the writer effectively establish the validity of his/her thesis to any greater degree than in the previous draft? Why or why not?

POSSIBLE STEP 8: Rewrite Opportunity

MINI LESSON 2:

The Test or Exam Essay
(Develop a thesis and support it)

While the "defend, refute, or qualify" essay prompt is popular among high school exam writers and standardized test makers, most of your course-related exam essays are likely to ask you simply to provide information. Explain what you learned. Demonstrate your understanding.

Still, do not allow a less structured prompt or question to trick you into thinking you do not need an essay. Unless you are specifically told to "list" or "list and explain," you must assume that at least part of the scoring criteria for your answer will be how well it is written.

Jonathan and Danae's History of the Western World final exam included this question, which was intended to encourage them to draw on material they had covered in several different units over the course of the full school year:

> Much of the study of history focuses not on people and events, but on the role of technology in instigating social, political, and cultural change. Considering the full span of the course this year, identify a past technological development and explore its role in the development of the "modern world."

As was the case in Mini lesson 1, students had a total of 3 hours (180 minutes) for the entire exam, allowing about an hour (60 minutes) for this essay.

The process for writing this essay is not very different from that for any other timed, on-demand essay for which you want to receive a top score.

STEP 1: Select a Topic (no more than 5 min. out of 60)

The prompt establishes three criteria for the technology to be chosen: It must reflect material covered during the course; it must be a "past technological development"; and it must have made a notable contribution to the "modern world."

Here is a recreation Jonathan's thoughts on his topic:

Printing press—Johannes Gutenberg, 1450. Reading more available; more people learn to read; more people write to supply reading material; the Bible, literacy, and the whole Protestant Reformation.

Gunpowder—not really a Western invention, but introduced to Europe during the 13th century. Changed warfare. (Well, it still took over 400 years to do away with armor and protective gear like that. Actually, cops and soldiers still wear a kind of armor—Kevlar, etc.).

> This kind of arguing against himself is an important part of the process so that Jonathan will not end up with an unworkable topic. He must remember not to spend too much time on this first step, however.

The invention of steam—transportation, the whole Industrial Revolution, exploitation of workers and the labor movement, the Bolshevik Revolution—all that because of steam.

Incandescent lightbulb—brighter homes; less fire hazard; safer city streets ...

> One error Jonathan is making is that he seems to equate "technology" with "invention," and therefore thinks that he must be prepared to discuss the impact of a single invention. If he broadened his understanding of the assigned topic, he might find it easier to develop workable concepts.

Here is Danae's:

Probably the most important invention in all of history is the printing press. Whatever else books and magazines end up looking like, the printing press made it necessary and possible for more and more people to learn to read. Twenty-first-century American democracy would not be possible if it weren't for the invention of the printing press back in 1450.

> Danae and Jonathan's teacher must have really stressed the printing press. Notice that Danae does bring her impact into the twenty-first century, the "modern world."

Before the printing press was the olive press, and olive oil has been very important to all societies in all of human history—diet, fuel, cosmetics, medicine, religion, trade.

TIME SPENT: 5 MIN.—TIME REMAINING: 55 MIN.

STEP 2: Draft a thesis (no more than 5 min out of 60)

We cannot stress this enough: even if the prompt does not specify that you need a thesis, even if you think you are to write a purely informative piece, *always* think in terms of a thesis and proof. Always take the stance that you are advancing an argument and need to convince your reader of the validity of your thesis.

Here are Jonathan's attempts at a thesis:

– The printing press is without a doubt one of the most significant inventions in human history.

– Johannes Gutenberg invented the printing press in 1450. Because of his invention, reading materials became more available, so that more people were able to learn how to read; more people wrote books to meet the new demand for material to read. When non-clergy people were able to read the Bible for themselves, the Protestant Reformation happened, and this led to revolts and revolutions all the way up to the Revolutionary War and American Independence.

> Jonathan tries to pack far too much into a single thesis. It also sets up a list of facts to verify rather than an argument to be supported.

– The invention of steam not only revolutionized transportation, but it cause the whole Industrial Revolution. This led to the exploitation of workers, which then caused the labor movement and the Bolshevik Revolution.

> Jonathan jams too much into this attempt as well. He is also a little careless in his choice of words and in overly generalized claims; he doesn't mean the "invention of steam" but the harnessing of steam power, and while the exploitation of workers was certainly an element in the Bolshevik Revolution, this one factor cannot be legitimately called the revolution's "cause."

– Even though Thomas Edison is given the credit for inventing the incandescent light bulb, it was actually the result of several people's work. What Edison did was successfully market his invention.

– The impact of the incandescent light bulb was enormous to the modern world. It was Thomas Edison, being God, and saying to the world, "Let there be light."

> This attempt is certainly creative, and a scorer might be seduced into rewarding Jonathan's boldness, but the essay itself must still demonstrate Jonathan's knowledge of the subject.

Danae feels she has so much she can say about the invention of the printing press that she doesn't consider any of her other topic ideas:

– By making information accessible to the common man, the invention of the printing press in 1450 is probably the single-most important invention in human history. Without it, the "modern world" as we know it could not possibly exist.

> Two of the main strengths of this possible thesis are that is focuses the essay on a single key impact—putting information into the hands of common people—and it addresses the requirement in the prompt to discuss the innovation in terms of the modern world.

TIME SPENT: 10 MIN.—TIME REMAINING: 50 MIN.

STEP 3: Brainstorm, jot notes (no more than 10 min out of 60)

Remember that you want every point you can earn. This essay has to be a thoughtful and thorough display of *both your knowledge and your ability to talk about it*. That will be the purpose of every exam you will ever take, from your first state assessment to the defense of your doctoral dissertation.

Here are Jonathan's notes:

Thesis: The invention of steam not only revolutionized transportation, but it cause the whole Industrial Revolution. This led to the exploitation of workers, which then caused the labor movement and the Bolshevik Revolution.

> Flawed as this thesis is, Jonathan is wise not to have been seduced.

Transportation = trains and steamships. Travel = easier and cheaper. Workers could live farther from work = rise of middle class "suburban" landowner (think: Forsythe Saga)

Easier transportation of goods = cheaper, more competition, not restricted to local

Manufacturing/Industrial Revolution = cheaper goods, change of lower class from rural poor to urban poor

Capitalism, exploitation of workers

Exploitation of workers eventually led to labor movement and revolutions.

Here are Danae's:

Thesis: By making information accessible to the common man, the invention of the printing press in 1450 is probably the single-most important invention in human history. Without it, the "modern world" as we know it could not possibly exist.

Cost of books; limited availability; limited subjects—religious works, some pre-Medieval classics (Aristotle, Greek and Roman comedies and tragedies)

Education controlled by church and some universities.

Only wealthy or those who entered the Church were taught to read, and what could be read was limited.

First printed was Bible—

Local parishes could afford a Bible

Local priest maybe was first time he'd read the Bible

Compare your own reading with what others say it says and means ... then extend this to other matters ... news, laws, etc. The printing press made it possible to everyone to be better informed, which changed the world.

> Some of Danae's notes actually sound like sentences that she might choose to use in her essay.

TIME SPENT: 20 MIN.—TIME REMAINING: 40 MIN.

STEP 3: Outline (no more than 5 min out of 60)

Jonathan:

Thesis: The invention of steam not only revolutionized transportation, but it cause the whole Industrial Revolution. This led to the exploitation of workers, which then caused the labor movement and the Bolshevik Revolution.

I. Transportation/trains and steamships.

   A. Travel = easier and cheaper.

   B. Workers could live farther from work

   C. Easier transportation of goods

      1. cheaper, , not restricted to local

II. Manufacturing/Industrial Revolution

  A. cheaper goods

III. Economics and social class

  A. Workers could live farther from work

  B. Rise of middle class "suburban" landowner (think: Forsythe Sage)

  C. Change of lower class from rural poor to urban poor

  D. Rise of Capitalism

   1. more competition for goods

  E. Exploitation of workers

IV. Exploitation of workers eventually led to labor movement and revolutions.

  A. Bolshevik Revolution

> If Jonathan had more time, or this were a longer essay assignment, he would want to take a second look at his intended organizational plan. For a timed, on-demand exam essay, however, this plan will serve him fine.

Danae:

Thesis: By making information accessible to the common man, the invention of the printing press in 1450 is probably the single-most important invention in human history. Without it, the "modern world" as we know it could not possibly exist.

> Because she feels her notes are already organized in a logical order, Danae has decided to save this time and go right to the writing step. This is advisable only if you are absolutely certain that your thoughts are organized and comprehensible to a reader.

> **TIME SPENT: 25 MIN.—TIME REMAINING: 35 MIN.**

STEP 4: Write your essay (30 min out of 60)

If you've paid sufficient attention to your preliminaries, especially creating your thesis, jotting down the information you know you can use, and then drafting your outline, this step should be the easiest part of the entire process. The 30 minutes you are allowing yourself is only to make sure you have enough time to physically write or keyboard the essay itself.

Here is Jonathan's essay:

Thesis: The invention of steam not only revolutionized transportation, but it caused the whole Industrial Revolution. This led to the exploitation of workers, which then caused the labor movement and the Bolshevik Revolution.

> It isn't required to state the thesis like this before an exam essay, but it won't hurt either.

Probably one of the most important inventions of the Modern World was the invention of steam. You could almost say that the invention of steam actually created the Modern World. Without steam power, there would not have been an Industrial Revolution. Capitalists would not have started to exploit their workers, and there would not have been a Bolshevik Revolution. The two main ways the invention of steam power created the Modern World are in transportation and manufacturing. The revolution in manufacturing is what caused the economic changes that brought about the Bolshevik Revolution.

In terms of transportation, steam made trains and steamships possible. Both made travel and the transportation of goods faster and cheaper. When travel became easier and cheaper, one of the biggest changes to society was that workers who used to have to live close to where they worked could move farther away. This allowed for the development of more residential neighborhoods, not too different from the Modern World's suburbs.

Jonathan's organizational plan is pretty obvious, but it should serve him well on this exam. More problematic is that he seems to really want to write about the Bolshevik Revolution when he claims that his focus is on the harnessing of steam power.

Everything Jonathan is saying so far is essentially correct, but he is providing too broad an overview of the topic to prove the type of familiarity with the subject that this exam probably demands. There is also evidence of an organizational problem in his introducing the socio-economic results of the harnessing of steam.

Of course, not every worker could afford a home in the country or the train fare to commute, so the poor ended up huddled in the cities while the middle class and the rich moved to the suburbs.

The transportation of goods also made it possible for the middle class to thrive. Merchants could sell their goods cheaper, and they were not limited to selling only local goods. Steamships made it possible to import exotic fruits and vegetables. Trains meant that crops grown in Italy could be sold in Germany, and so on. The transportation of goods and people also made the men who owned the railroads very rich. The Rail Barons.

It was also trains that allowed movements like the Bolshevik Revolution to gain momentum.

Again, Jonathan reveals a greater interest in the Revolution than in the assigned topic.

Manufacturing also improved with the invention of steam power. Before the Industrial Revolution, most manufactured items were made by hand by craftsmen. They were either sold by the craftsmen who made them, or they were commissioned by someone. Steam made the factory possible, and mass production, and the assembly line. Goods could be manufactured much faster, and the people making them did not need to be skilled. Even women and children could operate the machines that mass-produced the goods. This is what led to the exploitation of the workers and the creation of poverty and slums. The materials that made the goods could also be transported faster and cheaper, so a factory in Yorkshire could use coal from New Castle and wood from forests in Scotland and textiles from Leeds. Even mills, like textile mills, wood mills, and grain mills, could operate faster than when they relied on water power. And the mills could be built anywhere; they did not need to be near a source of water power.

If we can assume that these materials and cities were covered in class, then this is the closest Jonathan has come to detailed support for any of his summary claims.

All of these seeming improvements, however, created problems for the lowest classes of society.

When the middle and upper classes left the cities to live in the suburbs because transportation was easy and cheap, all that was left in the city were poor people. When farms and country villages were destroyed to make homes for these newly rich people, the peasants who lived on that land had no choice but to move to the cities. Because they had no skill or education, all they could do was operate the machinery in the factories. The men who owned the factories, the railroads, and the steamship lines did not want to lessen their profits by paying high wages or benefits like health insurance and pension plans, so the workers became exploited.

When they kept dying in factory fires and mine collapses, etc., the workers rebelled. Labor unions were formed, and in some countries like Russia, the workers rose up and took control of the government.

The workers were originally exploited because of the invention of steam and the rise of factories. Today we have a strong middle class. We can travel anywhere in the world that we want, and we can eat lettuce, tomatoes, and things like that all year long. In one way or another, all of this: the suburbs, travel, food, everything, is the result of the invention of steam power.

Again, what Jonathan is saying is not necessarily incorrect, but he refers to it too broadly and generally to prove a deep understanding of the subject matter.

In this exam essay, Jonathan demonstrates, at best, a general knowledge of his topic. The essay itself is fairly formulaic, but even with the five-paragraph formula as his basis, Jonathan's essay reveals lapses in organization and unity.

Analysis of Exam Essay

What is this writer's point? Jonathan's point is that the harnessing of steam led to a variety of social and economic consequences, both positive and negative: improvements in transportation and manufacturing, which improved the quality of life for the middle and upper classes, but also changes in the work, working conditions, and quality of life of the lower classes. He also wants to make the claim that the economic divide that resulted from the Industrial Revolution led to social and political movements like the Bolshevik Revolution.

In what way(s) does this thesis fulfill the requirements of the prompt? On the surface, Jonathan's thesis completely fulfills the requirements of the prompt. He identifies a technology: the harnessing of steam; and he traces a connection to the Modern World: labor unions and the middle class.

What information does the writer provide to demonstrate his understanding of the tested subject matter? Unfortunately, Jonathan does not provide much information at all. The bulk of his discussion is too broad and general, mentioning events and movements without showing any deep understanding of them.

What techniques has this writer used to present this information in a coherent, cohesive essay? Coherence and cohesion are problems for Jonathan. He seems so much more interested in the Bolshevik Revolution that this one element of his topic intrudes on the entire essay.

What type of score is this essay likely to receive? Why? Unfortunately, this essay is most likely to receive a failing—or the lowest possible passing—grade.

- After a successful thesis, this essay contains no substance to show what Jonathan knows and understands from the course.

- The organizational plan is compromised by Jonathan's lack of information and his apparent overriding interest in the Bolshevik Revolution.

Here is Danae's essay:

While not strictly conventional, Danae has chosen to begin her essay with her thesis. This might start her out on the right foot and keep her essay on track.

In addition to the fact that Danae repeats "ignorance" twice in one sentence, Danae's wording is excessive. Hopefully, she will not try to use style to mask insufficient content.

By making information accessible to the common man, the invention of the printing press in 1450 is probably the single-most important invention in human history. Without it, the "modern world" as we know it could not possibly exist. This invention lowered the cost of books, freed illiterate people from ignorance and superstition, and allowed peasants to rise above their poverty and ignorance.

The first impact of the invention of the printing press was the cost of books. Before, whatever books existed were all printed by hand. They were very expensive, and only the very wealthy could own them, and even they could only own a few. Only a few people knew how to read and write. There was no reason to learn since there was nothing to read. The invention of the printing press changed all that, however. Suddenly, many copies of the same book could be printed at the same time in much less time than it would have taken a single monk to make a single copy. As books became affordable, more people bought them, and more people learned to read because reading was available.

Before the printing press, the books that existed were mostly owned by the Church and Universities. They not only owned the books, but because they had the people who knew how to write, they controlled what books got copied and what books would be forgotten. They controlled knowledge.

The printing press took the control of knowledge out of the hands of a few and put it into the hands of the masses. A good example of this is that the first book Johannes Gutenberg, the inventor of the printing press chose to print was the Bible.

Before this, all of the Bibles that existed had been hand-copied. Very few people had ever seen a Bible, let alone been able to read one. Most local parishes did not have a single copy of the Bible. Most priests did not own one. That meant that they were preaching things they had been taught, but they never had the chance to study for themselves. Today, we take it for granted that if a teacher tells us something, we can verify it for ourselves. We can check the Bible, the textbook , the newspaper, or the Internet. Before the printing press, any corrupt official could lie about what the Bible or some other important document said, and no one would know any better.

The printing press, and the printing of the Bible, changed all this. Once copies of the Bible became more available, and more people read it,

So far, Danae's essay is not significantly better than Jonathan's. She seems to be providing a broad overview rather than a detailed and informed discussion.

things like the Protestant Reformation began to happen. With the ability to read the Bible for themselves, people were able to say they disagreed with official dogma, and they had the basis to argue back.

Knowledge is power, and the people who control sources of knowledge have the power to control other people. The best way for people to gain power over their own lives is to gain knowledge. This is what the invention of the printing press gave us.

This one concrete example is probably enough to rescue Danae's essay from the mediocre score that Jonathan's is likely to receive.

Danae's essay is generally more successful than Jonathan's in that Danae goes beyond vague generalities and offers as least the one concrete illustration of the cultural phenomenon she claims. Given that this is a timed essay in response to an essay question, this is probably enough for the essay to receive a safely passing score.

Analysis of Exam Essay

What is this writer's point? Danae's point is that the invention of the printing press contributed to the development of the modern world by making knowledge more accessible to the masses and, thus, broadening the base of what she calls power.

In what way(s) does this thesis fulfill the requirements of the prompt? The prompt requires students to:

- consider the full span of the course, and Danae has chosen a technology from the fifteenth century, presumably studied relatively early in the course;

- identify a past technological development, and Danae has chosen the invention of the printing press;

- explore its role in the development of the "modern world"; and Danae illustrates how the printing press opened up sources of knowledge to the masses.

What information does the writer provide to demonstrate her understanding of the tested subject matter? Danae uses the printing of the Gutenberg Bible as her primary example:

- prior to the printing press, copies of the Bible were handwritten and very expensive;

- few people—including most parish priests—owned, or had even read, a Bible;

- the fact that the Church's official teachings could not be called into question made corruption possible;

- the availability of Bibles contributed to the Protestant Reformation;
- in much the same way, other instances of the people taking power over their own lives has been the result of their being able to read and have access to information.

What techniques has this writer used to present this information in a coherent, cohesive essay? Danae has a clear thesis. She follows essentially a five-paragraph essay format, and she chooses to develop a single specific example rather than recite a string of generalities.

What type of score is this essay likely to receive? Why? This essay should receive a respectable passing score. Danae fully addresses the prompt, clearly understands the relationship between the technology and social change, and she chooses a single, strong example to illustrate her point. If she had had time to develop a second or third example, her essay might have received a top score.

> **TIME SPENT: 55 MIN.—TIME REMAINING: 5 MIN.**

STEP 5: Review, proof, and edit (5 min out of 60)

In an exam situation, you do not usually have time to complete a full second draft, but before you turn it in, you should give it one last quick read and correct any surface errors you find that might reduce your score. Misspellings of key words or prominent people's names are especially damaging.

Here is a portion of Danae's actual submission with its cross-outs and insertions:

> was invented
> Before the printing press, ^ the books that existed were mostly
> These powerful institutions
> owned by the Church and Universities. ~~They~~ ^ not only owned the
> books, but ~~because they had the people who knew how to write, they~~
> controlled what books got copied and what books would be forgotten.
> In short, they
> ~~They~~ controlled knowledge. The printing press took the control of

these

knowledge out of the hands of a ^ few and put it into the hands
of the masses. A good example of this is that the first book Johannes
Gutenberg, the inventor of the printing press chose to print was the
B   B
bible. Before this, all of the bibles that existed had been hand-copied.

been able to

Very few people had ever seen a Bible, let alone ^ read one. Most

P

local parishes did not have a single copy of the Bible. Most Priests did

even

not ^ own one. That meant that they were preaching things they had
been taught, but they never had the chance to study for themselves.
Today, we take it for granted that if a teacher tells us something,
we can verify it for ourselves. We can check the Bible, the textbook,
the newspaper, or the Internet. Before the printing press, any corrupt
official could lie about what the Bible or some other important document
said, and no one would know any better.

TIME SPENT: 60 MIN.—TIME REMAINING: 0 MIN.
Turn in your essay, or begin the next section.

PART IV:

The Research Projects

We come again to what are arguably the most important assignments in this series of books: the research reports. Regardless of your past experience with these crucial college and career skills, neither conducting the research nor composing the report should be a completely new skill for you.

Every time you check a newspaper or website for the scores of yesterday's games or to check tomorrow's weather, you are doing research. Every time you read more than one review—both positive and negative—of a movie you might see, a video game you might buy, or an event you might attend, you are doing research. And every time you ask another person for advice or compare the feedback you get from different people, you are doing research.

Research is nothing more than simply searching for and collecting information you need in order to answer a question, prove a point, or perform a task.

Last year, we focused on performing research to answer a question (or series of questions) and writing a paper to share that answer with others. The research paper was an informative piece, pure and simple. This year, we're going to begin to think more about arguing a point than merely answering a question. The point you are arguing is your **thesis**, just like the theses you've supported in many other assignments in this book.

As you know, your thesis must be arguable, that is, rooted in fact but not merely a statement of fact. There must be enough of a slant, a unique insight, an original inference, something new that you can bring to the conversation. Your research, then, becomes the search not only for information, but also for information that will help your reader understand your thesis and agree that it is a valid argument.

And the report is quite simply the presentation of your thesis and evidence.

It's important, but it's not difficult. Every time you make a reasoned and logical case for an increase in your allowance, for an extension of your curfew, for a coveted Saturday night off from work, you are doing just this sort of thing.

ASSIGNMENT 1:

Research Project—Non-ELA

STEP 1: Select a Topic

Just as the research paper is a slightly different concept as compared to other academic essays, the research topic is different as well. *Every* essay requires focus, a point, and an angle, but the research paper requires an even sharper *focus*. Whenever anyone with the least amount of curiosity goes off in search of information, without *focus*, it's all too easy for the poor researcher to find himself or herself mired in pages of trivia, contradictions, half-truths, and outright lies.

Don't forget that writing the research paper is also a strictly academic activity, so the topic must be academic in nature as well. It might be pleasant to share stories about your favorite pet or the day you learned how to ride a bicycle; reporting to your teacher or class on an interesting article you've read or reflecting on the social relevance of a short story in your literature anthology will help you learn to gain and share information, but neither the report nor the reflection approaches the breadth and depth of information necessary in a research paper.

When thinking about potential research paper topics that will keep your interest during the entire term of the project and result in a paper worth your reader's time to read it, you should consider the following:

Exploring Relationships...

Sources of... Many elements in J. R. R. Tolkien's *The Hobbit* and *The Lord of the Rings* are drawn from the ancient sagas and adventures stories of Iceland. From what elements did Tolkien draw? How did he use them? What might his purposes have been for choosing these and using them as he did? *What literary and historical evidence is there to evaluate the claims of such sources for Tolkien's plot, characters, settings, and themes?*

Influences on... President Barack Obama cites President Abraham Lincoln's personality, goals, and methods as strong role models for his own presidency. What aspects of Lincoln did Obama admire? In what ways were Lincoln's and Obama's situations similar? In what ways were they different? *What sociological, political, and historical evidence is there to make a case for or against a Lincoln influence on the Obama presidency?*

Inspirations for... Many critics believe that Sidney Carton's desperate love for the unattainable Lucy Darnay in Charles Dickens's *A Tale of Two Cities* was inspired by Dickens's own infatuation with the actress Ellen Ternan, who was twenty-seven years his junior. In what ways does Lucy resemble Ellen? How are Dickens's and Carton's situations similar? How are they different? What themes might Dickens be suggesting if Ellen really is the inspiration for Lucy? What literary and biographical evidence is there to support this kind of link?

Notice that considering all of these potential topics involves asking questions, especially those that open the topic up to academic research, rather than only reading, viewing, and reflection.

Other common relationships that lend themselves to academic research—and the types of topics these relationships might yield—include:

- Cultural, Political, and/or Social contexts ...
    † *political and social background of Chaim Potok's* The Chosen
    † *historical and social context in which Shakespeare wrote* The Tempest
    † *cultural and philosophical background to eighteenth-century documents like the Declaration of Independence and Thomas Paine's* Rights of Man

- Impact of an event, invention, or discovery on...

- *Impact of...*
    † *the publication of Harriet Beecher Stowe's* Uncle Tom's Cabin *on the abolitionist movement*
    † *electronic data-sharing on the entertainment and publishing industries*
    † *the invention of the printing press on European politics and/or religion*

- *Causes of...*
    † *the global economic collapse of (pick a year)*
    † *the Dust Bowl of the 1930s*
    † *the failure of the Soviet Union*

- *Events leading to...*
    † *the 1962 Cuban Missile Crisis*
    † *the call for a Federal Convention in 1789*
    † *the issuing of a* fatwa *against novelist Salman Rushdie by Ayatollah Ruhollah Khomeini*

- *Factors contributing to...*
  - † *the phenomenal success of J.K. Rowlings's* Harry Potter *series*
  - † *the Union's victory in the Civil War*
  - † *Toni Morrison's being awarded the Nobel Prize in Literature in 1993*

Remember that, immediately after Thanksgiving weekend, Maya's English teacher began assigning issue-based journal prompts to help her students generate possible topics for their second-semester social studies research projects. Maya was particularly interested in one of the prompts that asked students to argue whether funding of arts courses in public schools should be cut. Maya knew she had read and heard a few things about the importance of music and drawing to mathematics instruction, and she wrote a decent journal entry arguing for the maintenance of such programs. She has chosen as her socials studies research topic the relationship between instruction in the arts and higher achievement in other academic subjects.

Studying art in school helps students learn other subjects as well.

While the topic will be adapted and refined a number of times as Maya considers her thesis, outline, and drafts, there are a few fairly important problems indicated by how she has worded this topic. If she is thinking along the lines of "fact," she will have trouble finding something to argue. The goal of her paper is to be more than merely the verification of a fact, even if it is a little-known fact.

Remember, facts might need to be verified, but they cannot be argued with.

Maya is also thinking too vaguely, What does she mean by "art"? What "other subjects"? As she goes on to the next steps of her process, Maya will certainly want to remember and fix these weaknesses, or they will result in an unsuccessful report.

STEP 2: Draft a thesis

Studying art in school helps students learn other subjects as well. I think that's it. All I need to do is find some statistics to show this. Piece of cake.

> Maya is severely underestimating the depth of information her teacher is going to expect in the final draft of her paper.

STEP 3: Draft a Preliminary Outline

Remember, this is your shopping list. It is the planned menu of your dinner party, which will govern what stores you go to, what departments you visit, and what you end up buying. It will also, to a large extent, control what you do with the material once you get home from the "store."

Thesis: Studying art in school helps students learn other subjects as well.

I. Music courses

    A. Math

        1. fractions and ratios

        2. intervals

    B. Physics

        1. sound pitches and frequencies

        2. harmonics

    C. Language arts

        1. Reading and listening to music is like reading or listening to a language.

        2. Lyrics are poetry.

        3. The composer writes music that expresses the mood and meaning of the word.

II. Drama

    A. Seeing plays

        1. like being read to, can understand what someone else is saying even if you couldn't read it yourself

        2. exposure to a variety of literature

    B. Performing in plays

        1. reinforce reading for understanding and feeling

        2. exposure to literature

        3. get close to plot and characters

        4. understand theoretical concepts like plot elements, etc.

        5. help memory skills

C. Technical and other aspects of play production

    1. set design and construction

    2. costume design and construction

    3. business aspects

III. Fine arts

> Notice that some parts of this outline are better developed than others. This is a reflection of Maya's vague thinking about her topic and her weak thesis. You should also notice that, at this point, it seems as if Maya is going to try to cover *every benefit of every art course* a student could take.

STEP 4: Conduct Your Research

Remember that the academic purposes of the research project are to:

1. gather information from a variety of knowledgeable and authoritative sources,

2. develop your own understanding of, and insight into, your topic,

3. communicate your knowledge to others.

To ensure that your final project meets all of these purposes, you need to be intentional in your selection of potential sources and in the information you take from them.

All of the information must support your thesis and should be applicable to one part of your preliminary outline.

> There might, of course, be the rare exception when the bulk of information makes you question your original thesis or part of your plan. This situation will require you to make a judgment call: You may choose to keep your original thesis and plan, or you may amend them. Do not, however, allow this possibility to seduce you into rushing through the thesis and outline stages. Most of the time, a well-planned thesis and outline will be supportable with minimal revision.

The information you record in your notes—whatever form they take—must also reflect your ultimate goal, the reason you were assigned the research project to begin with:

- information drawn directly from a source: direct quotation, paraphrase, summary;

- interpretation, analysis, or explanation of information drawn directly from a source;

- response or reaction to your sources: agreement, disagreement, qualification;

- your own thoughts, ideas, realization, and insight.

Since your final project is supposed to communicate *your* knowledge and insight—explained and supported by your sources—it really is in your best interest to make certain your notes include your original ideas. Otherwise, you run the risk of turning your paper into little more than a review of your sources.

You must be prepared to add something to the conversation.

STEP 5: Write your first draft

Here is Maya's problematic first draft.

Studying art in school helps students learn other subjects as well. Students who participate in music courses do better in their math classes. Science classes like physics also benefit from students taking music. Students who study music and drama do better in their language arts classes. There are many reasons students should take art classes in school.

Students who participate in music courses do better in their math classes. A lot of this improvement has to do with the brain and how it develops. Most neuroscientists, people who study the brain's structure and function, agree that the brain continues to develop even years after birth. And studies clearly indicate that musical training actually helps the part of the left side of the brain that is known to deal with language to grow stronger.[1] In another study, students in two elementary schools in Rhode Island were given lessons in "sequential, skill-building music programs."[2] They showed "marked improvement in reading and math skills."[3] Even if the students in the test group started out behind students in the control group, they caught up with the control group in reading and passed them in math.[4] Students who

[1] National Arts in Education Research and Development Center. *Twenty Reasons Music Training is Good for your Brain.* (New York: New York University, 1997) 276.
[2] Faith Gardiner, Jeffrey Cormant, and Philip Knowles. "The Truth about Music and Math." *Nature's World,* (May 23, 1996), 12–13.
[3] Ibid.
[4] Ibid.

Maya commits a common error here, commonly called the "half-empty comparison." She states that students of music *do better in math*, but it is not clear *better than what?* Better at math than social studies? Music students do better than non-music students? Maya cannot simply assume her reader will arrive at the right inference.

Here is another half-empty comparison. Better in language arts *than what?*

Structurally, this introduction is sufficient. It introduces the thesis and the main claims that are going to be supported in the paper. In terms of content, however, it does not do its job of orienting the reader to the types of evidence that are going to be presented and to how the central argument is going to be developed.

While it's good that Maya is crediting her sources, she's quoting material that does not need to be quoted, and she's documenting conclusions and generalizations, not specific, meaningful information.

Notice that the form of Turabian we are following requires a full footnote. What needs to be included in these notes and how to format them are explained in Appendix 1.

Ibid is a short form of the Latin *Ibidem,* which means "the same place." In these uses, Maya is telling her reader that the information cited in notes 3 and 4 came from the same source as 2.

It is pretty apparent from these sentences that Maya is simply repeating sentences from her sources. Since she offers no explanation or additional insight, the reader might suspect that she does not understand what she is writing about. She also uses first person, which serves only to weaken her academic, authoritative tone.

participated in similar programs in New York City elementary and middle schools showed increases in self-esteem and thinking skills.[5]

"Spatial intelligence" is very important. It is how we see the world accurately and how we visualize things as they are described to us. It is the kind of intelligence that allows us to solve complex math problems and pack a suitcase.[6] Apparently, one way music helps students to learn is by listening to a familiar song while learning something new, the brain links the new material with the song, and this helps the child remember the new material.[7]

---

[5] National Arts in Education Research Center.
[6] Martin Shaw, Asher Rastikov, et al. "Music training enhanced temporal reasoning in preschoolers." *Journal of Neurological Research*, (Vol. 19, 1-8. February 1997), 17–20.
[7] National Arts in Education Research Center.

It's generally not acceptable to begin a sentence with digits.

This comparison is complete and correct.

Maya's word choice undermines her credibility. Unless there was only one study, and all three universities participated in it, it is not correct to say that UC Irvine and McGill did "the same" study as the unnamed elementary school.

Piano lessons are especially important. An elementary school had new computer software to teach math to second graders. 237 of them used the software <u>and</u> got piano lessons. They scored 27% higher on tests dealing with proportions and fractions than the children that used only the software.[12] The University of California at Irvine did the same study and showed that preschoolers who had eight months of piano lessons increased their spatial reasoning IQ by 46%.[13] They did the same study at McGill University, too. There they found that "pattern recognition and mental representation scores improved significantly for students given piano instruction of a three-year period."[14] They also found that the students who got piano lessons also showed higher self-esteem and musical skills.[15]

---

[12] Aimee Grandizzio, Matthew Peters, and Gordon Spitz, "Enhanced learning of proportions and mathematics through music and spatial-temporal training," *Journal of Neurological Research*, (Vol. 23 March 2001), 22–23.

13 Asher Rastikov, et al. <u>Music and Spatial Awareness: A Relationship of Cause and Effect</u>. (Irvine, CA: University of California, 1997), 453.

14 Gioccomo Costanza. "The Piano Project: Effects of piano instruction on children's cognitive abilities, academic achievement, and self-esteem." Paper presented at the meeting of the International Music Educators Annual Conference, Phoenix, AZ, April 1999.

15 Ibid.

Even the people who give us the SATs know that arts instruction is important:

In 2001, students participating in music education scored higher on the SATs than students who had no art participation did. Scores for students in music performance classes were 57 points higher (Verbal) and 41 points higher (Math). Scores for students in music appreciation classes were 63 points higher (Verbal) and 44 points higher (Math).[21]

21 The College Board. "College-Bound Seniors: National Report: Profile of SAT Program Test Takers." Princeton, N.J.: The College Entrance Examination Board, 2001.

From the beginning, Maya has said that her topic is arts instruction and its benefits for other disciplines. She is several pages into her report, however, and the only art she has discussed is *music*. Likewise, this quotation is the first mention of an academic subject that is not math. Thus, she is still in section I A of her outline. If she really intends to write the paper she outlined, it will be either terribly underdeveloped or terribly long.

Maya's first draft continues in much the same way.

Bibliography

The College Board. "College-Bound Seniors: National Report: Profile of SAT Program Test Takers." Princeton, N.J.: The College Entrance Examination Board, 2001.

Costanza, Gioccomo. "The Piano Project: Effects of piano instruction on children's cognitive abilities, academic achievement, and self-esteem." Paper presented at the meeting of the International Music Educators Annual Conference, Phoenix, AZ, April 1999.

Gardiner, Faith, Jeffrey Cormant, and Philip Knowles. "The Truth about Music and Math." Nature's World, May 23, 1996, 65-66.

Grandizzio, Aimee, Matthew Peters, and Gordon Spitz, "Enhanced learning of proportions and mathematics through music and spatial-temporal training," Journal of Neurological Research, Vol. 23, 22-32. March 2001.

National Arts in Education Research and Development Center. Twenty Reasons Music Training is Good for your Brain. New York: New York University, 1997.

Rastikov, Asher, Martin Shaw, et al. Music and Spatial Awareness: A Relationship of Cause and Effect. Irvine, CA: University of California, 1997.

Shaw, Martin, Asher Rastikov, et al. "Music training enhanced temporal reasoning in preschoolers." Journal of Neurological Research, Vol. 19, 1-8. February 1997.

Analysis of First Draft

What is this writer's purpose? Maya's stated purpose is to argue the importance of arts instruction in schools by illustrating how studying the various arts can improve students' learning and performance in non-art, academic subjects. However, Maya devotes most of her paper to the relationship between music instruction and mathematics success. She should consider narrowing her topic and thesis to this specific relationship.

What is his/her thesis? Her thesis is that the study of art in school improves student achievement in other subjects as well.

What key points has the writer identified to clarify his/her thesis? Maya does not seem to have *intentionally* chosen music as her representative art or math as her representative academic subject, but that is, in fact, how the majority of the paper plays out.

What key points has the writer identified to support his/her thesis? Each of these needs additional discussion, explanation, and some reflection on Maya's part, but she does offer the following information that she gathered in her research:

- reference to a study performed by the University of California, Irvine
- reference to a study performed by McGill University
- reference to less well-identified studies performed in Rhode Island, New York City, and on unspecified second-graders.

Does the writer effectively prove his/her thesis? Since Maya's current thesis deals with instruction in "the arts" and its impact on "academic subjects," she does not prove her thesis. However, if she were to narrow her focus to the relationship between music and math, she would certainly be headed in the right direction. As it stands now, however, this report is too dependent on the sources' conclusions with no examination of how those conclusions were reached. The paper is a summary of Maya's research, but does not provide any of Maya's own thoughts or insights.

NOW you will plan your own research report. You will probably find it helpful to follow the same process Maya has followed.

STEP 1: Select a Topic

Just as Maya chose to explore the relationship between studying art and success in other disciplines, you might also find it helpful to think in terms of relationships between ideas, persons, events, and so on in order to arrive at a workable topic. Remember that some of the most commonly studied relationships include:

Sources of...

historical and cultural sources of the concept of law in modern Western civilization

Influences on...

the influence of Athenian democracy on the Virginia Plan for the Constitution

Inspirations for...

historical and literary inspirations for the labor movement of the nineteenth and twentieth centuries

Cultural, Political, and/or Social contexts of...

political and cultural resistance to early vaccination movements

Impact of...

the discovery of penicillin on germ theory and medical science

Causes of...

the United States' failure in the Vietnam conflict

Events leading to...

the 1955 Montgomery, Alabama, bus boycott

Factors contributing to...

the rise of the "Women's Liberation Movement" of the 1960s and 1970s

---

STEP 2: Draft a Thesis

Make sure your thesis is arguable—rooted in facts and reasonable conclusions, not pure opinion.

Make certain you have or know you can find sufficient evidence in the facts and expert opinions your discovered in your research to explain and support your key points.

STEP 3: Draft a Preliminary Outline

STEP 4: Conduct Your Research

STEP 5: Write Your First Draft

STEP 6: Peer Edit

What is this writer's purpose?

What is his/her thesis?

What key points has the writer identified to clarify his/her thesis?

What key points has the writer identified to support his/her thesis?

What details, facts, etc., have been included to make this a thorough study of the topic and a convincing argument?

Does the writer effectively prove his/her thesis?

STEP 7: Revised/Final Draft

Here are Maya's peer editor's comments and analysis, as well as Maya's responses.

- Maya commits a common error here, commonly called the "half-empty comparison." She states that students of music *do better in math*, but it is not clear *better than what*? Better at math than social studies? Music students do better than non-music students? Maya cannot simply assume her reader will arrive at the right inference.

- Here is another half-empty comparison. Better in language arts *than what*?

- Structurally, this introduction is sufficient. It introduces the thesis and the main claims that are going to be supported in the paper. In terms of content, however, it does not do its job of orienting the reader to the types of evidence that are going to be presented and to how the central argument is going to be developed.

- While it's good that Maya is crediting her sources, she's quoting material that does not need to be quoted, and she's documenting conclusions and generalizations, not specific, meaningful information

- It is pretty apparent from these sentences that Maya is simply repeating sentences from her sources. Since she offers no explanation or additional insight, the reader might suspect that she does not understand what she is writing about. She also uses first person, which serves only to weaken her academic, authoritative tone.

- It's generally not acceptable to begin a sentence with digits.

- This comparison is complete and correct.

- Maya's word choice undermines her credibility. Unless there was only one study, and all three universities participated in it, it is not correct to say that UC Irvine and McGill did "the same" study as the unnamed elementary school.

- From the beginning, Maya has said that her topic is arts instruction and its benefits for other disciplines. She is several pages into her report, however, and the only art she has discussed is *music*. Likewise, this quotation is the first mention of an academic subject that is not math. Thus, she is still in section I A of her outline. If she really intends to write the paper she outlined, it will be either terribly underdeveloped or terribly long.

And here is Maya's reaction:

> A big factor seems to be discussing the stuff from my sources. I'll have to play around with that.
>
> I do want to narrow my focus. There is even more I found out about the connection between music and math that I didn't cover because I thought it would be too much.
>
> I need to review when to quote versus when to paraphrase versus when to summarize.

Analysis of First Draft

What is this writer's purpose? Maya's stated purpose is to argue the importance of arts instruction in schools by illustrating how studying the various arts can improve students' learning and performance in non-art, academic subjects. However, Maya devotes most of her paper to the relationship between music instruction and mathematics success. She should consider narrowing her topic and thesis to this specific relationship.

> Yes. I want to narrow my topic to only music and math.

What is his/her thesis? Her thesis is that the study of art in school improves student achievement in other subjects as well.

> New thesis: Students who study music do better in their mathematics courses and on mathematics tests.

This does narrow the focus, but as it is currently stated, it doesn't really invite much discussion or sharing of individual insight.

What key points has the writer identified to clarify his/her thesis? Maya does not seem to have intentionally chosen music as her representative art or math as her representative academic subject, but that is, in fact, how the majority of the paper plays out.

> Works for me. Especially with the new thesis.

What key points has the writer identified to support his/her thesis? Each of these needs additional discussion, explanation, and some reflection on Maya's part, but she does offer the following information that she gathered in her research:

- reference to a study performed by the University of California, Irvine
- reference to a study performed by McGill University
- reference to less well-identified studies performed in Rhode Island, New York City, and on unspecified second-graders.

> I guess they're suggesting I find more information about those unidentified studies?

Does the writer effectively prove his/her thesis? Since Maya's current thesis deals with instruction in "the arts" and its impact on "academic subjects," she does not prove her thesis. However, if she were to narrow her focus to the relationship between music and math, she would certainly be headed in the right direction. As it stands now, however, this report is too dependent on the sources' conclusions with no examination of how those conclusions were reached. The paper is a summary of Maya's research, but does not provide any of Maya's own thoughts or insights.

> *Okay, I have the new thesis. I'll make it a point to stick in some of my own ideas.*

Here is Maya's revised draft. While it is still not an *excellent* report, she has begun to address her peer editor's concerns.

Thesis: *Students who study music do better in their mathematics courses and on mathematics tests.*

Maya has narrowed her thesis, but this sentence is still an abrupt beginning for her report. She also has still not addressed her "half-empty comparison": better *than what?*

This is an interesting addition to Maya's introduction. While it is awkwardly worded, it does add a sense of purpose to the information Maya is going to present. She will have to be careful not to lose sight of this purpose.

Originally, Maya had a footnote here, but she has wisely taken it out because it is a conclusion, not the information that led to that conclusion.

Students who study music do better in their mathematics courses and on mathematics tests. Many studies show that students who are given music instruction, especially piano lessons, while they are young have increased spatial-temporal intelligence, which lets them do better in higher math. Based on this evidence, those who think that cutting arts courses or reducing the funding for arts courses would be a good way to save money and reduce spending deficits are sadly mistaken.

A lot of the connection between music study and success in math has to do with the brain and how it develops. Most neuroscientists, people who study the brain's structure and function, agree that the brain continues to develop even years after birth. And studies clearly indicate that musical training actually helps the part of the left side of the brain that is known to deal with language to grow stronger. Dr. Gottfried Schlaug, M.D., Ph.D., is the director of the Music and Neuroimaging Laboratory in Boston, Massachusetts. He has decided that certain regions of the brain, such as the corpus callosum and the right motor cortex, were larger in musicians who started their musical training before the age of 7.[1] In fact, most research shows that when children are trained in music at a young age, they tend to improve in their math skills.

In one study, students in two elementary schools in Rhode Island were given lessons in music instruction that emphasized sequential skills like playing scales, and games that sharpened their rhythm and pitch skills. They showed notable improvement in reading and math skills. Even if the students in the test group started out behind students in the control group, they caught up with the control group in reading and passed them in math.[2]

The right motor cortex, which Dr. Schlaug found to be larger in musicians than in non-musicians, is the part of the brain that manages spatial-temporal thinking. He found that, even in non-musicians, this part of the brain can be activated simply by listening to music.[3] This cortex is important because it is used in higher brain functions like the ones used in mathematics. Spatial-temporal intelligence controls our ability to see the world accurately and to visualize things that are described to us. It is the kind of intelligence that allows us to solve complex math problems, play chess, and plan what we will need next week on vacation so we can pack our suitcase. For example, in order to write a mathematical proof, the student must have a strong sense of sequences and be able to think ahead several steps. These abilities are examples of spatial-temporal thinking and come from the right motor cortex of the brain.

---

[1] Gottfried Schlaug, M.D., Ph.D. The Musician's Brain: A Model for Functional and Structural Adaptation. (New York: New York Academy of Sciences Press, 2001). 373.

[2] Faith Gardiner, Jeffrey Cormant, and Philip Knowles. "The Truth about Music and Math." Nature's World, (May 23, 1996), 12 – 13.

[3] Ibid.

While Maya's research is a little better here, she trivializes her source's research and studies by claiming that he simply "decided."

This is a considerably better treatment of this material than in Maya's first draft.

Maya is now doing a much better job explaining these difficult concepts as she understands them. Word choice and point of view, however, are still problems.

Most of the studies show that the children's math abilities improved after they had studied music for a certain period of time. The children were also young, and this suggests that maybe the music instruction must come early in order to help with math scores. The students the study described above from <u>Nature</u> scored much better in math than the other students did after they [the students who studied music] studied music for six months.[7]

Piano lessons seem to be especially important. Researchers found that children given regular piano lessons significantly improved in their spatial-temporal IQ scores.[8] One elementary school had new computer software to teach math to second graders, 237 of whom used the software and got piano lessons. They scored 27% higher on tests dealing with proportions and fractions than the children who used the software by itself did.[9] The University of California at Irvine did the same study and showed that preschoolers who had eight months of piano lessons increased their spatial reasoning IQ by 46%.[10] Researchers did the same study at McGill University, too. There they found that "pattern recognition and mental representation scores improved significantly for students given piano instruction of a three-year period."[11] They also found that the students who got piano lessons also showed higher self-esteem and musical skills.

There is still nothing wrong with Maya's information, and she is being very careful to credit her sources, but there is still no sense of what Maya understands or what she wants her reader to make of all this.

Ibid alone tells the reader that the cited information came from the same page in the same source as the previous note. *Ibid* plus a page number indicates the same source, but the page noted.

---

[7] Asher Rastikov, et al. Music and Spatial Awareness: A Relationship of Cause and Effect. (Irvine, CA: University of California, 1997), 453.

[8] Ibid 470.

[9] Aimee Grandizzio, Matthew Peters, and Gordon Spitz, "Enhanced learning of proportions and mathematics through music and spatial-temporal training," Journal of Neurological Research, (Vol. 23,. March 2001), 22 – 23.

[10] Rastikov et al. 502.

[11] Gioccomo, Costanza, "The Piano Project: Effects of piano instruction on children's cognitive abilities, academic achievement, and self-esteem." Paper presented at the meeting of the International Music Educators Annual Conference, Phoenix, AZ, April 1999.

And even though the strongest and longest lasting improvements in math were because the student played an instrument, actually learning and making the music, some studies show there might be even some benefit just from listening to music. This benefit is called "The Mozart Effect," named this because there is evidence that listening to an hour or two of music by the famous composer Mozart can increase the listener's creativity and concentration and actually make her analytical and problem-solving skills sharper. This phenomenon was first discovered by a French researcher, Alfred A. Tomatis. It was then studied by researchers at the University of California at Irvine who found that Mozart's music did indeed produce a short-term improvement of spatial-temporal reasoning.

Participants were asked to experience three different listening conditions, a spatial reasoning test after experiencing three different listening conditions—a Mozart sonata, nondescript "relaxation" music, and silence. After each listening condition, participants took a test of abstract spatial reasoning. What Rausch and her colleagues found was that the participants did score better on the IQ test after listening to the Mozart than they did after the other two conditions.[17] This does not mean that listening to classical music will make a student smarter. First, the UC researchers found improvement only in participants' spatial-temporal reasoning, not in their overall intelligence. Second, the improvement was found to be only temporary: none of the participants had an effect that lasted longer than fifteen minutes.[18]

---

[17] Rastikov et al., 453.
[18] Ibid 469.

Schools that think they can save money by cutting their arts funding, especially their music programs, had better think again. Society today is demanding better quality education. They don't want American students to score the lowest of every nation on international math tests. They don't want all of our jobs shipped overseas because American companies say Americans cannot do the work. So, if Americans really want smart and educated high school and college graduates, they might just want to consider increasing funding for music programs, especially in preschool and the early grades, and they should require every student to take piano lessons for at least six months. Only then will our math scores improve, and America can once again be proud as a nation.

This is certainly Maya's strongest conclusion so far, but it is actually a little excessive. She has completely lost her academic tone and has almost lost her focus in a political tangent.

Even the people who give us the SATs know that music instruction is important:

In 2001, students participating in music education scored higher on the SATs than students with no art participation did. Scores for students in music performance classes were 57 points higher (Verbal) and 41 points higher (Math). Scores for students in music appreciation classes were 63 points higher (Verbal) and 44 points higher (Math).[21]

It's funny that the College Board's studies show higher improvement in Verbal than in Math, but still it is undeniable that the scores improved after the students received instruction in music. Maybe the difference between the Verbal and Math is because the students received their music instruction too late to make that much difference in math.

Maya is making a fine effort to discuss the evidence she presents and share some of her own insight. Still, she cannot simply speculate. Her suspicion about the differences in Verbal and Math scores would be worth exploring to see whether there is any evidence to support it.

---

[21] The College Board. "College-Bound Seniors: National Report: Profile of SAT Program Test Takers." Princeton, N.J.: The College Entrance Examination Board, 2001.

The evidence is clear. Early instruction in music activates the parts of the brain that manage spatial awareness and abilities. This temporal-spatial intelligence is very important in performing higher mathematics. Therefore, music instruction given at a young age is an important component of a child's mathematics instruction.

This is a fairly weak conclusion. At this point, it doesn't have much more impact than a repetition of a verified fact. At the very least, Maya should remind her reader that her ultimate goal is to argue in favor of funding for music courses in school.

Bibliography

The College Board. "College-Bound Seniors: National Report: Profile of SAT Program Test Takers." Princeton, N.J.: The College Entrance Examination Board, 2001.

Costanza, Gioccomo. "The Piano Project: Effects of Piano Instruction on Children's Cognitive Abilities, Academic Achievement, and Self-esteem." Paper presented at the meeting of the International Music Educators Annual Conference, Phoenix, AZ, April 1999.

Gardiner, Faith, Jeffrey Cormant, and Philip Knowles. "The Truth about Music and Math." Nature's World, May 23, 1996.

Grandizzio, Aimee, Matthew Peters, and Gordon Spitz, "Enhanced Learning of Proportions and Mathematics through Music and Spatial-temporal Training," Journal of Neurological Research, Vol. 23, 22-32. March 2001. .

Jameson, Cynthia. "Music–Math Connection: A Neurobiological View." WebEssays, 16 May 2008. Web.

The Music Foundation. "Benefits of Music Education to Math, Reading, Language, and Spatial Intelligence."

National Arts in Education Research and Development Center. Twenty Reasons Music Training is Good for your Brain. New York: New York University, 1997.

Rastikov, Asher, Martin Shaw, et al. <u>Music and Spatial Awareness: A Relationship of Cause and Effect</u>. Irvine, CA: University of California, 1997.

Schlaug, Gottfried, M.D., Ph.D. <u>The Musician's Brain: A Model for Functional and Structural Adaptation</u>. New York: New York Academy of Sciences Press, 2001.

Shaw, Martin, Asher Rastikov, et al. "Music Training Enhanced Temporal Reasoning in Preschoolers." <u>Journal of Neurological Research</u>, Vol. 19, 1-8. February 1997.

Analysis of Revised Draft

What is this writer's purpose? Given the way she revised her introduction, Maya seems to suggest that her purpose is to defend the funding of music programs in school by establishing the connection between music instruction and increases in student mathematics achievements. She does, however, very quickly lose sight of this new purpose.

What is his/her thesis? Her narrowed thesis is that there is a strong connection between instruction in music and improvement in mathematics ability.

Has the writer's new draft strengthened his/her point? Yes. Maya does present additional support, and she is more aware of sharing her own insight, inferences, and conclusions.

Has the rewrite strengthened the case for his/her thesis? Yes. See above.

What new details, facts, etc., have been included to make this a more thorough study of the topic? Maya has introduced some new information about brain physiology and about the phenomenon that has come to be known as "The Mozart Effect."

Does the writer effectively prove his/her thesis to any greater degree than in the previous draft? Yes.

Now write your final draft.

POSSIBLE STEP 8: Rewrite Opportunity

Given the grade she received and her teacher's comments, Maya decided that it was worth taking her paper into a third draft.

The United States is experiencing what many think is the worst economic crisis in the nation's history since the Great Depression. State and local governments everywhere are debating budget cuts. Even schools are finding it necessary to cut their budgets. Teachers and aides are being fired, and educational programs are being cut. Defunded programs include "unimportant," "fluff" courses offered in schools' arts departments: art, music, drama, etc. The truth is, however, that arts courses are very important. For example, there is an entire body of evidence that shows that early music instruction helps children develop important parts of the brain that control the type of thinking necessary to learn and do mathematics. Given the evidence, it is clear that students who study music do better than others in their mathematics courses and on mathematics tests.

A lot of the connection between music study and success in math has to do with the brain and how it develops. Most neuroscientists, people who study the brain's structure and function, agree that the brain continues to develop even years after birth. Studies clearly indicate that musical training helps the part of the left side of the brain that is known to deal with language to grow stronger. Dr. Gottfried Schlaug, M.D., Ph.D., is the director of the Music and Neuroimaging Laboratory in Boston, Massachusetts. His research has found that certain regions of the brain, such as the corpus callosum and the right motor cortex, were larger in musicians who started their musical training before the age of 7.[1] In fact, most research shows that

[1] Gottfried Schlaug, M.D., Ph.D. The Musician's Brain: A Model for Functional and Structural Adaptation. (New York: New York Academy of Sciences Press, 2001). 373.

Maya has wisely returned to her original journal entry to revisit how she introduced the funding issue and tied it into the music-math connection. She has, of course, cleaned up her awkward sentence structure and word choice.

This is a much better introduction. It sets up both Maya's purpose and thesis and even suggests the type of evidence she is going to provide in the body of the paper.

This is a decent example of Maya trying to share some of her own insight with her reader.

Maya still needs to work on eliminating all first person and creating a formal, authoritative, and academic tone.

when children are trained in music at a young age, they tend to improve in their math skills.

In one study, students in two elementary schools in Rhode Island were given lessons in music instruction that emphasized sequential skills like playing scales and games that sharpened their rhythm and pitch. They showed notable improvement in reading and math skills. Even if the students in the test group started out behind students in the control group, they caught up with the control group in reading and passed them in math.[2] The fact that they showed more growth in math than in reading makes it seem as if music has a larger effect on the mathematical parts of the brain.

The right motor cortex, which Dr. Schlaug found to be larger in musicians than in nonmusicians, is the part of the brain that manages spatial-temporal thinking. He found that, even in non-musicians, this part of the brain can be activated simply by listening to music.[3] This cortex is important because it is used in higher brain functions like those used in mathematics. Spatial-temporal intelligence controls our ability to see the world accurately and to visualize things that are described to us. It is the kind of intelligence that allows us to solve complex math problems, play chess, and plan what we will need next week on vacation so we can pack our suitcase.[4] For example, in order to write a mathematical proof, the student must have a strong sense of sequences and be able to think ahead several steps. These abilities are examples of spatial-temporal thinking and come from the right motor cortex of the brain.

---

[2] Faith Gardiner, Jeffrey Cormant, and Philip Knowles. "The Truth about Music and Math." Nature's World, (May 23, 1996), 12 – 13.
[3] Ibid.

Most of the studies also show that, not only should the music instruction be started while the child is young, the children's math abilities also improved after they had studied music for a certain period of time. The students Gardiner and his colleagues describe in their article in <u>Nature</u> improved their math scores after they had studied music for six months.[7] Other studies also describe gains in math after the children have received music instruction for a specific period from three months to a year or two.

Piano lessons seem to be especially important. Researchers found that children given regular piano lessons significantly improved in their spatial-temporal IQ scores.[8] One elementary school had new computer software to teach math to second-graders, 237 of whom used the software and got piano lessons. They scored 27% higher on tests dealing with proportions and fractions than did the children that only used the software.[9] A very similar study was conducted at the University of California at Irvine and showed that preschoolers who had eight months of piano lessons increased their spatial reasoning IQ by 46%.[10] Similarly, researchers at McGill University in Montreal also found that "pattern recognition and mental representation scores" improved significantly for students who had piano instruction for at least three years.[11] The reader needs to realize that these studies reinforce the earlier findings that the music instruction should begin while the child is young and should continue for a specified period of time.

Nice transition.

This is a very important word choice change. Two different universities cannot do "the same" study unless there is only one study, and both are a part of it. Here, Maya is clarifying that there was more than one study, but that these studies were "similar." This is an important distinction and will affect how credible Maya remains as a serious student.

While this is not a startling realization, and Maya does not state it all too subtly, at least she does try to share an insight with her reader rather than just rehash information from her sources.

---

[7] Asher Rastikov, et al. <u>Music and Spatial Awareness: A Relationship of Cause and Effect</u>. (Irvine, CA: University of California, 1997), 453.

[8] Ibid 470.

[8] Aimee Grandizzio, Matthew Peters, and Gordon Spitz, "Enhanced learning of proportions and mathematics through music and spatial-temporal training," <u>Journal of Neurological Research</u>, (Vol. 23,. March 2001), 22 – 23.

[10] Rastikov et al. 502.

[11] Gioccomo, Costanza, "The Piano Project: Effects of piano instruction on children's cognitive abilities, academic achievement, and self-esteem." Paper presented at the meeting of the International Music Educators Annual Conference, Phoenix, AZ, April 1999.

And even though the strongest and longest lasting improvements in math were because the student played an instrument, actually <u>learning and making</u> the music, some studies show there might be even some benefit just from <u>listening</u> to music. This benefit is called "The Mozart Effect," named this because there is evidence that listening to an hour or two of music by the famous composer Mozart can increase the listener's creativity and concentration and actually make her analytical and problem-solving skills sharper. This phenomenon was first discovered by a French researcher, Alfred A. Tomatis. It was then studied by researchers at the University of California at Irvine who found that Mozart's music did indeed produce a short-term improvement of spatial-temporal reasoning.

Participants were asked to experience three different listening conditions, a spatial reasoning test after experiencing three different listening conditions—a Mozart sonata, nondescript "relaxation" music, and silence. After each listening condition, participants took a test of abstract spatial reasoning. What Rausch and her colleagues found was that the participants did score better on the IQ test after listening to the Mozart than they did after the other two conditions.[17] This does not mean that listening to classical music will make students smarter. First, the UC researchers found improvement <u>only</u> in participants' spatial-temporal reasoning, not in their overall intelligence. Second, the improvement was found to be only temporary: none of the participants had an effect that lasted longer than fifteen minutes.[18]

---

[17] Rastikov et al., 453.
[18] Ibid 469.

Schools and districts are misguided if they think they can save money by cutting arts funding. Society today is demanding a better quality education. That better quality must include a higher ranking than last on international mathematics tests. It must prepare workers to keep the United States economy strong. If Americans really want educated high school and college graduates, they should actually consider increasing funding for music programs, especially in preschool and the early grades. Rather than making music an elective and cutting its funding, schools should require every student to take piano lessons for at least six months. The research is clear and shows that learning music is crucial for brain development and for learning all of the other subjects Americans consider important.

This conclusion is less melodramatic than the previous one and, therefore, more successful. Once Maya works out her problems with word choice and tone, she will have a fine research paper.

Bibliography

The College Board. "College-Bound Seniors: National Report: Profile of SAT Program Test Takers." Princeton, N.J.: The College Entrance Examination Board, 2001.

Costanza, Gioccomo. "The Piano Project: Effects of Piano Instruction on Children's Cognitive Abilities, Academic Achievement, and Self-esteem." Paper presented at the meeting of the International Music Educators Annual Conference, Phoenix, AZ, April 1999.

Gardiner, Faith, Jeffrey Cormant, and Philip Knowles. "The Truth about Music and Math." Nature's World, May 23, 1996.

Grandizzio, Aimee, Matthew Peters, and Gordon Spitz, "Enhanced Learning of Proportions and Mathematics through Music and Spatial-temporal Training," Journal of Neurological Research, Vol. 23, 22-32. March 2001.

Jameson, Cynthia. "Music–Math Connection: A Neurobiological View." <u>WebEssays</u>, 16 May 2008. Web.

The Music Foundation. "Benefits of Music Education to Math, Reading, Language, and Spatial Intelligence." nd.

National Arts in Education Research and Development Center. <u>Twenty Reasons Music Training is Good for your Brain</u>. New York: New York University, 1997.

Rastikov, Asher, Martin Shaw, et al. <u>Music and Spatial Awareness: A Relationship of Cause and Effect</u>. Irvine, CA: University of California, 1997.

Schlaug, Gottfried, M.D., Ph.D. <u>The Musician's Brain: A Model for Functional and Structural Adaptation</u>. New York: New York Academy of Sciences Press, 2001.

Shaw, Martin, Asher Rastikov, et al. "Music Training Enhanced Temporal Reasoning in Preschoolers." <u>Journal of Neurological Research</u>, Vol. 19, 1-8. February 1997.

ASSIGNMENT 2:

Research Project—English Language or Literature Topic

The research project is an independent, third-quarter unit. The only requirement the teacher imposes is that the topic reflect something previously covered that year in class. **Danae** particularly enjoyed the class's study of the translation of a play or book to a film. For the study, they read *Romeo and Juliet* and watched large excerpts of several film interpretations, especially Franco Zeffirelli's lavish 1968 production and Leonardo DiCaprio's modernized 1996 rendering. Danae knows she must pick a different pair—one that she can study on her own.

STEP 1: Select a Topic

Books to film:

The Great Gatsby ... there's the Robert Redford movie, but the new Leonardo DiCaprio one might not be out in time.

The Scarlet Letter? Sleepy Hollow ... all they kept there was the title and the name of the main character, Ichabod Crane.

Vincent Price acted in a lot of movies on Edgar Allen Poe stuff.

Play to film:

Any Shakespeare: Othello to O

Roman Polanski's Macbeth ... they say it's really exciting, but kind of gross

But maybe Shakespeare is too obvious.

Our Town ... there's that awful movie version I saw, black and white, at the end Emily wakes up and screams, "I want to live! I want to live."

Hello Dolly was a play first ... but maybe that's too commercial, not "literary enough."

Danae is actually wise to worry whether a proposed topic is "literary" or "academic" enough. She is, after all, learning and practicing a skill she will apply in college and graduate school, so it is in her best interest to practice working with academic topics.

My Fair Lady was based on a play by George Bernard Shaw. I could find out which one.

> Danae is talking about George Bernard Shaw's *Pygmalion*. If she decides to pursue that topic, she won't have any trouble finding information on the adaptation of the play and the development of the film.

STEP 2: Draft a thesis

Students of literature know the artistic quality of the novels, plays, and movies they study, but they rarely pay any attention to the commercial aspects. I like this, especially the contrast of literary and commercial, but is this really an arguable thesis, or is it simply a verifiable fact?

Today, the plays of William Shakespeare are studied for their artistic quality, but popular film adaptations of his plays show they contain a strong commercial element as well. Well, this specifies the playwright, but it is still just a statement of fact.

An examination of director Roman Polanski's 1971 film adaptation of William Shakespeare's Macbeth... I'm not sure I want to do Shakespeare. But I can probably say the same thing about The Great Gatsby or that Shaw play.

> Danae is on the right track thinking about contrasting the artistic and commercial aspects of literature, but she needs to step back and do a little more research to make sure she chooses the book-to-film adaptation that will serve her purpose.

An examination of the two versions of Pygmalion show that George Bernard Shaw had to sacrifice a lot of his artistry as a playwright in order to sell a commercially popular play. This has the comparison I want, and it identifies the author and play, but it makes Shaw sound like a sell-out or something.

The process of translating George Bernard Shaw's 1914 stage play Pygmalion into a commercially successful 1938 film shows the conflict between art and commercialism.

The process of translating George Bernard Shaw's 1914 stage play Pygmalion into a commercially successful 1938 film shows the conflict between art and commerce.

> Notice that the evolution of Danae's thinking includes not only the broad ideas but also specific word choice, "commercialism" versus "commerce."

The process of translating George Bernard Shaw's 1914 stage play Pygmalion into a commercially successful 1938 film shows that, in the conflict between art and commerce, art is often the loser.

> Here Danae adds an important realization that also provides a sense of argument to her thesis.

An examination of the 1914 stage play and the 1938 film adaptation of George Bernard Shaw's Pygmalion and stories about the making of the two productions show that the story Shaw wanted to tell and the story the audience demanded were almost the opposite of each other.

> This version shows tremendous improvement in the clarity of Danae's thoughts. She is no longer relying on vague terms like "commerce" and "art" but is illustrating those ideas with direct reference to her specific topic.

An examination of the 1914 stage play and the 1938 film adaptation of George Bernard Shaw's Pygmalion and accounts of the making of the two productions suggest that the story Shaw intended to tell and the story the commercial audience demanded were nearly antithetical.

STEP 3: Draft a preliminary outline

Thesis: An examination of the 1914 stage play and the 1938 film adaptation of George Bernard Shaw's Pygmalion and accounts of the making of the two productions suggest that the story Shaw intended to tell and the story the commercial audience demanded were nearly antithetical.

I. The point Shaw wanted to make.

  A. Social commentary

    1. Lower class improves itself through education.

    2. Happiness is in the middle class.

  B. Creation of a human being

    1. Eliza as a "pillar of strength"

    2. Higgins likes her because she is strong enough to leave him.

II. Audience's desire

    A. Romantic comedy

    B. "Happy ending"

    C. Conflict between Tree and Shaw

        1. Tree's ending

        2. Shaw's "sequel"

III. Shaw gives in

    A. Demands complete control in film adaptation

    B. Includes Cinderella-like ball scene

    C. Writes romantic ending

IV. Long-term legacy

    A. My Fair Lady stage play and film

    B. Socialist theme exists only in the "sequel"

STEP 4: Conduct Your Research

As always, your research must include examining whatever primary sources are available to you, in this case the original text of Shaw's *Pygmalion* and access to the 1938 film. A research paper that contains only discussion of other people's thoughts, reactions, and findings cannot receive more than a low passing grade.

STEP 5: Write your first draft

Danae is now ready to write her first draft.

If Danae is going to make a point to state dates, then she should offer some explanation why the play opened nearly two years after it was written. Otherwise, the reader might be distracted from what is important by wondering about this trivial point.

> In the spring of 1912, playwright George Bernard Shaw wrote what would become his most popular, adapted, and enduring play. When it opened in London on April 11, 1914, it was an immediate hit, which didn't make its author

very happy. For Shaw, the play was too popular, and fame put him in a position he didn't like—where he had to do things he didn't want to do to please his audience. This is shown when Shaw wrote the screenplay for the movie. He felt his artistic vision was contradicted and his honesty questioned. An examination of the two versions of <u>Pygmalion</u> and stories about the making of the two productions show that the story Shaw wanted to tell and the story the audience demanded were almost the opposite of each other.

When he wrote the play in 1912, Shaw was a socialist. He did not want to write a romantic comedy. <u>Pygmalion</u> is the story of a statue that turns to life, and that's what Shaw wanted to write—the story of a woman who could take care of herself. From the opening of the play's first London production, however, no one got it. Instead, the director wanted a love story, and the audience wanted a happy ending. The record of <u>Pygmalion's</u> production and publication history records Shaw's attempts to save his original vision and his ultimate failure to do so. This failure is most evident in the plot of the movie, which Shaw wrote and approved.

But audiences were not satisfied. From opening night, Tree toyed with Shaw's ending, trying to make it closer to what the audience expected. Shaw had stormed angrily out of the opening night performance, but he returned for the play's milestone one-hundredth performance. According to Shaw's own account of the night, he was shocked to see Higgins run to the outdoor balcony at the back of the set and toss a bouquet of flowers to Eliza. When Shaw

---

Tone and voice are problems for Danae here. Word choice and sentence structure are almost childish, and her vague reference to "things he didn't want to do" is virtually meaningless. What *things*? *Didn't want to do* for what reasons? Why did he *have* to do them?

What movie?

Clearly, Danae wants to say something about how Shaw succumbed to popular demand when translating his stage play to film, but she is alluding to the issue as if she were mentioning something the audience already knows.

Word choice continues to be a problem. Her thesis is never made explicit.

There are a couple of problems in these sentences. In addition to telling us what Shaw did *not* want, it might be helpful to tell us what he *did* want to write. It also sounds as if being a socialist precludes writing romantic comedies, which is probably not what Danae means to imply.

"Got it" is too colloquial for a formal paper. It is also an unsubstantiated exaggeration to suggest that "no one" understood Shaw's intent.

In the last few sentences, Danae follows a simple formula that might prove helpful to her in her early draft. She will want to work to grow beyond mere formula writing. Still, she has finally identified the issue of the paper.

Danae introduced Sir Henry Beerbohm Tree, who directed the premier production, owned the theater at which the production was staged, and played Henry Higgins, in the paragraphs not shown above.

Readers who do not already know the issue will probably not understand why Higgins' tossing a bouquet of flowers to Eliza would be considered "damnable."

This is the second paragraph in a row that Danae begins with "but." This is a grammatically questionable and a stylistically poor choice. There is also the problem with Danae's use of "probably." This is a research paper, which does not allow for much speculation. Danae should limit her discussion to what she can support with evidence from the text and her other sources.

Because this is a paper on a literary topic for her English class, Danae is using MLA-style documentation, which favors in-text, parenthetical citation over footnotes.

Since the ending of the play and the continuation of the story comprise the key issues for this paper, Danae should devote more time to how Shaw wanted the story to end.

complained, Tree replied, "My ending makes money; you ought to be grateful." Shaw shot back, "Your ending is damnable; you ought to be shot" (<u>Collected Letters</u> 527).

But Higgins probably never stopped tossing Eliza the flowers, and when Shaw prepared <u>Pygmalion</u> for publication as a book, he added an essay he called "Sequel: What Happened Afterwards," which begins:

> The rest of the story need not be shown in action, and indeed, would hardly need telling if our imaginations were not so enfeebled by their lazy dependence on the ready-mades and reach-me-downs of the ragshop in which Romance keeps its stock of 'happy endings' to misfit all stories.

This is the "Afterword" that tends to be included in most textbook versions of the play (Martinski 372). It completes the story of Eliza and Freddie. Eliza does <u>not</u> return to Higgins, and the two do <u>not</u> end up together.

This Sequel is not the only evidence of Shaw's dislike of Tree's ending or the audience's desire for a "happy ending." In a letter to Mrs. Patrick Campbell (Beatrice Stella Tanner), the actress who was playing Eliza opposite Tree's Higgins, Shaw tried to clarify his character's emotional and psychological motivations:

> When Eliza emancipates herself—when Galatea comes to life—she must not relapse. She must retain her pride and triumph to the end. When Higgins takes your arm on 'consort battleship' you must instantly throw him off with implacable pride; and this is the note until the final 'Buy them yourself.' He will go out on the balcony to watch your departure; come back triumphantly into the room; exclaim 'Galatea!' (meaning that the statue has come to life at last); and—curtain. Thus he gets the last word; and you get it too. (Ferguson 34)

There is no written or printed copy of the play that ends like this, but Shaw's instructions to his actress make his intention clear. Eliza is too strong and independent a person to crawl back to Higgins. Even Higgins can be happy only when he knows that his Eliza "needs" no one, even him. If Sir Henry Beerbohm Tree thought he needed to "soften" the ending to make money Shaw could still have the last word about what was <u>really</u> going on in his play.

Or so he thought.

Twenty-four years later, Hungarian producer Gabriel Pascal approached Shaw for permission to produce a film version of <u>Pygmalion</u>. Shaw demanded and got full control over the adaptation, and his name appears on the opening credits as the writer of the screenplay. But his "full control" did not seem to include restoring his vision of how Eliza and Higgins' story should end. In the movie, not only does Higgins <u>not</u> triumphantly cry out "Galatea" as he watches Eliza walk from his life. He doesn't even just throw her flowers as she walks away. In the 1938 film, "Screenplay and Dialogue [by] Bernard Shaw" (<u>Pygmalion</u>, film, 0:31), Eliza returns to Higgins, who abuses her just as he did before she threatened to leave (1:34:33). This ending is practically the opposite of what Shaw intended.

Another drastic change in the screenplay occurs between what would have been Acts III and IV in the play. While every production and edition of the play jumps in timeline from the disastrous scene at Mrs. Higgins' house to the argument on the evening after Eliza's triumph at the garden party, the 1938 film dramatizes the triumphant ball scene. There is

Some instructors might protest the use of a single-sentence paragraph or the use of a structural fragment as a complete sentence, but stylistically, it creates a nice sense of contrast for Danae's reader.

Danae's overuse of this construction suggests it is not a stylistic choice as much as a default or habitual use.

Danae's sentence structure and word choice are confusing here. The first "sentence" is actually a sentence fragment that causes the reader to ask, "Not only ... what?" Her saying "He doesn't even" in the second sentence suggests that this was a compromise Shaw might have agreed to.

Danae raises a valid point, but she doesn't complete it. Why is it significant that the movie's ending is so antithetical to Shaw's intention? What insight into Shaw and the process of translating the playwright's vision to commercial success and then to film does Danae want to share with her reader?

In order to be true to her thesis about the tension between author vision and audience expectation, Danae needs also to explore why Shaw would have chosen not to include this scene.

Sentence structure problem: Including the party scene would not have destroyed the expense of sets and costumes.

It is unclear here whether Danae is telling us what Shaw believed or preaching to us what she believes.

This is certainly a strong statement, but it is also a severe oversimplification of the material that Danae herself presents in her paper.

only one reason for the audience's desire to see this scene.

The audience wanted romance. They wanted the story of Eliza and Higgins to be a modern-day Cinderella story. And they wanted to see Cinderella at the ball (Martinski 184). Including the party scene would destroy the five-act plot structure as well as the expense of an additional set, costumes, and stage extras. There was no need to show Eliza's brush with the upper class. Shaw's point is proven in the next Act: there is no difference between the high and the low that education and training cannot fix. Cinderella's rise from servant to princess is not a happy ending. The happy ending lies in the middle class.

It was the screenplay of this 1938 film and not Shaw's original 1912 play that became the basis of <u>My Fair Lady</u>, the popular 1956 Broadway musical and 1964 movie musical (<u>Collected Letters</u> 733).

The differences in ending between George Bernard Shaw's stage play <u>Pygmalion</u> and movie <u>Pygmalion</u> proves that the playwright's purpose doesn't really matter. All that counts is the audience's desire and the director's profit.

Works Cited

"The Instinct of An Artist: Shaw and the Theatre." Catalog for "An Exhibition from The Bernard F. Burgunder Collection," 1997. Cornell University Library.

Martinski, Andrea. "Audiences Rule, Writers Drool." <u>Alternative Views of Award-Winning Books and Authors. Ed.</u> by Aloysius DeMarco. New York: Marginal Press, 1969.

<u>Pygmalion.</u> Prod. Gabriel Pascal. Perf. Leslie Howard, Wendy Hiller, 1938. Film.

Shaw, Bernard. <u>Androcles and the Lion; Overruled; and Pygmalion.</u> New York: Brentano, 1916.

Shaw, George Bernard. <u>The Collected Letters of G.B. Shaw.</u> Ed. David A. Laurents. London: Asquith and Heron, 1987.

Analysis of First Draft

What is this writer's purpose? Danae intends to illustrate the frustrations playwright George Bernard Shaw experienced trying to preserve his artistic integrity and tell a story with a strong personal and social theme.

What is his/her thesis? Her thesis is that the history of the first London production of Shaw's *Pygmalion* and the changes made in adapting the 1914 play for the big screen in 1938 suggest a victory of commercialism over artistic vision.

What key points has the writer identified to clarify his/her thesis?

- the distinction between a romantic comedy and a social commentary

- a comparison between this story and "Cinderella"

- the description of a scene written for the film but not shown on stage

- a clear comparison of why Shaw would not have included this scene and why the audience wanted it.

What key points has the writer identified to support his/her thesis?

- a letter from Shaw to the actress creating the role of Eliza explaining to her the reason Higgins cannot suggest a romantic interest in Eliza

- a portion of a letter from Shaw condemning the slight changes his London director made to the staging of the end of the play

- a passage from the "sequel" written by Shaw for the print publication of the play

- the fact that the 1938 film—and every subsequent remake or adaptation of the play—ends in the precise way Shaw said it must not.

Does the writer effectively prove his/her thesis? For the most part, she does. There are a few areas that could be further expanded, and her conclusion needs work, but the information presented and alluded to in this draft do a nice job to support her thesis.

NOW you will plan your own research report. You will probably find it helpful to follow the same process Danae has followed.

STEP 1: Select a Topic

In her paper, Danae explored the relationship between an original work and a film adaptation of that work. You will probably also find it helpful to think in terms of relationships between ideas, persons, and events.

Sources of…

> *historical and mythological sources for plot events or characters in J.R.R. Tolkien's* Lord of the Rings.

Influences on…

> *the influence of Aristotle's* Poetics *on Elizabethan and Jacobean tragedies*

Inspirations for…

> *historical and literary inspirations for characters and situations in Kathryn Stockett's* The Help

Cultural, Political, and/or Social contexts of…

> *nineteenth-century political and cultural background to Nathaniel Hawthorne's* The Scarlet Letter

Impact of…

> *the characters and situations in many of Charles Dickens's novels on Victorian awareness of social and economic injustice*

Causes of…

> *the early and numerous challenges to including J.D. Salinger's* Catcher in the Rye *in high school curricula*

Events leading to…

> *Virginia Woolf's 1941 suicide*

Factors contributing to…

> *the emergence of Naturalist and Realist literature in the late nineteenth and early twentieth centuries*

STEP 2: Draft a Thesis

Make sure your thesis is arguable—rooted in the literary text, not pure opinion.

Make certain you have or know you can find sufficient evidence in the text of the literature to explain and support your key points.

STEP 3: Draft a Preliminary Outline

STEP 4: Conduct Your Research

STEP 5: Write your first draft

STEP 6: Peer Edit

What is this writer's purpose?

What is his/her thesis?

What key points has the writer identified to clarify his/her thesis?

What key points has the writer identified to support his/her thesis?

What aspects of the literary text, in terms of language, imagery and voice, does the author cite to support his/her thesis?

Does the writer effectively prove his/her thesis?

STEP 7: Revised/Final Draft

Here are Danae's peer editor's comments and analysis, as well as Danae's responses.

- If Danae is going to make a point to state dates, then she should offer some explanation why the play opened nearly two years after it was written. Otherwise, the reader might be distracted from what is important by wondering about this trivial point.

- Tone and voice are problems for Danae here. Word choice and sentence structure are almost childish, and her vague reference to "things he didn't want to do" is virtually meaningless. What things? Didn't want to do for what reasons? Why did he have to do them?

- What movie?

- Clearly, Danae wants to say something about how Shaw succumbed to popular demand when translating his stage play to film, but she is alluding to the issue as if she were mentioning something the audience already knows.

- Word choice continues to be a problem. Her thesis is never made explicit.

- There are a couple of problems in these sentences. In addition to telling us what Shaw did *not* want, it might be helpful to tell us what he *did* want to write. It also sounds as if being a socialist precludes writing romantic comedies, which is probably not what Danae means to imply.

- "Got it" is too colloquial for a formal paper. It is also an unsubstantiated exaggeration to suggest that "no one" understood Shaw's intent.

- In the last few sentences, Danae follows a simple formula that might prove helpful to her in her early draft. She will want to work to grow beyond mere formula writing. Still, she has finally identified the issue of the paper.

- Readers who do not already know the issue will probably not understand why Higgins' tossing a bouquet of flowers to Eliza would be considered "damnable."

- This is the second paragraph in a row that Danae begins with "but." This is a grammatically questionable and a stylistically poor choice. There is also the problem with Danae's use of "probably." This is a research paper, which does not allow for much speculation. Danae should limit her discussion to what she can support with evidence from the text and her other sources.

- Since the ending of the play and the continuation of the story comprise the key issues for this paper, Danae should devote more time to how Shaw wanted the story to end.

- Some instructors might protest the use of a single-sentence paragraph or the use of a structural fragment as a complete sentence, but stylistically, it creates a nice sense of contrast for Danae's reader.

- Danae's overuse of this construction suggests it is not a stylistic choice as much as a default or habitual use.

- Danae's sentence structure and word choice are confusing here.

- Danae raises a valid point, but she doesn't complete it. Why is it significant that the movie's ending is so antithetical to Shaw's intention? What insight into Shaw and the process of translating the playwright's vision to commercial success and then to film does Danae want to share with her reader?

- In order to be true to her thesis about the tension between author vision and audience expectation, Danae needs also to explore why Shaw would have chosen not to include this scene

- Sentence structure problem: Including the party scene would not have destroyed the expense of sets and costumes.

- It is unclear here whether Danae is telling us what Shaw believed or preaching to us what she believes.

- This is certainly a strong statement, but it is also a severe oversimplification of the material that Danae herself presents in her paper.

And here is Danae's reaction:

> I can find out all the specifics of the dates, names of actors, director, producer, etc.
>
> It was an issue of artistic integrity. Shaw wanted to show the folly of the upper class and the solid satisfaction of being in the productive middle class. I guess I need to made that more explicit. Colloquial and non-academic language seem to be big problems I need to work on.
>
> I need to make my thesis clear and specific. Shaw wanted a social commentary; the audience wanted a fairy tale.

Analysis of First Draft

What is this writer's purpose? Danae intends to illustrate the frustrations playwright George Bernard Shaw experienced trying to preserve his artistic integrity and tell a story with a strong personal and social theme.

> Yes.

What is his/her thesis? Her thesis is that the history of the first London production of Shaw's *Pygmalion* and the changes made in adapting the 1914 play for the big screen in 1938 suggest a victory of commercialism over artistic vision.

> Yes. I like the way "commercialism over artistic vision" is phrased.

What key points has the writer identified to clarify his/her thesis?

- the distinction between a romantic comedy and a social commentary

- a comparison between this story and "Cinderella"

- the description of a scene written for the film but not shown on stage

- a clear comparison of why Shaw would not have included this scene and why the audience wanted it.

> It really seems as if most of my problems are with language and maybe giving more support. My reader does seem to have gotten what I wanted her to get.

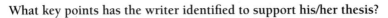

What key points has the writer identified to support his/her thesis?

- a letter from Shaw to the actress creating the role of Eliza explaining to her the reason Higgins cannot suggest a romantic interest in Eliza

- a portion of a letter from Shaw condemning the slight changes his London director made to the staging of the end of the play

- a passage from the "sequel" written by Shaw for the print publication of the play

- the fact that the 1938 film—and every subsequent remake or adaptation of the play—ends in the precise way Shaw said it must not.

> Yes.

Does the writer effectively prove his/her thesis? For the most part, she does. There are a few areas that could be further expanded, and her conclusion needs work, but the information presented and alluded to in this draft do a nice job to support her thesis.

> So I need to give more support, and maybe I should also discuss the point and the support more.

Here is Danae's revised draft. Notice how she has clarified her thesis.

Thesis: An examination of the 1914 stage play of George Bernard Shaw's _Pygmalion_, the 1938 film adaptation, and accounts of the making of the two productions illustrate the often conflicting desires of playwright and commercial audience. This examination further reveals that, in such a conflict, the playwright does not always prevail.

In the spring of 1912, playwright George Bernard Shaw wrote what would become his most popular, adapted, and enduring play. Due to illness and conflicts, <u>Pygmalion</u> didn't open in London until April 11, 1914. It was an immediate hit, but its popularity and the demands of fame on Shaw's artistic integrity frustrated and infuriated the playwright. In 1938, a film version of Shaw's <u>Pygmalion</u> was released. Although Shaw himself wrote the screenplay for this film, which would serve as the basis of the award-winning Broadway and Hollywood musical <u>My Fair Lady</u>, he still felt his vision to be challenged and his integrity compromised. An examination of the two versions of <u>Pygmalion</u> and accounts of the making of the two productions show that the story Shaw intended to tell and the story the commercial audience demanded were nearly antithetical. These differences are especially apparent in a comparison of the 1914 play and the 1938 film.

When he wrote the play in 1912, Shaw intended to write a social commentary, not a romantic comedy. He hoped to illustrate the creation of a strong and independent human being, not one half of a romantic couple. From the opening of the play's first London production, however, no one accepted Shaw's vision. Instead, the director wanted a love story, and the audience wanted a happy ending. The record of <u>Pygmalion's</u> production and publication history records Shaw's attempts to save his original vision and his ultimate failure to do so. This failure is most evident in the plot of the 1938 film, which Shaw wrote and approved.

But theatergoers did not want lessons in economics and socialist theory; they wanted comedy and romance. They wanted a happy ending. From opening night, Tree toyed with Shaw's ending, trying to make it closer to what the audience expected. Shaw had stormed angrily out of the opening night performance, but he returned for the play's milestone one-hundredth performance. According to Shaw's own account of the night, he was shocked to see Higgins run to the outdoor balcony at the back of the set and toss a bouquet of flowers to Eliza after she has left, "disdainfully" telling Higgins to run errands he had just ordered her to run himself. Shaw complained that this gesture of Higgins clearly insinuated a romantic relationship between Eliza and him. Tree replied, "My

Here is Danae's thesis.

This paragraph is still strongly formulaic, but Danae has managed to bring her content more to the front and allow her formula to withdraw more to the background.

This statement provides a smooth transition from Danae's discussion of audience expectations, which is not included here, to her point about the story's happy ending.

- 310 -

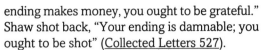

ending makes money, you ought to be grateful." Shaw shot back, "Your ending is damnable; you ought to be shot" (<u>Collected Letters</u> 527).

Tree was not shot, however, and Shaw apparently was grateful for the money because there is no record that later performances did not end with Higgins tossing Eliza the flowers. Shaw was not completely satisfied, however, because when he prepared his most popular and commercially successful play for publication as a book, he added an essay he called "Sequel: What Happened Afterwards," which begins with the sarcastic tirade:

> The rest of the story need not be shown in action, and indeed, would hardly need telling if our imaginations were not so enfeebled by their lazy dependence on the ready-mades and reach-me-downs of the ragshop in which Romance keeps its stock of 'happy endings' to misfit all stories. (Shaw 257)

This is the "Afterword" that tends to be included in most anthology textbook versions of the play (Martinski 372). In it, Shaw completes the story of Eliza and Freddie, explaining that, after the two lovers marry and flounder for a while, Colonel Pickering gives them the money to open the flower shop that was Eliza's goal at the beginning of the play. Freddie opens a greengrocer's shop next door, and after a few years of hard work and financial help from the Colonel, they succeed. Eliza does not return to Higgins, and the two do not end up as some sort of couple, romantic or otherwise.

This Sequel is not the only evidence of Shaw's dislike of Tree's ending or the audience's desire for a "happy ending." In a letter to Mrs. Patrick Campbell (Beatrice Stella Tanner), the actress who was playing Eliza opposite Tree's Higgins, Shaw tried to clarify his character's emotional and psychological motivations—and salvage his intended social theme:

> When Eliza emancipates herself—when Galatea comes to life—she must not relapse.

She must retain her pride and triumph to the end. When Higgins takes your arm on 'consort battleship' you must instantly throw him off with implacable pride; and this is the note until the final 'Buy them yourself.' He will go out on the balcony to watch your departure; come back triumphantly into the room; exclaim 'Galatea!' (meaning that the statue has come to life at last); and—curtain. Thus he gets the last word; and you get it too. (Ferguson 34)

There is no written or printed copy of the play that ends like this but Shaw's instructions to his actress make his intention clear. The woman whom his Higgins has created is too strong and independent a person to crawl back to the man who could only lord his position as Creator over her. Even Higgins can be happy only when he knows that his Eliza "needs" no one, even him. If Sir Henry Beerbohm Tree thought he needed to "soften" the ending to make money Shaw could still have the last word about what was <u>really</u> going on in his play.

Or so he thought.

Twenty-four years later, however, when Hungarian producer Gabriel Pascal approached Shaw for permission to produce a film version of <u>Pygmalion</u>, Shaw agreed on the condition that he retain full control over the adaptation. His name appears on the opening credits as the writer of the screenplay. What is interesting, however, is that Shaw's "full control" did not include restoring his vision of how Eliza and Higgins's story should end. The end of the 1938 film, starring Leslie Howard as Higgins and Wendy Hiller as Eliza, should have enraged Shaw, rather than receiving his approval. Not only does the move not end as Shaw had originally wanted—Higgins does <u>not</u> triumphantly cry out "Galatea" as he watches his creation walk from his life—it doesn't even end suggesting romance by having Higgins toss flowers to Eliza. In the final sequence of the 1938 film, "Screenplay and Dialogue [by] Bernard

Danae has succeeded in making the progression of hateful-to-Shaw endings clearer.

- 312 -

Shaw" (<u>Pygmalion</u>, film, 0:31), Eliza returns to Higgins, repeats an earlier line of dialogue that stands for her status as a lowly creature of the gutter, and Higgins demands, "Where the devil are my slippers, 'Liza?" (1:34:33). This ending is practically the opposite of what Shaw intended. Allowing his name to appear on the credits must have represented to him the final surrender of his vision and a severe compromise of his principles.

Here is an example of the discussion, the personal insight that Danae was told was missing in her first draft.

Another drastic change in the screenplay occurs between what would have been Acts III and IV in the play. While every production and edition of the play jumps in timeline from the disastrous scene at Mrs. Higgins's house to the argument on the evening after Eliza's triumph at the garden party, the 1938 film shows the triumphant scene but sets it at a formal ball. There are many reasons that Shaw would not have wanted to dramatize this scene, but there is only one reason for the audience's desire to see it.

Danae has taken her editor's advice and indicated to her reader that she will discuss Shaw's desire as well as the audience's.

The audience wanted romance. They wanted the story of Eliza and Higgins to be a modern-day Cinderella story. And they wanted to see Cinderella at the ball (Martinski 184). For Shaw the playwright, to have included the party scene would have required him to alter his five-act plot structure and would have required the expense of an additional set, costumes, and stage extras. For Shaw the socialist, there was no need to show Eliza's brush with the upper class. His point would be proven in the next Act: there was no difference between the high and the low that education and training could not fix. And his "happy ending" did not involve a poor girl's rise to the noble class. His happy ending was the poor girl's "rise" and the gentleman's "descent" to the middle class where they become happy and productive members of society. How willing was Shaw to create a

Simply adding the two phrases, "For Shaw the ..." points out the two perspectives from which Shaw was working that were at odds with what a commercial audience wanted.

This is a much clearer explanation of Danae's point.

scene that was unnecessary and might actually distract his audience from the point he wanted them to take home is not recorded, but the changes made to the story and script of the 1938 film clearly insinuate a defeat for Shaw and his artistic and social vision.

It is ironic, and possibly sad for those who admire the man George Bernard Shaw was, that it was the screenplay of this 1938 film and not Shaw's original 1912 play that became the basis of <u>My Fair Lady</u>, the popular 1956 Broadway musical and 1964 movie musical (<u>Collected Letters</u> 733).

The transition of George Bernard Shaw's <u>Pygmalion</u> from popular stage play to even more popular film reveals an interesting balance of pleasing the money-paying audience, respecting the actors' and directors' visions, and fulfilling the goals and purposes of the playwright. The transition of <u>Pygmalion</u> from stage play to film also seems to show that, when all things are taken into consideration, the playwright's purpose may not be the only, or even the most important value that governs the transitional process.

Works Cited

"The Instinct of an Artist: Shaw and the Theatre." Catalog for "An Exhibition from The Bernard F. Burgunder Collection," 1997. Cornell University Library. http://rmc.library.cornell. edu/EAD/pdf guides/RMM04617 pub.pdf

Martinski, Andrea. "Audiences Rule, Writers Drool." <u>Alternative Views of Award-Winning Books and Authors Ed.</u> by Aloysius DeMarco. New York: Marginal Press, 1969.

<u>Pygmalion</u>. Prod. Gabriel Pascal. Perf. Leslie Howard, Wendy Hiller, 1938. Film. http://www.youtube.com/watch?v=ToMYoE1O-Ew&feature=related

Shaw, Bernard. <u>Androcles and the Lion; Overruled; and Pygmalion</u>. New York: Brentano, 1916.

Shaw, George Bernard. <u>The Collected Letters of G.B. Shaw</u>. Ed. David A. Laurents. London: Asquith and Heron, 1987.

Analysis of Revised Draft

What is this writer's purpose? Danae illustrates the frustrations playwright George Bernard Shaw experienced trying to preserve his artistic integrity and tell a socially relevant story instead of a trivial romance.

What is his/her thesis? An examination of the 1914 stage play and the 1938 film adaptation of George Bernard Shaw's *Pygmalion* and accounts of the making of the two productions illustrate the often conflicting desires of playwright and commercial audience. This examination further reveals that, in such a conflict, the playwright does not always prevail.

Has the writer's new draft strengthened his/her point? Yes. Danae provides a good bit more specific information and has taken the time to discuss this information to lead her reader to the point she is trying to establish.

Has the rewrite strengthened the case for his/her thesis? Yes. See above.

What new details, facts, etc., have been included to make this a more thorough study of the topic? Not necessarily new information as much as a shift in focus, so that Eliza is also seen as Higgins's creation and what he intends that creation to be. Higgins is seen as the man who both created and abused his creation. By looking at Higgins and Eliza, not only as characters but as character types, Danae has been able to see beyond the audience's limited vision and appreciate what Shaw originally wanted to do.

Does the writer effectively prove his/her thesis to any greater degree than in the previous draft? Yes.

Now write your final draft.

APPENDIX 1

Samples of MLA and Turabian Citation and Documentation

All citation and documentation formats serve the same purpose: to allow the writer to share with the reader the sources from which information and ideas were gathered. It's a matter of both credit and credibility:

- as an academic, a researcher, you *must* give credit to the men and women whose prior work assisted you, whose ideas helped you shape yours, whose observation, experimentation, and discovery of information made your research possible;

- as a student who is not yet a recognized expert in your field, you *must* refer to those whose expertise is acknowledged to reassure your reader that you are knowledgeable in the subject, and your findings and insights can be trusted.

Once you understand those basic ideas, questions of what information to document and what sources to cite become easier to answer.

The question of *how* to cite your sources and document your information is not difficult either. For the most part, a documentation format will be assigned to you. Most likely, the assigned format will be determined by the discipline or subject matter of the class for which you are writing the paper.

This series of books has focused on the three most commonly used formats, the three that you are most likely to be using in college and beyond.

The **MLA style** is developed by the Modern Languages Association, and is the format you will use in the vast majority of your humanities, language, and arts courses.

The **Turabian** style is a modified form of the **Chicago** style developed by Kate Turabian, the late graduate school dissertation secretary and editor of official publications at the University of Chicago from 1930 to 1958. It is the form of citation and documentation most often used in the humanities, social sciences, and natural sciences. It is often recommended as the style to use when you're not sure which style is appropriate.

The **APA** style is developed by the American Psychological Association. It is used primarily in the social sciences (especially psychology and education).

Because there is considerable overlap in the disciplines for which both Turabian and APA can be used, it is never a bad idea to check with your instructor as to which format is preferred. You should know, however, that APA will almost never be acceptable for a literature paper, and MLA will probably not be accepted by a psychology or economics professor.

MLA:

Danae's *Pygmalion* paper was on a literary topic and written for her English class, so she used MLA style documentation.

In an MLA-style paper, the **list of sources** is called the **"Works Cited" page**. Regardless of its name or particular format, this portion of the research paper serves the same purpose—to provide your reader with a complete list of sources from which you got information. Regardless of the type of source, every entry provides your reader with all of the data he or she would need to locate it.

Between your **Works Cited Page** and **parenthetical documentation**, you are giving your reader everything he or she would need to locate the source and verify the information you claim to have gotten from it.

While there might seem to be countless forms and variations (one for each type of source), they are all variations of the **basic format**.

Author last name, First name and middle initials. *Title*. City of publication: Publishing Company, copyright date.

In all of the following samples, the necessary punctuation has been **increased in size and bolded** for emphasis:

Formats for books:

Shaw, Bernard. *Androcles and the Lion; Overruled; and Pygmalion*. New York: Brentano, 1916.

Books with more than one author:

1st author last name, First name and middle initial, **and** 2nd First and last names. Title and publishing information as above.

Shaw, Bernard, and Roger Raintree. ...

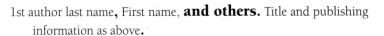

1st author last name, First name, **and others.** Title and publishing
   information as above.

Shaw, Bernard, **et al.** …

Periodicals:

Author(s). "Title of Article." *Title of Periodical* Day Month Year: pages.
   Medium of publication.

Martinski, Andrea. "What Do You Do if the Playwright's Wrong." *Theatre
   from a Different Angle* Apr 2012: 22-27. Print.

Gladstone, Paula, and Marshall Kent. "Don't Go to the Movies and Look for
   a Play." *The Adapter's Quarterly.* Jan.-Mar 1987: n.p. Electronic.

Website:

Editor, author, or compiler name (if available). *Name of Site.* Version number.
   Name of institution/organization affiliated with the site (sponsor or
   publisher), date of resource creation (if available). Medium of publication.
   Date of access.

Snowden, Nicholas. "A Collection of Plans and Activities to Teach Pygmalion to
   High Schoolers." Playnerd.Com, Web. 10 May 2012.

For references to a source within the body of the paper, MLA style prefers in-
text, parenthetical citation to footnotes or endnotes. The basic form for these
parenthetical citations provides simply the author's name and the page
number from which the information was drawn:

(Martinski 184)

(Ferguson 34)

(Shaw 257)

If there is no stated author, then use an abbreviated form of the title, along
with the page number:

(Collected Letters 527)

If, in the course of your paper, you cite more than one source by the same
author or editor, your note will also contain an abbreviated form of the title of
the source you are citing.

If you refer to the same source two or more times in a row, the second and
third (etc.) consecutive citations contain only the page number.

There are a few minor variations to the basic form, depending on how you present the information and the source:

If you name the author in the text:

> Martinski credits Tree with thrusting Shaw into fame, despite the playwright's protests **(163)**.

If you name the author *and source* in the text:

> In his "alternative study" of well-known works, Andrea Martinski insists that Shaw would have been long forgotten had it not been for Tree's adaptations to *Pygmalion* **(163)**.

If the source does not provide the typical information required in a citation, simply cite whatever information is available to you that is likely to be helpful to your reader.

For example, when Danae wants to cite information that can be verified by viewing the film, she notes the film on her Works Cited page and provides the film's timer marking in her parenthetical citation:

> In the final sequence of the 1938 film, "Screenplay and Dialogue [by] Bernard Shaw" **(Pygmalion, film, 0:31)**, Eliza returns to Higgins, repeats an earlier line of dialogue that stands for her status as a lowly creature of the gutter, and Higgins demands, "Where the devil are my slippers, 'Liza?" (1:34:33).

Websites also often do not provide authors' names, page numbers, traditional publishing information, and so on. If you work to understand the principles that govern the Works Cited Page and your parenthetical citations, you should be able to work out a form that meets your and your reader's needs and adheres to the spirit of the MLA conventions.

Turabian:

Maya's paper is about a non-language topic, and her social studies teacher specifically assigned that she follow Turabian style in her citations and documentation.

The **basic format** of a Turabian-style **Bibliography** is similar to MLA's:

> Author last name**,** First name and middle initials**.** *Title***.** City of publication**:** Publishing Company, copyright date**.**

Formats for books:

> Schaug, Gottfried, M.D., Ph.D. *The Musician's Brain: A Model for Functional and Structural Adaptation.* New York: New York Academy of Sciences Press, 2001.

Books with more than one author:

> 1st author last name, First name and middle initial, **and** 2nd First and last names. Title and publishing information as above.

> Shaw, Martin and Asher Rastikov. ...

> 1st author last name, First name, 2nd First and last names, **and** 3rd First and last names.

> Shaw, Martin, **et al.** ...

Periodicals:

> Author(s). "Title of Article." *Title of Periodical,* Day Month Year, pages.

> Gardiner, Faith, Jeffrey Cormant, and Philip Knowles. "The Truth about Music and Math." *Nature's World* May 23 1996, 65-66.

Website:

> Author. copyright. Title of Article or Website. Producer of cite. Universal Resource Locator (URL).

> "Music–Math Connection: A Neurobiological View." WebResearch. Cynthia Jameson, 2008. http://www.WebResearch.net/wiki/music_math/jameson.html.

To refer to a source within the body of the paper, Turabian style allows both in-text, parenthetical citation and **footnotes** or endnotes. The **basic form** for **footnotes** essentially duplicates the information in bibliographical entries with a few variations in punctuation:

First citation of a source:

> **Footnote number from body of text** Author's name (first and last), *Title of Book* (City of Publication: Publisher, copyright date), page number.

> **1.** Gottfried Schlaug, M.D., Ph.D. *The Musician's Brain: A Model for Functional and Structural Adaptation* (New York: New York Academy of Sciences Press, 2001), 373.

2. Faith Gardiner, Jeffrey Cormant, and Philip Knowles, "The Truth about Music and Math," *Nature's World*, May 23, 1996, 12– 3.

A second (and third, etc.) citation of the source just cited:

3. Ibid.

4. Ibid 255.

(*Ibid* establishes that the current note refers to the same page of the source just cited. *Ibid* and the page number refers to the same source but the stated page.)

Later citation of a source previously cited:

15. Schlaug 227.

19. Gardiner **et al.** 15.

Since the purpose of footnotes, parenthetical citations, and the bibliography is to help your reader locate your sources and verify the information in your paper, it's more a matter of understanding the principle than it is trying to memorize a format. If you are uncertain about the appropriate form to cite a certain type of source, and you cannot find a model to follow (there are literally dozens available on the Internet), let your common sense guide you as you improvise a form that will both meet the needs of your reader and maintain the integrity of your Turabian documentation.

APPENDIX 2

A Side-by-Side Comparison of the Grade 9 and 10 Rubrics

TOPIC: *Choosing and narrowing your topic is absolutely fundamental to successful writing. It would not be completely unfounded to say that, without a good topic, none of the other qualities of your essay matter. Choosing and narrowing a topic is also probably one of the earliest traits you learned and practiced in elementary school; you should have it pretty well mastered by now.*

Grade 9

5 • **Topic is clear and sufficiently narrow** for the nature of the writing.
Even at the ninth-grade level, the goal is for the topic to be "sufficiently narrow." Is there any expectation that a topic that is not "sufficiently narrow" can result in a top-scoring piece of writing?

• Topic is **suitable** to fulfilling the **purpose** of the writing (e.g., persuasive versus informational).

4 • **Topic is clear and sufficiently narrow** for the nature of the writing.
• Topic is **suitable** to fulfilling the **purpose** of the writing (e.g., persuasive versus informational).
Suitability of topic will expand in tenth grade and above to include suitable complexity. Even at this point, the writer should be encouraged to strive for topics that are not too simple or too complex for the assignment.

Grade 10

5 • **Topic is clear and sufficiently narrow** for the nature of the writing.
The wording of this descriptor is identical to the same score-point at grade 9 to indicate that "clear and sufficiently narrow" are the goals for the workable topic. As the writers progresses from ninth through twelfth grade, other traits might need to become more sophisticated, but the need for the topic to be clear and sufficiently focused will not change.

• Topic is **sufficiently complex** and is **suitable** to fulfilling the **purpose** of the writing (e.g., persuasive versus informational). *"Sufficiently complex" reflects the increased sophistication of the topic as the student progresses through school.*

4 • **Topic is clear and sufficiently narrow** for the nature of the writing.
• Topic is **sufficiently complex** and is **suitable** to fulfilling the **purpose** of the writing (e.g., persuasive versus informational).
Complexity of topic has implication for other aspects of the writing, including development and elaboration, differentiating the writer's claims from others, and so on. An overly simple or generalized topic will not yield a rich and thorough examination or discussion.

3 • **Topic** is **clear** and reveals a **strong attempt** to **narrow** it sufficiently for the nature of the writing.

Clarity and specificity of the topic are essential to a successful piece of writing. Clarity is an easier goal to achieve, so writing at this score point indicates a writer still working toward mastery of the narrowed-down topic.

• Topic may be **too simple or general** for **the purpose** of the writing (e.g., persuasive versus informational).

Possibly the simplicity of the topic is a consequence of the writer's struggle to narrow it sufficiently.

2 • **Topic** is **clear** but either **too broad or too narrow** for the nature of the writing.

• Topic may be **too simple or general** for **the purpose** of the writing (e.g., persuasive versus informational).

1 • **Topic** is **clear** but either **too broad or too narrow** for the nature of the writing.

Writing that does not have a clear topic is simply not acceptable.

• Topic may be **too simple or general** for **the purpose** of the writing (e.g., persuasive versus informational).

---

3 • **Topic** is **clear** and reveals a **strong attempt** to **narrow** it sufficiently for the nature of the writing.

• Topic may be **too simple or general** for **the purpose** of the writing (e.g., persuasive versus informational).

Possibly the simplicity of the topic is a consequence of the writer's struggle to narrow it sufficiently.

2 • **Topic** is **clear** but either **too broad or too narrow** for the nature of the writing.

• Topic may be **too simple or general** for **the purpose** of the writing (e.g., persuasive versus informational).

1 • **Topic** is **clear** but either **too broad or too narrow** for the nature of the writing.

• Topic may be **too simple or general** for **the purpose** of the writing (e.g., persuasive versus informational).

The simple truth is that, even for younger and relatively less experienced writers, a weak topic will result in a weak piece of writing.

CRAFTSMANSHIP: *Few, if any, writers, even extremely successful ones, produce final-draft quality work without planning and effort. Writing is a craft that can be improved with practice. Proficient, college-and-career-ready writers appreciate this fact and are in control of their craft.*

5 • **Writing** is **competent**. Tone **and style** are **appropriate** to the topic, purpose, and audience of the piece.

   At this grade and score level, the student writer has a command of grammar and mechanics and is developing a speaking and writing vocabulary sufficient to communicate his or her knowledge and perceptions.

• **All claims** or points being explored are **expressed clearly**. *This is an absolutely fundamental function of an introduction.*

• The **distinctions** between the student's ideas and those from other sources **are clearly suggested**.

• **All claims** (both the student's and others') are **presented accurately**, with **strong evidence** of an **attempt** to present **others' claims fairly**.

5 • **Writing** is **competent and confident**. Tone **and style** are **consistent and appropriate** to the topic, purpose, and audience of the piece.

   At this grade and score level, grammar and mechanics are no longer issues. Students' expanding vocabulary provides them with the growing sense that they know what they want to say, and they are willing to discover how best to say it.

• **All claims** or points being explored are **expressed clearly**.

• The **distinctions** between the student's ideas and those from other sources **are evident**.

   For students to present someone else's claims without acknowledging the source—to tacitly suggest that the claims are their own—is a form of plagiarism. These concepts are not difficult to grasp and should be established habits by grade 10.

• **All claims** (both the students' and others') **are presented accurately**, with **strong evidence** of an **attempt** to present **others' claims fully and accurately** as appropriate to the topic, audience, and purpose.

- If appropriate to the topic, audience, and purpose, **narrative techniques are used purposefully.**

  One key phrase that appears throughout this rubric is "if appropriate." Not every technique is appropriate for every purpose and audience. Created dialogue and excessive figurative language would be as out of place in a highly academic research paper as would clinical and scholarly language in an informal personal narrative.

  A writer at this level is not afraid to experiment with wordplay or figurative language when appropriate.

4 • **Writing** is **competent.** Tone and style are **generally appropriate** to the topic, purpose, and audience of the piece.
- **All claims** or points being explored are **expressed clearly.**
- **Distinctions** between the student's ideas and those from other sources **are clearly suggested.**
- **All claims** (both the students' and others') are **presented accurately,** with **strong evidence** of an **attempt** to present **others' claims fairly.**

  Even as students understand the need to address other views and to address those views objectively, the actual achievement of that objectivity might pose a challenge that will require continued practice and feedback.

- If appropriate to the topic, audience, and purpose, **narrative techniques are used purposefully.**

- If appropriate to the topic, audience, and purpose, **narrative techniques are used for variety and effect.**

  The key difference between grades 9 and 10 is that the student has developed enough expertise with various narrative techniques that their use is more intentional and less experimental.

4 • **Writing** is **competent. Tone and style are consistent and appropriate** to the topic, purpose, and audience of the piece.
- **All claims** or points being explored are **expressed clearly.**
- The **distinctions** between the student's ideas and those from other sources **are evident.**
- A **strong attempt to present all claims** (both the students' and others') is apparent, and there is **evidence** of an **attempt** to present **others' claims fully and accurately** as appropriate to the topic, audience, and purpose.

  While expressing all claims should not pose much of a challenge to the writer, being thorough and accurate in expressing claims of others might be more difficult to master. Certainly a piece of writing that reveals a flawed attempt at completeness and objectivity cannot receive the highest score, but it should not be dismissed as a failure either.

- If appropriate to the topic, audience, and purpose, **narrative techniques are used for variety and effect.**

3 • **Writing** is **adequate. Tone and style** are, **for the most part, appropriate** to the topic, purpose, and audience.

The writer at this level is not committing grievous errors, but the writing is simplistic. There may be lapses in tone that suggest a lack of full control.

• **Most claims** or points being explored are **expressed**, while **some can be inferred.**

• A **strong attempt** to **distinguish the student's ideas from those of other sources** is evident.

• A **strong attempt** to present **both the students' and others' claims** is evident.

• **Some attempt** to present **the claims of others accurately and fairly** is evident.

This mid-level score point separates the presentation of others' claims and the accuracy and fairness of that presentation into two descriptors in order to reflect the probability that objectivity will be more difficult to achieve than the simple awareness of addressing others' claims.

• If appropriate to the topic, audience, and purpose, **narrative techniques are used.**

2 • **Writing** is **uneven. Tone and style** seem **unplanned** and **not necessarily demanded** by the topic, purpose, and audience.

---

3 • **Writing** is **adequate. Tone and style** are **consistent** and **appropriate** to the topic, purpose, and audience.

The key difference between a 3 and a 4 is the element of competence. The writer at this level is not committing grievous errors, but the writing does reveal less control, less ease with words and constructions that make writing better than "good enough."

• **Most claims** or points being explored are **expressed**, while **some** may be **suggested or implied.**

• The **distinctions** between the student's ideas and those from other sources **are usually apparent.**

• The writing exhibits **some effort** to present **all claims** (both the students' and others') **accurately.**

"Some effort" suggests that the writer knows he or she needs to be accurate and thorough, but might not know how to handle claims he or she does not fully understand or cannot discuss as thoroughly as others. The tenth-grade writer might not yet have developed the judgment to edit or perform additional research before writing.

• **Omissions** in either strengths or limitations **suggest bias** and/or **faulty reasoning.**

• If appropriate to the topic, audience, and purpose, **narrative techniques are used for variety** and **effect.**

2 • **Tone and style** are, for the **most part, appropriate** to the topic, purpose, and audience with a **few minor lapses.**

At score point two, borderline unacceptable, the writer is not in complete control.

- **Some claims** or points being explored **are specified**, but **many are implied** or are **stated ambiguously**.

- The writing suggests **attempts to distinguish** between the student's ideas and those from other sources.
  As the distinctions between the writer's claims and those of his or her sources become less clear, the writer risks being accused of plagiarism.

- The writing suggests **tentative attempts to** present both the **students' and others' claims**.

- **Omissions** in either strengths or limitations **suggest bias** and/or **faulty reasoning**.
  At this score point, the writer's difficulty in achieving objectivity results in more than an unsuccessful attempt but a noticeably flawed piece of writing.

- **Narrative devices** that would make the writing clearer or more powerful **are missing**.
  This writer is either afraid of taking the narrative risk or does not realize the impact the use of such devices can have on his or her writing.

1 • **Writing is flawed. Tone and style are inconsistent** or **apparently unrelated to** the topic, purpose, and audience.

- **Claims** or points being explored **are often omitted or expressed ambiguously**.

- **Some claims** or points being explored **are specified**, but **many are implied** or are **stated ambiguously**.
  The distinctions between "most" and "some" and "some" and "many" might seem arbitrary, but the distinction between a 3 and a 2 is in the reader's overall impression: is the writer "telling the whole story" and telling it fully and objectively, or are there noticeable gaps?

- **The distinctions** between the student's ideas and those from other sources **are usually apparent**.
  As the distinctions between the writer's claims and those of his or her sources become less clear, the writer risks being accused of plagiarism.

- The writing suggests **tentative attempts to present its claims** (both the students' and others') **accurately**.

- **Obvious omissions** in either strengths or limitations and **uneven treatment of some claims suggest bias and/or faulty reasoning**.

- **Narrative devices** that would make the writing clearer or more powerful **are missing**.
  This writer is either afraid of taking the narrative risk or does not realize the impact the use of such devices can have on his or her writing.

1 • **Tone and style are inconsistent.**
  Inconsistency indicates a lack of control.

- **Some claims** or points being explored **are specified**, but **many are implied** or are **stated ambiguously**.
  As noted earlier, this is a habit that should be well established by this grade level.

- There is **minimal to no clear distinction** between the student's ideas and those from other sources.

  Whether intentional or accidental, not to identify for the reader what ideas are the writer's own and what are from other sources is plagiarism and unacceptable.

- The writing suggests **minimal to no attempt to** present both the **students' and others' claims.**

- There is **no attempt** to use **narrative devices** that might be appropriate to the topic, audience, and purpose.

- There is **minimal distinction** between the student's ideas and those from other sources.

  Whether intentional or accidental, not to identify for the reader what ideas are the writer's own and what are from other sources is plagiarism and unacceptable.

- The writing suggests **minimal attempts to present all claims** (both the students' and others') **accurately.**

- **Narrative devices** that would make the writing clearer or more powerful **are missing.**

ELABORATION, DEVELOPMENT, AND SUPPORT: *A valid point is not enough to convince a reader. A good default position to assume in everything you write is that your readers either do not understand what you are saying, or they disagree. In either case, it is your responsibility as writer to explain and support all sides of an issue to help your readers see the validity of your point.*

5 • **All claims**, inferences, and analyses are **supported with evidence** from literary or informational texts, as appropriate to the topic, audience, and purpose.
Other descriptors will deal with the nature and quality of the evidence, but a ninth-grade writer should know that he or she must have evidence to support every claim.
• **Facts**, examples, and/or details are **relevant and sufficient to establish the purpose** of the writing and meet the needs of the audience.
This is the top score for this component, an "A" if you will, so it is not unreasonable to expect both relevancy and sufficiency. A piece of writing that achieves one or the other might be acceptable, but it cannot be evaluated as "excellent," even in the ninth grade.
• When appropriate to the topic, audience, and purpose, elaboration of the topic includes **vivid images and impressions.**

4 • **For the most part, claims**, inferences, and analyses are **supported with evidence** from literary or informational texts, as appropriate to the topic, audience, and purpose.

5 • **All claims**, inferences, and analyses are **supported with evidence** from literary or informational texts, as appropriate to the topic, audience, and purpose.
Other descriptors will deal with the nature and quality of the evidence, but a tenth-grade writer should know that he or she must have evidence to support every claim.
• **Facts**, examples, and/or details are **well-chosen, relevant, and sufficient to establish the purpose** of the writing and meet the needs of the audience.
• When appropriate to the topic, audience, and purpose, **sensory language** helps to create desired **images and impressions.**
This descriptor acknowledges that the writer at this level is experimenting with a new awareness. Score point 5, however, reflects relatively successful "experimentation," not merely the use of sensory words.

4 • **For the most part, claims**, inferences, and analyses are **supported with evidence** from literary or informational texts, as appropriate to the topic, audience, and purpose.

"For the most part" suggests an overall quality or impression. Rather than tallying supported and unsupported claims, the reader has a sense of general satisfaction after reading the piece.

- **Facts**, examples, and/or details are, **for the most part, relevant** and **generally sufficient to establish the purpose** of the writing and meet the needs of the audience.

"For the most part" suggests the writer understands the ideas of relevance and sufficiency and is working toward achieving those goals.

- When appropriate to the topic, audience, and purpose, elaboration of the topic includes **vivid images and impressions**.

3 • **Most claims**, inferences, and analyses are **supported with evidence** from literary or informational texts, as appropriate to the topic, audience, and purpose.

- **Facts**, examples, and/or details are **generally relevant** and **help to establish the** purpose of the writing and meet the needs of the audience. **Some irrelevancies** are present, but these **do not severely detract** from the overall effectiveness of the writing.

This writer is struggling to discern the relevant from the irrelevant. Some of the irrelevancies are probably the result of the writer's attempt to include sufficient evidence or details to achieve the purpose of the writing.

- When appropriate to the topic, audience, and purpose, elaboration of the topic includes **images and impressions**.

"For the most part" suggests an overall quality or impression. Rather than tallying supported and unsupported claims, the reader has a sense of general satisfaction after reading the piece.

- **Facts**, examples, and/or details are **well-chosen, relevant, and sufficient to establish the purpose** of the writing and meet the needs of the audience.

- When appropriate to the topic, audience, and purpose, **sensory language** helps to create desired **images and impressions**.

3 • **Most claims**, inferences, and analyses are **supported with evidence** from literary or informational texts, as appropriate to the topic, audience, and purpose.

- **Facts**, examples, and/or details are **well-chosen and relevant** and **help to establish the purpose** of the writing and meet the needs of the audience.

At this mid-level score point, the quality of the evidence that is provided contributes to that overall sense of completeness that defines a score point 4.

- **A strong attempt to use appropriate sensory language** contributes to the creation of desired **images and impressions**. **Sensory language** may **occasionally give way** to less powerful **adjectives and adverbs**.

2 • **Claims**, inferences, and analyses are **generally supported with evidence** from literary or informational texts, as appropriate to the topic, audience, and purpose of the writing.
Failing to support all claims with at least some evidence is a more egregious error than failing to sort out irrelevant facts and details in finding support for every claim.

• **Facts**, examples, and/or details **may be generally relevant, but are insufficient to establish the purpose** of the writing and/or meet the needs of the audience.
At this score point, there is simply not enough to build a strong case or provide a thorough discussion.
Ninth-grade writing at the score point of 2 generally exhibits one or the other of the two qualities above. Evidence that is insufficient in both quality and quantity will suggest a score point of 1.

• When appropriate to the topic, audience, and purpose, elaboration of the topic includes an **attempt at images and impressions.**

2 • **Most claims**, inferences, and analyses are **supported with evidence** from literary or informational texts, as appropriate to the topic, audience, and purpose

• **Facts**, examples, and/or details are generally relevant with **occasional minor irrelevancies.**
One distinction between a 3 and a 2 is in the quality of the evidence. Writers at this score point are still working on finding and selecting the most useful and relevant support.

• **Facts**, examples, and/or details may be generally relevant, but are **insufficient to establish the purpose** of the writing and/or meet the needs of the audience.
Another distinction between a 3 and a 2 is in the quantity of the evidence. There simply is not enough to build a strong case or provide a thorough discussion.
Tenth-grade writing at the score point of 2 generally exhibits one or the other of the two qualities above. Evidence that is insufficient in both quality and quantity will suggest a score point of 1.

• **Images and impressions** generally rely on **commonplace adjectives and adverbs.**

1 • **Lack of adequate support** for one or more claims, inferences, or analyses **weakens the overall impact** of the writing.
   • **Evidence** is characterized by **trivial or irrelevant** facts or details. Examples may be **tangential**.
   • **Development and elaboration** of the topic are **limited to factual statements** or **general observations**.

This final descriptor at all score points reflects the occasional need, especially in personal writing or narrative nonfiction to recreate experiences or convey emotions. In grades 10 and above, the use of sensory language will become a requirement in order to address this provision in the Common Core Standards.

1 • **Lack of adequate support** for one or more claims, inferences, or analyses **weakens the overall impact** of the writing.
   • **Evidence** is characterized by **trivial or irrelevant** facts or details. Examples may be **tangential**.
   • **Development and elaboration** of the topic are **generally limited to factual statements** or **general observations**. **Ineffective use or overuse of common adjectives and adverbs** undermines attempts to create images and impressions.

ORGANIZATION: *Whether you're writing a simple five-paragraph essay, a book-length narrative divided into chapters, or a research paper divided into major headings and sub-headings, you must determine the structure and the order of ideas that are going to be most effective at achieving your purpose and communicating so that your reader will understand and appreciate what you have to say.*

5
- **Introduction**, thesis, lead, etc., **orients** the reader to the **nature and purpose** of the piece to follow.
- **Conclusion follows logically from** the information presented and **clearly ends** the piece of writing.
- **Relationships** between elements of the piece of writing (**claims and reasons, reasons and evidence, claims and counterclaims**) are **logical** and **clear** and suggested by the **order of ideas.**

4
- **Introduction**, thesis, lead, etc., **orients** the reader to the **nature and purpose** of the piece to follow.
- **Conclusion follows logically from** the information presented and **clearly ends** the piece of writing.
- **Relationships** between elements of the piece of writing (**claims and reasons, reasons and evidence, claims and counterclaims**) are **logical** and **clear** and suggested by the **order of ideas.**

3
- **Introduction**, thesis, lead, etc., **suggests** the **nature and purpose** of the piece to follow.
  Whether it's called an introductory paragraph, lead, thesis statement, or whatever, this is not a new element to even an early ninth-grader. An introduction that does not orient the reader is unacceptable.
- **Conclusion follows logically from** the information presented and **ends** the piece of writing.

5
- **Introduction**, thesis, lead, etc., **orients** the reader to the **nature and purpose** of the piece to follow.
- **Conclusion follows logically from** the information presented and **clearly ends** the piece of writing.
- **Order** of ideas and the use of **transitional elements** establish the relationships between **claim(s) and reasons**, between **reasons and evidence**, and between **claim(s) and counterclaims.**

4
- **Introduction**, thesis, lead, etc., **orients** the reader to the **nature and purpose** of the piece to follow.
- **Conclusion follows logically from** the information presented and **clearly ends** the piece of writing.
- **Order** of ideas and the use of **transitional elements** establish the relationships between **claim(s) and reasons**, between **reasons and evidence**, and between **claim(s) and counterclaims.**

3
- **Introduction**, thesis, lead, etc., **orients** the reader to the **nature and purpose** of the piece to follow.
- **Conclusion follows logically from** the information presented and **clearly ends** the piece of writing.

- • **Relationships** between elements of the piece of writing (claims and reasons, **reasons and evidence, claims and counterclaims**) are **apparent.**

  "Apparent" indicates that the reader can sense the author's intent and the relationships between the elements even if not all relationships are evident in the writing itself.

- • **Attempts** to **order ideas are evident** and contribute to the reader's understanding of the **relationships.**

2 • The **nature and purpose of the piece can be inferred** from the **introduction**, thesis, lead, etc.

  The characteristic that distinguishes a 2 from a 3 is the level of clarity or explicitness. If the nature and the purpose of the piece are all ambiguous to the reader, the entire piece is weakened.

- • **Conclusion follows logically from** the information presented and **suggests that the piece** of writing **has ended.**

- • **Relationships** between elements of the piece of writing (**claims and reasons, reasons and evidence, claims and counterclaims**) are **unclear.**

- • Attempts to **order ideas** are evident, though the **order** might **not be logical or consistently controlled.**

  Looking at Organization as a whole, the unacceptable piece of writing is characterized by a lack of logic, consistency, and clarity or definition. The reader is left to infer a great deal that is not made explicit in the writing itself.

- • **Order** of ideas ... **suggests the relationships** between **claim(s) and reasons**, between **reasons and evidence**, and between **claim(s) and counterclaims.**

  Even at the tenth-grade level, these are pretty fundamental qualities for acceptable writing. Students have practiced such patterns as chronological order, order of magnitude, and so on. They have also been instructed and drilled in the use of transitional elements. Even a mid-scoring piece of writing, then, reveals that these techniques are already well established.

2 • **Introduction**, thesis, lead, etc. **suggests** the **nature and purpose** of the piece to follow.

  The characteristic that distinguishes a 2 from a 3 is the level of clarity or explicitness. If the nature and the purpose of the piece are all ambiguous to the reader, the entire piece is weakened.

- • **Conclusion is largely drawn from** the information presented and **clearly ends** the piece of writing.

- • **Relationships** between claims and reasons, between reasons and evidence, and between claims and counterclaims **can be inferred.**

- • **Order of ideas is unclear** or **illogical.**

  Looking at Organization as a whole, the unacceptable piece of writing is characterized by a lack of clarity or definition. The reader is left to infer a great deal that is not made explicit in the writing itself.

1 • **Introduction**, thesis, lead, etc., leaves the **nature and purpose** of the piece unclear.

• **Conclusion follows logically from** the information presented but **does not establish** that the piece of **writing is definitely finished.**

• **Relationships** between elements of the piece of writing **(claims and reasons, reasons and evidence, claims and counterclaims) are unclear.**

• There **is minimal evidence** of a **logical, consistent,** and **intentional ordering of ideas.**

1 • **Introduction**, thesis, lead, etc., leaves the **nature and purpose** of the piece unclear.

• **Conclusion essentially recaps** the information presented.

• The **apparent relationships** between claims and reasons, between reasons and evidence, and between claims and counterclaims **are not necessarily supported** by the **order** of ideas or the use of **transitional elements.**

• **Order of ideas** is **unclear or illogical.**

FORMS AND CONVENTIONS: *For the most part, forms like paragraph, essay, etc., should be well established. The tenth-grade student who is preparing for college or entry into his or her career after high school cannot be still spending a significant amount of classroom and homework time learning and practicing the conventions of written English.*

5 • **Word choice** is **careful and accurate** and clearly conveys the student's meaning.

• When appropriate, **academic and domain-specific words and phrases** are used **accurately**.

• **Writing** is **free of** spelling and/or typographical **errors**.

Even at this grade level, the student should know how and when to use the tools available: dictionaries, spell check, and so on. The final draft should be carefully proofed before it is submitted, so there is no "acceptable level" of errors of this nature.

• **Writing** is **free of** grammatical and **mechanical errors**.

Again, for top-scoring writing, there really is no "acceptable level" of basic errors.

• The piece **clearly reflects the student's own thinking** and writing, with **all material** or ideas derived **from outside sources clearly identified** and **carefully cited**.

Knowing to cite all outside sources should not be a new concept, even to a ninth-grade writer; nor is it that difficult a skill to master.

• **All citations** and notations **conform** to the teacher's or school's prescribed style manual (MLA, APA, Turabian, etc.).

4 • **Word choice** is **careful and accurate** and clearly conveys the student's meaning.

5 • **Word choice** is **intentional and precise** and clearly conveys the student's meaning.

• When appropriate, **academic and domain-specific words and phrases** are used **accurately and effectively**.

• **Writing** is **free of** spelling and/or typographical **errors**.

• **Writing** is **free of** grammatical and **mechanical errors**.

• The piece **clearly reflects the student's own thinking** and writing, with **all material** or ideas derived **from outside sources clearly identified** and **carefully cited**.

• **All citations** and notations **conform** to the teacher's or school's prescribed style manual (MLA, APA, Turabian, etc.).

4 • **Word choice** is **intentional and precise** and conveys student's meaning.

- When appropriate, **academic and domain-specific words** and phrases are used **accurately**.
  - **Writing** is **free of** spelling and/or typographical **errors**.
  - **Writing** is **free of** grammatical and mechanical **errors**.
  A piece of writing that contains basic errors like these simply cannot be evaluated as "excellent."
- The piece **clearly reflects the student's own thinking** and writing, with **all material** or ideas derived **from outside sources clearly identified** and **carefully cited**.
- **All citations** and notations **conform** to the teacher's or school's prescribed style manual (MLA, APA, Turabian, etc.).

3 • **Word choice is accurate** and conveys the student's meaning.
- When appropriate, **attempts to use academic and domain-specific words** and phrases **are evident**.
An important part of one's education in any discipline is learning to speak and write in the language of that discipline.
- Spelling and/or typographical **errors** are **infrequent** and **do not interfere** with the reader's ability to understand the writing.
- Grammatical and mechanical **errors** are **infrequent** and **do not interfere** with the reader's ability to understand the writing.
- The piece **clearly reflects the student's own thinking** and writing, with **all material** or ideas derived **from outside sources clearly identified** and **carefully cited**.

- When appropriate, **academic and domain-specific words** and phrases are used **accurately and effectively**.
  - **Writing** is **free of** spelling and/or typographical **errors**.
  - **Writing** is **free of** grammatical and mechanical **errors**.
- The piece **clearly reflects the student's own thinking** and writing, with **all material** or ideas derived **from outside sources clearly identified** and **carefully cited**.
- **All citations** and notations **conform** to the teacher's or school's prescribed style manual (MLA, APA, Turabian, etc.).

3 • **Word choice is careful and accurate** and conveys the **student's meaning**.
- The use of **academic and domain-specific words** and phrases **reflects a growing understanding** of the term's meaning or appropriate application.
An important part of one's education in any discipline is learning to speak and write in the language of that discipline.
- Spelling and/or typographical **errors** are **minor and infrequent**.
- Grammatical and mechanical **errors** are **minor and infrequent**.
- The piece **clearly reflects the student's own thinking** and writing, with **all material** or ideas derived **from outside sources clearly identified** and **carefully cited**.

- **All citations** and notations **conform** to the teacher's or school's prescribed style manual (MLA, APA, Turabian, etc.).
  "Give credit to your sources" and "follow the assigned model" are not difficult concepts to master.

2 • **Word choice** is **mostly adequate** to convey the **writer's meaning.** Use of **ambiguous or vague words** and **occasional misuse of key words** contributes to **reader confusion.**
Writers at this grade level and score point should be increasingly aware of the importance of careful and precise word choice, but their working vocabularies are not completely up to the task of communicating their ideas. Some writers at this level are working to improve their vocabularies, but they have fallen into the trap of choosing words that "sound smart" and, as a result, misuse words they do not yet completely understand.

- **Academic and domain-specific words** and phrases are used **unnecessarily** or **incorrectly.**

- Spelling and/or typographical **errors** are **infrequent** and **do not interfere** with the reader's ability to understand the writing.
- Grammatical and mechanical **errors are noticeable** but **do not interfere** with the reader's ability to understand the writing.

- **All citations** and notations **conform** to the teacher's or school's prescribed style manual (MLA, APA, Turabian, etc.).
  "Give credit to your sources" and "follow the assigned model" are not difficult concepts to master.

2 • **Word choice** is **mostly adequate** to convey the **writer's meaning.** Use of **ambiguous or vague words** and **misuse of key words** contributes to **reader confusion.**
Writers at this grade level and score point are probably aware of the importance of careful and precise word choice, but their working vocabularies are not completely up to the task of communicating their ideas. Some writers at this level are working to improve their vocabularies, but they have fallen into the trap of choosing words that "sound smart" and, as a result, misuse words they do not yet completely understand.

- **Academic and domain-specific words** and phrases are used **unnecessarily** or **incorrectly.**
As is the case with word choice, this descriptor addresses the writer who does not yet understand the words' meaning or application and is trying to "sound smart" as much as communicate precisely.

- Spelling and/or typographical **errors** are **infrequent** and **do not interfere** with the reader's ability to understand the writing.
- Grammatical and mechanical **errors are distracting** but **do not interfere** with the reader's ability to understand the writing.

- The piece clearly reflects the student's thinking and writing, with material and ideas derived from outside sources identified and cited with only occasional lapses.

  Failure to cite information and credit outside sources is essentially plagiarism. Even if committed unintentionally, it can have disastrous academic consequences and should be strongly discouraged from the beginning of the writer's education.

- All citations and notations conform to the teacher's or school's prescribed style manual (MLA, APA, Turabian, etc.).

  Imitating a model for citation and documentation is likewise not a higher-level skill. Any failure to conform to a prescribed style manual is essentially inexcusable.

1 • Word choice is adequate to convey the student's meaning.

  If the word choice were not at least adequate, the writing would be essentially incomprehensible.

- Academic and domain-specific words and phrases are used unnecessarily or incorrectly, or they are not used when their application is indicated.

- Spelling and/or typographical errors are infrequent but distracting.

- Grammatical and mechanical errors are infrequent but distracting. *It does not matter whether these errors are infrequent. If they distract the reader, they severely weaken the overall effectiveness of the writing, thus lowering its quality.*

- The piece clearly reflects the student's thinking and writing, with material and ideas derived from outside sources identified and cited with only occasional lapses.

  Failure to cite information and credit outside sources is essentially plagiarism. Even if committed unintentionally, it can have disastrous academic consequences and should be strongly discouraged from the beginning of the writer's education.

- All citations and notations conform to the teacher's or school's prescribed style manual (MLA, APA, Turabian, etc.).

  Imitating a model for citation and documentation is likewise not a higher-level skill. Any failure to conform to a prescribed style manual is essentially inexcusable.

1 • Word choice is barely adequate to convey the student's meaning. Frequent ambiguities and misused key words cause reader confusion.

  If the word choice were not at least adequate, the writing would be essentially incomprehensible.

- Academic and domain-specific words and phrases are used unnecessarily or incorrectly, or they are not used when their application is indicated.

- Spelling and/or typographical errors are distracting but do not interfere with the reader's ability to understand the writing.

- Grammatical and mechanical errors are distracting and may interfere with the reader's ability to understand the writing.

- Material and/or ideas derived from **outside sources** are **identified and cited carelessly** and **erratically**.
- **Citations** and notations **generally conform** to the teacher's or school's prescribed style manual.

- Material and/or ideas derived from **outside sources** are **identified and cited carelessly and erratically**.
- **For the most part, citations** and notations **conform** to the teacher's or school's prescribed style manual.

This descriptor is not talking about severe or egregious errors. The writer's notations and citations are "mostly right." However, if the writer is indeed following a model, there is no good reason that citations are not "completely right."

APPENDIX 3

Common questions about the interpretation and use of the rubric as an instructional and evaluation tool

How should this rubric be read?

It is virtually impossible to adequately describe a non-linear, three-dimensional process like evaluating a piece of writing in one-dimensional and linear language. Ideally, this rubric will be read holistically, each component being considered in the context of every other, no one being valued at the exclusion of any another.

For example, while control of style can be examined as evidence of a writer's *craftsmanship*, one cannot evaluate a writer's *command of conventions* without examining certain elements of style like word choice and sentence structure.

Similarly, the *craftsmanship* quality of presenting and supporting both claims and counterclaims accurately cannot be evaluated completely independently of *elaboration's* providing appropriate and sufficient evidence.

A familiarity with all of the elements and descriptors at every score point will help the scorer judge, not how accomplished a sample of student writing is in each individual trait, but as a unified whole, examining the contribution each makes to the writing's overall success.

How should this rubric be used? Are you suggesting each piece of writing receive a separate score for each of the five elements or qualities?

Again, the intent of the rubric is to help the scorer attain an overall or holistic evaluation of the student's work, an assessment of the overall success of a piece of writing. For example, a lively style and vivid word choice should not mislead the scorer into evaluating an argumentative piece filled with questionable claims and spurious support as accomplished. By the same token, however, a fully adequate—but dully or inarticulately written—argument is not fully accomplished either.

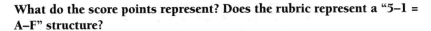

What do the score points represent? Does the rubric represent a "5–1 = A–F" structure?

It would not be completely unthinkable to equate an overall score of 5 with an A and an overall score of 1 with an F. It is important, however, to remember that whatever type of score or grade is given should be a holistic score and not the result of a simple average of the "scores" assigned to individual qualities.

One strategy that has proven effective in both improving student writing and helping to establish good writing habits in students is to interpret a *holistic score* of 2 or 1, not as an occasion to give the writing a failing grade, but to require the student to rewrite the piece until it meets the criteria of at least a 3.

Is there a way to fairly and consistently determine a reportable holistic grade from the combination of individual trait scores?

There are a number of methods. Here is one that has proven helpful (though not necessarily simple):

1. Weight each trait according to its relative value to the overall writing. For example, you might decide that a clear and narrow *topic* is worth 1% of the overall grade, while *organization*, *elaboration*, and *craftsmanship* are each worth 30% of the grade, and so on.

Make sure the total of the five weightings is 100%.

Note: If an entire school or district is using this rubric, it would be a good idea for everyone to agree on a uniform weighting scale, so that all students' work is evaluated fairly and consistently.

2. Multiply the essay's rubric score for each trait by its weighted value. For example:

Topic	3 [rubric score] x 1 [weighted value]	= 3
Craftsmanship	3	x 30	= 90
Elaboration	4	x 30	=120
Organization	2	x 30	= 60
Conventions	3	x 9	= 27

3. Add the products and divide the total by 100. For example, Step 2 above yields a total of 300. This total divided by 100 yields an overall score of 3 for the essay being scored.

While cumbersome at first (you may want to construct a spreadsheet to do all of the necessary calculations, so all you have to do is input the rubric scores), this process accomplishes several goals.

- It allows you or your department to agree on the standards by which your students' grades are going to be determined.

- It provides a means of communicating those standards clearly to your students, their parents, or any other interested parties.

- It ensures that the rubric and your anchor papers really are the bases of your students' grades.

This rubric seems awfully rigorous. Many common, relatively minor errors result in scores of 1 or 2. Why is that?

There are several reasons for the rigor of this rubric, some of which reflect "conventional wisdom" that is all too often ignored, and some of which do reflect a necessary paradigm shift from the traditional cant of what students cannot do to a sincere exploration of what they can.

1. This is the Grade 10 rubric. Its language is not intended to reflect the work of an introductory student. The language is intended to hold the tenth-grader working toward college and career readiness accountable to knowledge and skills attained in previous years. Students whose writing will be assessed by this rubric are nearly halfway through high school. They are not laying the foundation of their educations; they are within a year or two of their Advanced Placement exams, their college application essays, and possibly their states' high-stakes graduation exams. The work evaluated by this rubric should reveal progress toward mastery, not an ongoing struggle with fundamental language or composition elements.

2. This is a rubric to assess the writing of students working toward *college and career readiness* as described by the Common Core State Standards Initiative. Without dismissing or criticizing other post-secondary goals, the Common Core Standards and this rubric focus on this one.

Why is there so much repetition in the wording of the rubric? Even among the upper end, the wording does not change as the score progresses from a 3 to a 4 and a 5.

For the most part, this repetition is intended to emphasize the rigorous expectations of the college and career readiness standards, clarifying which qualities should be well established by a particular level and which are still in development.

Spelling, for example, should not be a significant issue for tenth graders. Certainly students will inevitably encounter the occasional spelling demon or make the occasional typographical error, but the "college-and-career-ready" sophomore knows to use the necessary references to ensure correct spelling, and a good proofreading session or two will help identify and eradicate typos.

Similarly, the "command of the conventions of standard English grammar and usage"(L. 9-10.1) that the student is required to demonstrate should be mastered as early in his or her schooling as possible. Certainly, by tenth grade, we cannot admit to an "acceptable number" of subject-verb or pronoun-antecedent agreement problems or unintentional sentence fragments. Such problems should be, for the most part, eradicated before the student has reached high school.

Where the language does change from one score point to the next, we hope to describe the increase in sophistication that should accompany a student's progress from grade to grade. We also hope to describe the qualities that distinguish an accomplished piece of writing from a merely adequate one and an adequate piece from an unacceptable one.